Rights of Nature

Rights of nature is an idea that has come of age. In recent years, a diverse range of countries and jurisdictions have adopted these norms, which involve granting legal rights to nature or natural objects, such as rivers, forests, or ecosystems. This book critically examines the idea of natural objects as right-holders and analyzes legal cases, policies, and philosophical issues relating to this development.

Drawing on contributions from a range of experts in the field, *Rights of Nature: A Re-examination* investigates the potential for this innovative idea to revolutionize the concepts of rights, standing, and recognition as traditionally understood in many legal systems. Taking as its starting point Stone's influential 1972 article "Should Trees Have Standing?," the book examines the progress rights of nature have made since that time by identifying central themes, unifying principles, and key distinctions in how rights of nature discourse has been operationalized in the disciplines of law, philosophy, and the social sciences. These themes and principles are illustrated through a wide variety of examples, including ecosystem services, indigenous thinking, and ecological restoration, demonstrating how the relationship between humanity and the natural world may be transforming.

Taking a philosophical, political, and legal perspective, this book will be of great interest to students and scholars of environmental law and policy, environmental ethics, and philosophy.

Daniel P. Corrigan is Assistant Professor of Philosophy at Marymount University.

Markku Oksanen is Senior Lecturer in Philosophy in the Department of Social Sciences, University of Eastern Finland.

Routledge Explorations in Environmental Studies

The Environmental Impact of Overpopulation
The Ethics of Procreation
Trevor Hedberg

Riverlands of the Anthropocene
Walking Our Waterways as Places of Becoming
Margaret Somerville

An Environmental History of Australian Rainforests until 1939
Fire, Rain, Settlers and Conservation
Warwick Frost

Daoism and Environmental Philosophy
Nourishing Life
Eric S. Nelson

Ecological Law and the Planetary Crisis
A Legal Guide for Harmony on Earth
Geoffrey Garver

From Environmental to Ecological Law
Kirsten Anker; Peter D Burdon; Geoffrey Garver; Michelle Maloney and Carla Sbert

Climate Change Temporalities
Explorations in Vernacular, Popular, and Scientific Discourse
Edited by Marit Ruge Bjærke, Anne Eriksen and Kyrre Kverndokk

Rights of Nature
A Re-examination
Edited by Daniel P. Corrigan and Markku Oksanen

For more information about this series, please visit: https://www.routledge.com/Routledge-Explorations-in-Environmental-Studies/book-series/REES

Rights of Nature

A Re-examination

Edited by Daniel P. Corrigan and Markku Oksanen

Routledge
Taylor & Francis Group
LONDON AND NEW YORK
earthscan
from Routledge

First published 2021
by Routledge
2 Park Square, Milton Park, Abingdon, Oxon OX14 4RN

and by Routledge
605 Third Avenue, New York, NY 10158

Routledge is an imprint of the Taylor & Francis Group, an informa business

British Library Cataloguing-in-Publication Data
A catalogue record for this book is available from the British Library

Library of Congress Cataloging-in-Publication Data
Names: Corrigan, Daniel P., editor. | Oksanen, Markku, 1966-editor.
Title: Rights of nature: a re-examination/edited by Daniel P. Corrigan and Markku Oksanen.
Description: Abingdon, Oxon; New York, NY: Routledge, 2021. | Series: Routledge explorations in environmental studies | Includes bibliographical references and index.
Identifiers: LCCN 2020052995 (print) | LCCN 2020052996 (ebook) | ISBN 9780367479596 (hardback) | ISBN 9780367479589 (ebook)
Subjects: LCSH: Rights of nature. | Natural resources–Law and legislation.
Classification: LCC K3478 .R54 2021 (print) | LCC K3478 (ebook) | DDC 344.04/6–dc23
LC record available at https://lccn.loc.gov/2020052995
LC ebook record available at https://lccn.loc.gov/2020052996

ISBN: 978-0-367-47959-6 (hbk)
ISBN: 978-0-367-77497-4 (pbk)
ISBN: 978-0-367-47958-9 (ebk)

Typeset in Bembo
by Deanta Global Publishing Services, Chennai, India

Contents

Contributors

J. Michael Angstadt is Assistant Professor of Environmental Studies at Colorado College. He researches the intersection of global environmental politics and international environmental law, emphasizing domestic actors' interactions with global environmental norms.

Patrik Baard is a postdoctoral researcher in ethics at the Department of Global Political Studies, Malmö University, Malmö, Sweden. He has previously been a postdoctoral researcher at the Swedish Biodiversity Centre, Swedish University of Agricultural Sciences, Uppsala, Sweden. He conducted his Ph.D. studies in philosophy at the Royal Institute of Technology, Stockholm, Sweden. He has published on different forms of uncertainty in climate change adaptation, environmental ethics, and biodiversity in journals such as *Ethics, Policy & Environment*, *Ethics & the Environment*, and *Journal of Agricultural and Environmental Ethics*, in addition to several anthology contributions.

Daniel P. Corrigan is Assistant Professor of Philosophy at Marymount University. His research focuses on human rights, political and legal philosophy, environmental ethics, and business ethics. He has published on topics such as environmental human rights, business and human rights, and other issues in human rights theory.

Alfonso Donoso is Associate Professor of political philosophy at the Institute of Political Science, Pontificia Universidad Católica de Chile. His current research and publications focus on animal and environmental ethics, in particular on the normative gap between these two areas of inquiry.

Andreas Gutmann is a research fellow at the Center of European Law and Politics (ZERP), University of Bremen, Germany, and a member of the international project "Nature as a Legal Person," funded by the German Research Fund (DFG). His fields of research are environmental law, postcolonial legal theory, Latin-American constitutional law, assembly law, and police law.

Marion Hourdequin is Professor of Philosophy at Colorado College. Her current research focuses on environmental philosophy, climate ethics, and relational approaches to ethics. She is the author of *Environmental Ethics: From Theory to Practice* (2015), and editor (with David Havlick) of *Restoring Layered Landscapes* (2016).

Anne Kumpula is Professor of Environmental Law at the University of Turku, Finland.

Linnea Luuppala is a Doctoral Candidate at the University of Helsinki. In her Ph.D. thesis she examines ecological restoration through conceptual analysis and explores its ethical implications.

Markku Oksanen is a Senior Lecturer in Philosophy at the University of Eastern Finland. He has published widely on green political theory and environmental ethics, including *Environmental Human Rights* (edited with Ashley Dodsworth and Selina O'Doherty, Routledge 2018).

Francine Rochford is Associate Professor in the School of Law, La Trobe University, Australia. She researches water law and environmental law along with the legal and governance aspects of universities and the law of torts. Her current projects include the relationship between soft regulation, risk, and tort law and the relationship between markets and law.

Giulia Sajeva is a Marie Skłodowska Curie Fellow at the University of Strathclyde Centre for Environmental Law and Governance. She has conducted research on the rights of local communities and indigenous peoples, with particular focus on biocultural rights. She has published a book on this topic, *When Rights Embrace Responsibilities: Biocultural Rights and the Conservation of Environment* (2018).

Mihnea Tănăsescu is a research fellow in the Political Science department, Free University of Brussels (VUB), Belgium. He works in the multidisciplinary field of political ecology and has focused on the rights of nature and conceptions of political representation, as well as the politics of nature conservation. He is currently working on a book on the concept of mutualism, as well as a general introduction to the theory and practice of rights for nature.

Acknowledgments

This volume developed out of a workshop on rights of nature that was convened in Lucerne, Switzerland in July 2019. The workshop was a part of the International Association for Philosophy of Law and Social Philosophy (IVR) biennial conference. Based on fruitful and animated discussions, and the high quality of the papers that were presented, we decided to pursue a joint publication in book format. In addition to a selection of papers from the workshop, we invited a couple of further contributions to fill gaps in the content. We would like to thank our contributors for their dedication and professionalism, as well as the other workshop participants who took part in our discussions.

Daniel would also like to thank Marymount University for support through a faculty development grant, which provided extra time to complete work on this project.

Daniel P. Corrigan
Markku Oksanen

1 Rights of Nature: Exploring the Territory

Daniel P. Corrigan and Markku Oksanen

Introduction

Rights of nature (RoN) involve the idea that nature, or natural entities and possibly natural processes, are in a position to be recognized as right-holders and taken into consideration in both our actions and our attitudes. While this is not an entirely new idea, it has been evolving gradually over the past few decades, especially since the turn of the millennium.

The ideas that inspire the current development of RoN, at least in some cases, can be found in the philosophies of indigenous peoples. However, the concept of "rights" is typically not native to these philosophies. According to conventional historiography or "a textbook narrative,"[1] rights are a Western and individualistic construct: "rights are typically conceived of as *possessed* or *owned by* or *belonging to* individuals [...]," as the famous legal philosopher H.L.A. Hart put it (1955, 182, original emphasis). Rights are often found in national constitutions, in the form of fundamental or basic rights that belong to human beings, and enable their social, political, and economic activities. However, as far back as the Roman legal system, the range of right-holders included municipalities, corporations, and other collective entities. Today, we are discussing new group rights, such as the rights of indigenous peoples (on group rights, see e.g. Jones 2016). RoN might be understood as combining the Western concept of rights with indigenous ideas or cosmologies, which hold that nature or natural entities themselves have some kind of value or moral importance, and thus are deserving of respect and protection.[2] Since RoN will tend to constrain economic and other types of human activities that affect nature, they may come into conflict with the rights of humans.

History

Many contemporary ideas and models of the environmental movement originated in the United States. As far as we know, this is also true of RoN in its literal sense, although the *idea* underlying RoN can be found and has been put into practice without the language of rights. For example, rather than the concept of "rights," some environmental movements have used concepts such as responsibility, duty, virtue, and care, or have painted a picture of human agents acting as guardians or stewards of nature. It is a matter of debate whether rights are conceptually, historically, or practically reducible to some other fundamental normative concept and how fundamental normative concepts overlap and are ranked.

According to environmental historian Roderick Nash, the earliest explicit mention of RoN can be found in a passage from John Muir (Nash 1989). In 1867, Muir, the Scottish-born American author and early environmentalist, wrote the following:

> How narrow we selfish, conceited creatures are in our sympathies! How blind to *the rights of all the rest of creation*! With what dismal irreverence we speak of our fellow mortals! Though alligators, snakes, etc., naturally repel us, they are not mysterious evils. They dwell happily in these flowery wilds, are part of God's family, unfallen, undepraved, and cared for with the same species of tenderness and love as is bestowed on angels in heaven or saints on earth.
>
> (Muir 1916, 98–99, emphasis added)

Aldo Leopold, the author of *A Sand County Almanac* (1949), also endorses the language of rights. According to him, species have a "biotic right" to existence that is independent of their economic value or "disvalue" (211). Thus, "A land ethic of course cannot prevent the alteration, management, and use of these 'resources,' but it does affirm their right to continued existence in a natural state" (204). Some commentators (e.g. Lehmann 1981) have read Leopold as an anthropocentrist who emphasizes "enlightened self-interest" in our dealings with nature, but the mainstream reading understands Leopold as an ecocentrist. It seems the same divide persists in the current debates about RoN since this framework is sometimes married with the language of sustainability (e.g. La Follette & Maser 2020), which was originally an explicitly human-centered, or anthropocentric, approach as formulated in the Brundtland Commission report *Our Common Future* (WCED 1987).

The idea of RoN became an issue of nuanced legal discussion with the publication of Christopher D. Stone's (1972) landmark article "Should Trees Have Standing?" For Stone, RoN began as a thought experiment, and he makes no mention of either Muir or Leopold. However, when a proposed development project threatened a pristine natural area in California, Stone employed this idea as a practical response to the project. Environmental advocacy groups fought the development project in the courts (as *Sierra Club v. Hickel*), and the case eventually made its way up to the U.S. Supreme Court (as *Sierra Club v. Morton*). In hopes of influencing the case, Stone published his article just prior to the Court's decision. While the majority did not decide to recognize RoN, the idea (and Stone's article) was cited in the dissenting opinion. In this volume, Oksanen and Kumpula offer an in-depth examination of Stone's article.

In the decades since this case, the idea that we should recognize the legal rights of nature or natural entities has begun to make progress. Examples of this progress can be found in a diverse range of nations around the world. Ecuador and Bolivia have adopted the Rights of Mother Earth, with Ecuador incorporating these rights into its constitution in 2008. New Zealand has legally recognized the rights of two rivers, a national park area, and a mountain in 2017 and 2018. The Supreme Court of Colombia recognized the rights of a river in 2016, and later recognized the rights of the Colombian Amazon in 2018. A court in India recognized the rights of two rivers in 2017, but the decision was later overturned by a higher court. In 2019, the High Court of Bangladesh recognized the rights of a river and held that this decision applies to all rivers in the country. A number of municipalities and Native American groups in the United States have adopted RoN, including a small town in Pennsylvania that successfully invoked these rights to overturn a permit for a fracking waste-injection well (Nobel 2017, 2020). The manner in which these rights have emerged and developed varies considerably. Some result from controversial court decisions, while others come from constitutional changes submitted to referenda, from agreements between national governments and indigenous peoples, or from local political initiatives. On the surface, these cases do not have much in common, apart from the fact that they result from human actions, with the potential implication that (legal) RoN differ from natural rights. Is this impression correct? It is an issue of ongoing debate whether RoN are based upon pre-existing ethical norms or are a matter of convention; some contributors in this volume approach RoN as moral rights, while others treat them as conventional legal norms.[3]

While the idea of RoN has certainly made progress, and these rights have begun to be institutionalized in various jurisdictions, many questions remain. In the cases mentioned above, the adoption of legal RoN is fairly recent. At this point, there has been little adjudication of these rights, which means their application and the jurisprudence relating to them is still very nascent. Beyond issues relating to the adoption and implementation of legal RoN, there are many underlying philosophical and political questions that have yet to be fully addressed or resolved. In the remainder of this introduction, we will briefly discuss a number of these issues, and mention the contributions in this volume that deal with them.

Justification

An initial issue concerns the justification of RoN. From a philosophical perspective, we can ask whether nature or natural objects are the types of things that should have rights. The idea of rights has emerged and evolved in a fundamentally anthropocentric context, and therefore the received wisdom is that humans are the only appropriate bearers of rights (and historically the range of right-holders has been even narrower and tied to citizenship, that is, to adult males with sufficient wealth).[4] Non-anthropocentric ethical approaches open the possibility of non-human entities becoming right-holders. The animal rights movement has attempted to extend rights to (at least some) non-human animals (Salt 1892; Regan 1983). Biocentric approaches could potentially extend the scope of right-holders to all living things, although there is no systematic presentation of this view within the deontological tradition (Taylor 1986 rejects non-human rights). Holistic approaches recognize the rights of entire ecosystems or the biosphere, although defenders of this view are typically pluralists who also defend the rights of non-human individuals. In cases of conflict, they may argue that the rights of "wholes" override the rights of individuals. While these non-anthropocentric views are not necessarily committed to a rights-based approach for all, or even some, of the entities to which they ascribe value or view as significant in some other sense, they each provide an account of the types of entities that have moral value or standing, and on those grounds may become a candidate for holding rights.

In this volume, Corrigan attempts to identify a link between an anthropocentric framework (human rights) and the natural environment, which could justify the recognition of RoN on anthropocentric grounds. Gutman examines indigenous philosophies and whether these are capable of justifying RoN. Sajeva discusses the prospects of rights that have a dual basis in the value of both humans and nature, known as biocultural rights, which offer a sort of hybrid between human rights and RoN. She examines the ways in which this dual basis may create internal tensions for these rights, thereby undermining one basis or the other. Luuppala offers an ecosystem-centric approach to RoN that appeals to the value of nature itself as justification for these rights. Finally, both Baard and Donoso raise challenges for RoN, based on various problems with trying to combine rights and natural objects. Donoso proposes an alternative understanding of RoN that treats them as group rights that belong to animals, while Baard argues that ultimately RoN cannot be justified.

An issue relating to the justification of RoN is what makes it reasonable to talk about non-human rights. It is often held that even if right-holders do not necessarily have to be full-fledged agents who are responsible for their actions, they must at least have interests (Stone 1972; Feinberg 1974). It is respect for, or protection of, these interests that justifies the ascription of rights. Stone claims that we are able to determine the "wants" or "needs" of natural entities, which provides the basis for determining their interests.[5] Nevertheless, he suggests this controversial claim can be avoided entirely by relying on the concept of "intactness." RoN need not depend on determining the interests of natural entities, but can instead be based on the concept of maintaining the intactness of these entities, which is a physical-based, rather than interest-based, standard. The concept of "intactness" is used by governments when they recover restoration costs and use the funds to restore a natural environment—as far as possible—to its state before damage (Stone 2012, 101–102). Baard touches on this issue, and our purported inability to determine the interests of nature, as a reason for rejecting RoN.

Stone's initial proposal for RoN is based on what we now call the interest theory of rights. According to the interest theory, the function of rights is to protect and advance the needs and well-being of the right-holder. The rival theory of rights is known as the will theory, which holds that the function of rights is to enable right-holders to exercise their autonomy. Traditionally, will theorists have been skeptical about extending rights even to human infants, not to mention animals, plants, and other non-human entities (e.g. Hart 1955, 181), since they do not have autonomy. However, when guardians or other representatives exercise RoN on behalf of natural entities, this may in some way embody an exercise of autonomy as understood by the will theory.

Personhood and Agency

RoN is conceptually related to the issue of legal personhood and agency. Let us begin with personhood. Ngaire Naffine, an Australian law professor, writes that

> Every time a right is recognized or denied, legal personality is implicitly brought into issue. For the creation of a legal right, and its corresponding duty, necessarily means that the two parties to this legal relation are constituted as persons. They are then capable of acting in law.
>
> (Naffine 2008, 885)

In his 1972 article, Stone pointed out that historically and as a matter of fact, legal personhood has been granted to a range of entities that lack personhood in a conventional philosophical sense, that is, having sophisticated mental properties of a competent human adult. Examples include collective entities like corporations, universities, municipalities, and states, and individual entities that lack legal competence like infants and adults with significant intellectual disabilities. Collective entities are deemed legal persons whose rights, duties, and responsibilities are not reducible to natural persons or human individuals. The idea is that legal personhood, which provides the basis for ascribing legal rights, can be independent of the philosophical concept of personhood. Difficulties with granting legal personhood to nature, or natural entities, provides an additional reason for Baard's rejection of RoN, while Rochford touches on this issue, and much like Stone, finds little problem with granting legal personhood to natural entities, such as a river.

A related issue involves the idea that with rights comes responsibility. It has sometimes been argued that only those capable of bearing responsibilities can hold rights. This implies that right-holders must be agents, who can act intentionally and bear responsibilities, and whose actions are evaluated in the light of valid moral and legal norms.[6] So, a possible way to distinguish the concept of an agent from the concept of a legal person is the idea that agency depends on the intrinsic qualities of an individual, whereas the concept of a person (in law) is a fully relational term. Thus, to understand the concept of agency, one has to assess whether an individual or a collective[7] meets the criteria of an active and deliberative entity that is capable of acting according to norms. If one believes that infants, the intellectually disabled, animals, etc. can have rights, then one rejects the idea that right-holders are restricted to those who are agents. Rochford briefly touches on this idea in the case of RoN, asking whether if nature or natural entities are granted rights, they should also have responsibilities. For example, if a river is granted rights, does the river bear responsibility if it happens to flood and cause damage to the property of others? If a human agent must act on behalf of the RoN, presumably this person could also act to meet any responsibilities that the right-holder would bear, which raises our next issue.

Since nature itself does not have agency and is incapable of exercising rights, the question arises as to *who* can exercise the RoN. In some countries that have adopted RoN, such as Ecuador, everyone is entitled to exercise these rights (e.g. bring legal action on behalf of the natural entity) and encouraged to do so. In contrast, other systems confine the power to exercise these rights to certain people or representatives. In New Zealand and Australia, certain bodies or committees have been appointed to oversee and exercise RoN. Tănăsescu discusses the case of New Zealand, while Rochford discusses the case of Australia. Sajeva discusses the case of biocultural rights in Colombia, which have a dual basis as both (indigenous) human rights and RoN. These rights can be exercised by the indigenous groups to whom they are granted. Other arrangements may also be possible. For example, Stone proposed that courts or other authorities could appoint representatives to exercise these rights, which would most likely involve the appointment of an attorney to act on behalf of the right-holder. See Oksanen's and Kumpula's discussion of Stone's proposal.

Composition of Right-Holders

Here we have followed Stone in adopting the object/entity approach to the entities that hold RoN. Alternatively, or in addition, this could be approached in terms of natural processes and whether such processes should have rights—for example, whether natural selection and evolution have a right to continue in plants and animals or whether the great wildebeest migration on the West-African savannah has a right to take place without human interference. In Luuppala's chapter on the right to restoration, the element of process comes up when restoration is understood in terms of the recovery process.

More generally, a key question concerns the composition of the right-holders: what types of entities are right-holders in the case of RoN? The title of Stone's article, "Should Trees Have Standing?" seems to raise the question of whether individual trees can have rights. The RoN that have been adopted and implemented in actual legal systems do not grant rights to entities as small as individual trees (despite the fact that the use of individual trees can be regulated by law and local customs); rather these rights have been granted to objects such as rivers, forests, or nature as a whole. As mentioned previously, this approach may come closer to the holistic view in environmental ethics, which suggests ecosystems or the biosphere as a whole are the appropriate right-holders. In the case of RoN, identifying and delineating right-holders can be a particularly challenging and politically contentious issue. Corrigan attempts to provide a rough sketch as to how we can divide up nature and identify particular right-holders. Donoso rejects the idea that we can assign rights to individuated parts of nature, on the grounds that nature is constituted by a non-individualistic biotic community. Gutmann discusses whether rights are compatible with the Andean indigenous concept of *Pachamama*, which includes all of nature. Other authors examine the legal RoN that have been granted to particular rivers, national park areas, and other natural entities.

The identification of particular right-holders raises a related issue, which concerns whether RoN are cosmopolitan in nature (like human rights)—that is, universal rights held by natural entities everywhere in the world—or alternatively, are domestic rights that may be recognized only within particular legal systems or held only by particular natural entities. This latter possibility should be divided into two issues: first, are these rights merely domestic norms, which may be recognized within a particular country, locality, or jurisdiction, and (legitimately) not recognized elsewhere?[8] Second, can these rights belong to only a particular natural entity, such as a particular river that may be deemed especially important for one reason or another (e.g. traditionally significant for a certain indigenous group), or do all natural entities of this type (e.g. all rivers) deserve rights? Indigenous philosophies, which have inspired some RoN, can differ on this issue. As Whyte points out, unlike conservationists who focus on the preservation of all species, some indigenous peoples focus on the particular species or natural entities that have ecological, economic, or cultural importance for their lives and communities (Whyte 2017). This sort of indigenous view suggests what we have called a "domestic" approach to RoN, which might recognize rights within a particular jurisdiction or for particular natural entities, but not others. Examples of this approach may be found in the case of the White Earth Band of Ojibwe, located in northwestern Minnesota, who in 2018 adopted rights for wild rice (or Manoomin), a plant species that provides a central source of food and is deeply rooted in their tradition, and the case of New Zealand granting rights to two rivers, a national park area, and a mountain which have particular significance for the Maori peoples, as part of a treaty settlement. However, other indigenous philosophies may suggest what we have called the "cosmopolitan" approach to RoN. For example, in Ecuador and Bolivia RoN have been inspired by the indigenous concept of *Pachamama* (Mother Earth), which views the whole of nature as sacred. This approach suggests that nature in general should have rights, and led Bolivia to draft and propose the Universal Declaration of the Rights of Mother Earth in 2010.

It is important to recognize that environmental problems do not observe national or jurisdictional boundaries. As Rochford points out, under the current regime there is almost no legal recourse for trans-national environmental harms. Thus, if RoN are to protect right-holders against all types of environmental threats or harms, the domestic rights approach will not be sufficient. For RoN to function in a manner equivalent to human rights, adoption of international legal norms is required, in addition to establishing international RoN tribunals or other enforcement mechanisms. Some authors deal with this issue at a general level. For example, Corrigan, Luuppala, and Donoso attempt to sketch the outlines of a cosmopolitan account of RoN. Other authors discuss the RoN that have been adopted and developed within particular legal frameworks, implicitly dealing with RoN as domestic legal norms.

Moral and Legal Rights

Let us return to the distinction between moral and legal rights. There can be a relation between these two types of rights, but this is not necessarily the case. The relation between these two normative domains, law and morality, and how they relate to each other depends on larger theories in moral and legal philosophy. If moral RoN are justified, this likely offers a reason in favor of recognizing and implementing legal RoN. However, it will not provide a definitive reason for adopting and implementing legal RoN, because legal rights involve numerous practical considerations that moral rights do not. These practical considerations can include issues such as whether the rights are justiciable, the costs of implementation, their effectiveness as policy instruments, and so forth. In addition, there is a general principle that not all moral norms should be instituted as legal norms since it would be inappropriate or unfeasible to legally codify some moral norms. Thus, even if moral RoN are justified, further justification will be needed to show that corresponding legal RoN should be adopted and implemented. For example, while people may have a general moral right that promises made to them be kept, it would not be appropriate to make all promises legally enforceable. While animals may have a moral right not to be eaten, it may be unfeasible to implement this right or create a universal legal duty to follow a vegan diet. Similarly, if plants have a moral right not to be eaten, it would certainly be futile to attempt to constrain herbivores' choices.

Looking at the other side, there may be reasons to adopt legal RoN, even if it is not possible to justify moral RoN. For example, we may be unable to provide a philosophical justification for moral RoN, but there could nevertheless be practical reasons for adopting and implementing legal RoN. Some authors, such as Luuppala, focus on moral RoN and their justification. Many of Baard's and Donoso's challenges to RoN seem to apply to both moral and legal rights, while others apply to legal rights in particular. The other authors primarily discuss legal RoN.

Conflicts of Rights and Other Norms

Whether we are considering moral or legal RoN, they can come into conflict or tension with other norms. This raises the question of the normative weight of RoN. In Stone's original article, he emphasizes that RoN will not preclude us from cutting down an individual tree. This implies that humans can permissibly act upon nature, so either RoN do not apply to all parts of nature, or RoN are sometimes defeated by other norms or values. The issue of normative weight concerns the latter possibility and involves the relative importance of RoN in relation to other norms. Any set of rights will encounter conflicts of norms, whether among the rights themselves or between the rights and other norms. These conflicts must be resolved either by defining the rights in a way that avoids any conflicts or by assigning weights that determine which norm takes precedence over another.

A key area of conflict will involve the inevitable tensions between human rights and RoN. However, just as with human rights, there could also be intra-rights conflicts within the RoN framework itself. For example, suppose a river threatens to flood a neighboring landscape. If both of these entities have rights, which entity's right should prevail? As this example illustrates, the issue of normative weight involves not merely determining the relative weight or importance of RoN in relation to other types of norms (e.g. human rights), but also determining the relative weight or importance among RoN themselves.[9] Some critics of RoN have seen these conflicts between rights as highly problematic. Bryan Norton argued that "if one assigns rights to individual mountains, there seems to be no basis for deciding which mountain is to be sacrificed for a four-lane highway through the range …." (1982, 35). A natural response might be that no highway should be built if building it violates some entity's right. This shows the potential of the RoN framework to offer an alternative to developmentalist ideology, however, one can ask whether the cost would be too great.

RoN will not merely conflict with other rights, but may also have compatibility with, or even provide support to, other rights. Once again, this can be true both with regard to other types of rights (e.g. human rights) and also among RoN themselves. Support between rights can occur when a certain right helps to realize or secure the enjoyment of another right. This support can be of a causal, epistemic, morally legitimating, or perhaps some other nature. Corrigan attempts to sketch an argument that demonstrates a supporting relation between RoN and human rights, where RoN help to secure the necessary conditions for the enjoyment of certain human rights. Donoso interprets RoN, or more specifically a right to a healthy biotic community, as a group right that is derived from the aggregate interests of non-human animals. One can debate whether Donoso's proposal actually refers to RoN, since the right-holder is non-human animals as a group, rather than some natural entity or object. Within RoN themselves, we may also find examples of how securing the rights of some natural entity (e.g. a wilderness area) helps to secure the rights of another natural entity (e.g. a river), so that there is a supporting relation among RoN.

Content of the Rights

In order to determine how RoN may conflict with or support other norms, the content of these rights and corresponding obligations for duty-bearers must be determined. It is common to divide the obligations corresponding to human rights into duties to respect, protect, and fulfill (and sometimes to promote) these rights. A similar set of duties may be used to understand obligations relating to RoN. Precisely which duties correspond to the RoN will depend on the content of these rights and on the nature of right-holders, which might vary from sentient animals[10] to plants and—in the eyes of modern science—to non-sentient and inanimate sites like rock formations and rivers. The content of the right refers to the entitlements that it grants to the right-holder. On some accounts, RoN may simply entitle a natural entity not to be damaged, degraded, or interfered with. In this case, RoN will entail a duty of respect, which involves a negative obligation to refrain from damaging, degrading, or interfering with the right-holder. Typically, rights will also entail a duty for some agent (e.g. government) to protect them. Duties of protection involve a positive obligation to ensure that others are complying with the duty to refrain from damaging, degrading, or interfering with the right-holder. This sort of entitlement, and corresponding duties, is perhaps a minimalist conception of RoN.

Other accounts of RoN could be more demanding and might entitle the right-holder to restoration. Here we should distinguish two types of restoration. The first type is compensatory restoration. This could arise from the previously mentioned right against damage, degradation, or interference. If someone violates the right, then the perpetrator may have a duty to restore the right-holder on compensatory grounds. However, the second type of restoration would be equivalent to a duty to fulfill the right. For example, suppose a right-holder is damaged through an act of nature (e.g. a windstorm, flood, etc.). In this case, there is no agent responsible for violating the duty to respect the right. Rather, the right-holder has been damaged or degraded through a natural event.[11] A more robust account of RoN could entitle the right-holder to restoration even in this type of case. Here the duty of restoration would be a positive obligation to fulfill the entitlement to be restored. For example, a government might have an obligation to restore a right-holder that has been damaged by fire, an invasive species, or some other cause. Luuppala develops an account of the right to restoration, while Sajeva discusses positive obligations to take actions that protect nature.

Purpose of the Rights

A final issue concerns the purpose of RoN, which can relate to questions about the function and/or justification of these rights. Given the different social and political contexts in which (legal) RoN have been adopted and implemented, we are unlikely to find one common function of RoN across all of these cases. However, even within a given social or political context, there may not be one agreed-upon function of these rights. For example, consider the case of New Zealand. The government of New Zealand may have agreed to grant

RoN to several natural entities as a means of settling long-standing disputes with the indigenous Maori people. From this perspective, RoN may function as a means of treaty settlement. By contrast, the Maori people may understand these same rights as a means of facilitating the moral respect and protection that is due to natural entities they hold to be sacred. In this case, different agents or groups who were party to the agreement understand the rights as having different functions. Tănăsescu discusses the case of RoN in New Zealand and the potentially political nature of these rights.

Angstadt and Hourdequin examine competing views about the function of RoN, and whether these rights serve as merely a pragmatic tool for realizing certain existing environmental aims or function instead as a paradigm shift in political and legal approaches to the natural environment. Corrigan's argument points to the role of RoN in protecting biodiversity, which can be seen as a necessary element for the enjoyment of certain human rights. Donoso understands existing RoN to serve the function of protecting the stability and integrity of the biotic community from harm.

Structure of This Book

The book at hand consists of ten chapters. We begin with Angstadt's and Hourdequin's systematic review of discussions about RoN in social science and law. In the next two chapters, Gutmann and Rochford consider the RoN adopted in Ecuador and Australia, respectively. This is followed by Tănăsescu's argument that RoN are essentially political rights. Next, Sajeva and Corrigan examine RoN in relation to human rights. Sajeva discusses biocultural rights, which offer a hybrid between (indigenous) human rights and RoN, while Corrigan considers the potential for a supporting relation between RoN and human rights and how this might be developed to offer a justification for RoN. Luuppala focuses on a particular RoN, the right to restoration, and develops an account of this right within the context of debates about the ethics of environmental restoration. Next, Donoso offers some objections to RoN as commonly understood, and instead offers an alternative proposal for "rights of the biotic community," which is a group right held by non-human animals. In the following chapter, Baard questions RoN in general, by raising an array of different challenges to the very idea that nature can have rights. The book concludes with a chapter by Oksanen and Kumpula, which takes a closer look at Stone's classic article from 1972 that began the modern, legally sophisticated discussion of RoN.

Notes

1 Halme-Tuomisaari & Slotte 2015. Whether this Eurocentric historiography of (human) rights is correct or not, we leave for others to discuss; see e.g. Slotte & Halme-Tuomisaari 2015.

2 In some cases, indigenous philosophies include the animistic or pantheistic views that nature or natural entities are living beings.

3 In a wider debate, some approaches to RoN emphasize that "The Universe is the primary law-giver, not human legal systems" (Cullinan 2011, 17); whereas Stone's position has been understood as conventionalist, in which the legal rights of nature do not rest on any pre-existing natural rights (Lehmann 1981, 133–36).
4 There are anthropocentric ethical theories that do not explicitly recognize rights or treat them as having secondary value or being of a derivative nature. For example, a classic defense of animal rights by Henry S. Salt begins with recognizing the conditionality of claims about right-holders: "Have the lower animals 'rights?' Undoubtedly—if men have" (1980, 1).
5 For example, Stone makes the following claim: "The lawn tells me that it wants water by a certain dryness of the blades and soil—immediately obvious to the touch—the appearance of bald spots, yellowing, and a lack of springiness after being walked on" (Stone 1972, 471).
6 In environmental philosophy, there have been discussions about how the concept of agent (and person) should be understood. The mainstream position is that of Tom Regan (1988, 151–52) and Paul W. Taylor (1986, 14–24), for whom moral agents have sophisticated psychological abilities, making it meaningful to assess their dispositions and behaviors; thus "normal adult human beings" are moral agents, as Regan puts it. The rival positions vary from Mark Rowlands' (2012) recognition of animals' moral tendencies to Bruno Latour's (e.g. Latour 2014) ecumenical, or agency-without-responsibility, conception of agency in nature.
7 When it comes to collective entities, the concept of a legal person is a fully individuated entity whereas the concept of a collective agent can be used less tightly, varying from formally recognized legal persons to loosely connected individuals with shared intentions and legally unrecognized collectives or "collectivities" (see e.g. Cripps 2013).
8 Human rights are held to be universally justified norms. A particular legal system may not recognize human rights, but that is thought to be a failure and an illegitimate aspect of that legal system.
9 This latter issue is unlikely to arise unless RoN become much more widespread and extensive than they are at present.
10 It is not clear whether the idea of animal rights falls under the label "rights of nature." The issue is complicated, especially the question as to whether we should expand the rights of animals to include rights to property or habitat (cf. Hadley 2015).
11 Anthropogenic global warming complicates this distinction, since human agents are ultimately responsible for the "natural" events that may cause damage.

References

Cripps, E. (2013) *Climate Change and the Moral Agent. Individual Duties in an Interdependent World*. Oxford University Press, Oxford.

Cullinan, C. (2011) "A History of Wild Law" in Burdon, P. ed, *Exploring Wild Law: The Philosophy of Earth Jurisprudence*. Wakefield Press, Kent Town, SA, 17–24.

Feinberg, J. (1974) "The Rights of Animals and Unborn Generations" in Blackstone, W.T. ed, *Philosophy and Environmental Crisis*. University of Georgia Press, Athens, GA, 43–68.

Hadley, J. (2015) *Animal Property Rights: A Theory of Habitat Rights for Wild Animals*. Lexington Book, Lanham, MD.

Halme-Tuomisaari, M. and Slotte, P. (2015) "Revisiting the Origins of Human Rights: Introduction" in Slotte, P. and Halme-Tuomisaari, M. eds, *Revisiting the Origins of Human Rights*. Cambridge University Press, Cambridge, 1–36.

Hart, H.L.A. (1955) "Are There Any Natural Rights?" *The Philosophical Review*, 64, 175–191.

Jones, P. (2016) "Group Rights" in Zalta, E.N. ed, *Stanford Encyclopedia of Philosophy* (Summer 2016 Edition), https://plato.stanford.edu/archives/sum2016/entries/rights-group/

La Follette, C. and Maser, C. eds. (2020) *Sustainability and the Rights of Nature in Practice.* CRC Press, Boca Raton, FL.

Latour, B. (2014) "Agency at the Time of the Anthropocene" *New Literary History*, 45, 1–18.

Lehmann, S. (1981) "Do Wildernesses Have Rights?" *Environmental Ethics*, 3, 129–46.

Leopold, A. (1989) *A Sand County Almanac.* Oxford University Press, New York (orig. publ. 1949).

Muir, J. (1916) *A Thousand-Mile Walk to the Gulf.* Houghton & Mifflin, Boston, MA.

Naffine, N. (2008) "Person" in Cane, P. and Conaghan, J. eds, *The New Oxford Companion to Law.* Oxford University Press, Oxford, 885–886.

Nash, R. (1989) *The Rights of Nature A History of Environmental Ethics.* University of Wisconsin Press, Madison, WI.

Nobel, J. (2017) "The Rights of Nature Movement Goes on Trial" *Rolling Stone.* https://www.rollingstone.com/politics/politics-news/how-a-small-town-is-standing-up-to-fracking-117307/

Nobel, J. (2020) "Nature Scores a Big Win against Fracking in a Small Pennsylvania Town" *Rolling Stone.* https://www.rollingstone.com/politics/politics-news/rights-of-nature-beats-fracking-in-small-pennsylvania-town-976159/

Norton, B.G. (1982) "Environmental Ethics and Nonhuman Rights" *Environmental Ethics*, 4, 17–36.

Regan, T. (1988) *The Case for Animal Rights.* Routledge, London (orig. publ. 1983).

Rowlands, M. (2012) *Can Animals Be Moral?* Oxford University Press, Oxford.

Salt, H.S. (1980) *Animals' Rights.* Centaur Publishing, London (orig. publ. 1892).

Slotte, P. and Halme-Tuomisaari, M. eds. (2015) *Revisiting the Origins of Human Rights.* Cambridge University Press, Cambridge.

Stone, C.D. (1972) "Should Trees Have Standing?: Towards Legal Rights for Natural Objects" *Southern California Law Review*, 45, 450–501.

Stone, C.D. (2012) "Response to Commentators" *Journal of Human Rights and the Environment*, 3, 100–120.

Taylor, P.W. (1986) *Respect for Nature. A Theory of Environmental Ethics.* Princeton University Press, Princeton, NJ.

WCED (World Commission on Environment and Development) (1987) *Our Common Future.* Oxford University Press, Oxford.

Whyte, K.P. (2017) "Our Ancestors' 'Dystopia Now': Indigenous Conservation and the Anthropocene" in Heise, U.K., Christensen, J. and Niemann, M. eds, *The Routledge Companion to Environmental Humanities.* Routledge, London, 206–215.

2 Taking Stock of the Rights of Nature

J. Michael Angstadt and Marion Hourdequin

Introduction

The origins of the "rights of nature" ("RoN") discourse are often traced to legal scholar Christopher Stone's influential 1972 article, "Should Trees Have Standing?" Stone's intervention was provoked by a legal case, *Sierra Club v. Morton*, in which the Sierra Club sued the U.S. federal government to stop a ski resort development in a national forest at the edge of California's Sequoia National Park. The Sierra Club's efforts were initially rebuffed by the courts due to lack of legal standing: the club had failed to show that the organization or its members would be harmed by the development. While the Sierra Club gathered testimony from its members to demonstrate standing, Stone penned an article arguing that the *forest itself* should be granted standing: courts should not only consider injury from environmental damage in terms of effects on human beings; they should consider harms to and endangerment of natural objects themselves.

Stone's argument attracted the attention of the court, and Judge William O. Douglas cited it in a dissenting opinion, giving some judicial credibility to Stone's proposal. However, the idea—though widely cited in the scholarly literature and taught in environmental ethics and environmental law classes for decades—gained relatively little traction in practice until the turn of the 21st century. Over the last 15 years, however, on-the-ground interest in the rights of nature has experienced a resurgence, with Bolivia, Colombia, Ecuador, India, Mexico, New Zealand, the U.S., and other jurisdictions establishing versions of these rights through the law (Kauffman & Sheehan 2019, see also https://celdf.org/advancing-community-rights/rights-of-nature/rights-nature-timeline/). Although academic research analyzing these developments has begun to emerge, the literature is fragmented within and across disciplines, including anthropology, communication, environmental studies, indigenous studies, law, political science, policy studies, and sociology. Interestingly, although many researchers describe RoN initiatives as representing a potentially significant philosophical shift and although the discussion of animal rights is flourishing, recent philosophical research on this topic has been limited (but see Tănăsescu 2014, 2015; Knauß 2018; conceptual and philosophical issues are also discussed in many of the legal articles on the rights of nature). Much of the literature emphasizes descriptive case studies (how were RoN provisions written into the Ecuadorian constitution? How do the RoN provisions in New Zealand, Colombia, and India compare?), and there has been relatively little synthesis of the academic literature across disciplines.

This chapter seeks to identify central themes, common principles, and key distinctions in existing rights of nature discourse, focusing on literature in law and the social sciences. We pursue this effort through a review of existing literature. Given the diffuse nature of this scholarship, we utilized academic databases to develop a descriptive, qualitative account of the state of the literature. While this approach primarily surveys English-language publications that appear in scholarly and legal journals, we believe that our effort enables us to examine three questions:

1) to what extent do legal and social science approaches envision the RoN approach as a paradigm shift, a pragmatic tool, or both?,
2) what are the central institutional and practical concerns that have emerged in relation to the RoN (e.g. "flooding the courts," representation, relief, conflicting rights)?, and
3) how have specific communities and diverse cultural, spiritual, and philosophical perspectives shaped rights of nature discourses, and to what degree does the existing literature present and address compatibilities and tensions between these perspectives and the discourse of rights?

Ultimately, this chapter's evaluation of the diversity and implications of existing scholarship complements other efforts within this volume to generate a clearer picture of how RoN discourse has been operationalized (e.g. Tănăsescu) and of associated implications in practice.

The Significance of Rights of Nature Movements: Paradigm Shift, Pragmatic Tool, or Both?

Rights of nature movements and proposals have been examined in diverse disciplines, including philosophy, law, and the social sciences. Together, these various accounts suggest an overarching question: how should RoN developments be viewed? To some, the movement may most accurately be characterized as an opportunity to fundamentally re-envision the balance of interests between humans and nonhuman nature—a fundamental ontological shift that is reflected by broad changes to societal and legal structures. To others, the movement might better be characterized as another pragmatic or strategic tool that can advance environmental protection without upending the dominant socio-legal framework—a way to highlight natural interests within legal systems, or a novel approach to advance a particular environmental lawsuit, without reshaping society. Still others may perceive the movement as enshrining both paradigmatic and pragmatic elements—a procedural approach that, in time and with broader adoption, can fundamentally reorder legal or societal understandings of human–nature relations. Many existing scholarly accounts offer clues regarding those authors' perceptions of the implications of nascent RoN movements.

Because legal scholars have generated much of the existing RoN literature, the publications that we reviewed may reflect legal foci and disciplinary conventions. Even still, however, there is considerable variation among scholarly accounts, and existing publications interpret rights of nature implications in three main ways. First, many authors emphasize the paradigm-changing potential of the RoN approach. Second, some researchers suggest that RoN movements may hold broad implications for various environmental issues, even if they do not yield a paradigm shift. Third, some pieces offer a contrasting perspective and suggest that, for multiple reasons, RoN movements situated within dominant societal and legal frameworks are unlikely to yield paradigmatic change.

First, as noted above, many existing pieces emphasize, either implicitly or explicitly, the paradigmatic potential of RoN approaches. Collectively, they emphasize the potential for RoN to support reimagined social and legal relationships linking humans and nature. Several pieces highlight this view by exploring the application and implications of RoN approaches within specific issue regimes, with riverine systems receiving particular focus. There, scholars utilize existing cases to note the expanding adoption of RoN approaches and underscore their paradigm-shifting potential. For instance, Clark et al. (2019) note the "profound bond" between rivers and life, suggesting river systems as an ideal starting point for an ontological shift in approaches to the human–nature relationship (791). Parenteau (2019) offers a similar assessment by noting that early RoN efforts have yielded fundamental shifts in some countries' river management approaches, even as they have fallen short in the United States (185–187).

Some pieces complement these regime-specific accounts by suggesting that a rights of nature approach could reshape entire legal disciplines. For instance, Taylor (1998) suggests that international law could more broadly embrace rights of nature alongside human rights and that doing so would support a widespread evolution from anthropocentrism to ecocentrism. Those examining the systems-level implications of an RoN approach similarly emphasize the movement's broad potential. For example, Borrás (2016) notes the opportunity for biocentric approaches to raise holistic environmental awareness and consciousness; elsewhere, Athens (2018) echoes and extends many of Stone's (1972) early contentions, analogizing the emancipatory potential of an RoN approach to the change realized amidst the women's suffrage movement. Collectively, these scholars appear to acknowledge the challenges inherent in institutionalizing RoN (e.g. White 2018, 165), but they also emphasize the potential for systemic change that it offers.

While this first group of accounts emphasizes how RoN movements could yield paradigmatic change, a second body of literature suggests that even limited applications of RoN could hold important environmental implications. For instance, Babcock (2016) identifies focused legal arguments and approaches that could permit rights of nature claims to enjoy greater success in the American legal system. However, she argues that these focused, strategic operationalizations of rights of nature have important implications, and could ultimately reflect "the only way to protect our disappearing natural resources," given challenges including "the intransigence of Congress, and the over-crowded agenda of the Executive Branch" (1). Likewise, assessments of subnational rights of nature movements emphasize that even focused, domestic efforts can hold transnational environmental implications (e.g. Valladares & Boelens 2017, 1031).

While most accounts emphasize the paradigmatic potential of the RoN movement, a third body of existing scholarship offers a more tempered assessment and suggests that RoN claims may instead serve initially as a more limited, pragmatic tool of environmental lawyers. These accounts note how legal and societal structures may limit the RoN movement. For example, scholars including Garver (2019) seem to recognize the challenges associated with operationalizing a revolutionary ideal while constrained by existing legal landscapes. As he notes, "resolving conflicts between rights of nature and human rights, including private property rights, requires criteria that inevitably will reflect a hierarchy of normative principles and values" (Garver 2019, 432).

Accordingly, many existing publications appear to acknowledge that early manifestations of the RoN movement might be more limited than wholesale reinventions of societal and legal systems. These pieces extend Stone's early arguments, which emphasized that granting rights to nature could represent a less revolutionary legal evolution than it might seem. As Stone (1972) noted,

> Throughout legal history, each successive extension of rights to some new entity has been, heretofore, a bit unthinkable. We are inclined to suppose the rightlessness of rightless 'things' to be a decree of Nature, not a legal convention acting in support of some status quo.
>
> (453)

Nevertheless, Stone emphasized that incremental evolution can yield significant change. He suggested that by distinguishing "legal-operational" considerations surrounding RoN movements from the "socio-psychic" aspects, advocates could first resolve procedural objections and only later undertake a broader reconsideration of the hierarchy between human interests and those of "natural objects" (458 et seq.).

Stone's early contention that an incremental RoN approach could support much broader changes in environmental consciousness now appears in multiple contemporary pieces. For example, as Houck (2018) argues,

> Properly viewed, rights of nature need not be a separate regulatory system, raising obvious difficulties with redundancy and conflicts. It need not be

> a system at all, but rather a pulse-check in the nature of due process that ensures decisions from line agencies also meet standards fundamental to the earth as a whole.
>
> (41–42)

In Houck's conception, this procedural step provides an opportunity to infuse emotion and "a powerful link to the human heart" into decision-making (2018, 50), offering a check to anthropocentrism, all without supplanting dominant frameworks. Others offer similar assessments. Gordon (2018) underscores that corporate personhood is a widely accepted legal fiction which, by its existence, does not diminish the personhood accorded to corporeal beings. Moreover, she underscores that defining legal personhood is "not binary; it is not a yes-or-no proposition," and she notes that granting corporate personhood is only a first step in determining "how much that legal, practical, rhetorical entity… should be allowed to claim the rights of other shades of personhood" (Gordon 2018, 50). To these authors, rights of nature can be introduced to existing legal frameworks without upending dominant legal paradigms.

The preceding paragraphs demonstrate that existing literature offers varying assessments of the paradigmatic or pragmatic potential of RoN movements. A final body of literature cautions that existing societal and legal frameworks may prevent a fundamental shift in human–nature relations, even if one is intended. For example, Garver (2019) suggests that seeking to grant rights to nature "in a globalized world still operating according to a growth-insistent narrative and worldview will lead to their erosion and dilution" (432). Additionally, at least one contemporary account provides evidence of active resistance to RoN efforts. In a detailed account of environmental trusteeship efforts in New Zealand, Prior (2016) offers multiple indicia that the government sought to limit the revolutionary potential of the oft-cited Whanganui River personhood case. Prior highlights the many ways that the Crown government incorporated indigenous Māori worldviews when adjudicating Whanganui River treaty settlements, but also emphasizes the ongoing resonance of economic imperatives. As she notes, "The Crown was careful to retain ownership of minerals (and the right to mine them)" (2016, 46–47). Moreover, she identifies resistance to RoN by governmental officials, including New Zealand's Attorney General, who noted that "the legal personality concept ought not to travel the country, and should not be replicated across other environmental areas of New Zealand" (Prior 2016, 47 [see note 214]).

In sum, much of the existing literature suggests a broad potential for rights of nature movements to fundamentally shift human–nature relationships and socio-legal frameworks. However, the scholarship does so in a nuanced fashion, noting both its paradigmatic promise and potential limitations.

Institutional and Practical Considerations

While the preceding section demonstrates that many scholars support the development of the RoN concept, numerous accounts have also identified potential institutional and practical challenges. While many of these reflect tension between RoN objectives and the dominant, deeply anthropocentric legal framework, their foci largely reflect one of three broad themes: considerations of "access," considerations of "implementation," and considerations of "outcome."

Access

Among existing research, many existing accounts raise questions of access to institutions that can adjudicate and enforce rights of nature. Legal accounts have primarily explored this theme by evaluating how RoN claims might best be framed to gain access to courts. Many of these procedural issues shape the broader field of environmental law. However, they are particularly resonant in this context, since many RoN claims employ novel legal arguments that, if successful, could set an expansive legal precedent and upend settled practice. While there are numerous potential challenges facing RoN claimants who seek access to courts, existing accounts emphasize questions surrounding jurisdiction, the definition of legal personhood, and how best to characterize the parties to an RoN claim.

First, an RoN claim can only succeed when a court clearly possesses the authority to hear a dispute. However, a court's jurisdiction is not guaranteed; in most instances, it must be demonstrated by a party to the dispute (see *Black's Law Dictionary*). Among the many dimensions of jurisdiction, those seeking to bring a dispute forward must establish that they have the authority to do so and that a specified court is empowered to hear those claims. In the context of RoN, neither of these jurisdictional bases are straightforward or guaranteed, since claims a) generally seek to name nature itself, rather than a human plaintiff, as the injured party, and b) often present holistic, rather than focused, claims of injury.

In recognition of these very real procedural hurdles, scholars have explored various potential mechanisms for establishing jurisdiction. In some existing cases, the forums that have claimed jurisdiction may be perceived as less legitimate; for example, the International Rights of Nature Tribunal hears relevant disputes but, as a peoples' tribunal, cannot issue legally binding decisions (Maloney 2016). Elsewhere, researchers have explored how RoN claims might be successfully brought in more formal governmental forums. For example, Colón-Ríos (2014) explores how cases of serious environmental harm in Ecuador could be addressed by permitting claims under universal jurisdiction—an arrangement that would permit any citizen to bring suits on behalf of nature.

Alongside jurisdictional considerations, researchers have highlighted the many practical considerations that would accompany a move to expand legal personhood to include nature. Many authors, including Stone (1972), emphasize that, through this process, nature would join a suite of other non-human interests already granted legal personhood. For example, corporations in the

United States enjoy an expansive suite of legal rights—"speech, religion, freedom from government searches, and unlimited campaign contributions"—all based upon their status as legal persons (Houck 2018, 26–27). Relatedly, Gordon (2017) explores how the concept of legal personhood could be made meaningful in the context of natural objects and ecosystems. She argues that, just as legal personhood is interpreted situationally and flexibly in disputes involving corporations, courts might do the same for disputes involving nature: legal personhood can be conceived as a continuum, with an entity receiving some rights and not others (Gordon 2017).

Alongside efforts to identify bases for justifying an extension of legal rights to nature, more practice-oriented pieces have explored how, specifically, personhood might be demonstrated within existing legal systems. Much of this scholarship has originated in the United States, where recent lawsuits, including an unsuccessful effort to extend RoN protections to the Colorado River system, have enjoyed mixed outcomes. At least two researchers have explored how RoN claims can better satisfy the legal "standing" requirements under current United States law; these include the burden of demonstrating that an actual or imminent injury will result if a court does not provide relief. Many concerns motivate the strict standing requirements of current U.S. law, but in an RoN context, these include 1) fear that courts could be overwhelmed by the many new claims that result from natural entities' newfound legal standing and 2) the potential for courts to pass judgment on policy questions more appropriately determined by other governmental branches (Babcock 2016, 45–48). In response, Babcock (2016) suggests that these concerns could be mitigated by applying certain stringency criteria, such as only permitting cases concerning "irreplaceable" ecosystems. Elsewhere, Miller (2019) argues that, despite recent setbacks, RoN claims are not fundamentally incompatible with existing U.S. standing requirements. Indeed, Miller (2019) suggests that if legal arguments in the 2017 *Colorado River Ecosystem* case had emphasized the specific factual elements required to prove standing, rather than deeper normative concerns, the case might have been decided in favor of the river as plaintiff (368–373).

In addition to researchers emphasizing questions of jurisdiction and legal personhood for RoN, a third set of publications considers how to identify and define the guardians who would, or should, bring claims to court on behalf of natural objects and ecosystems. As Prior (2016) notes, a move toward Earth trusteeship provides an opportunity to help states codify moral obligations to nature (49). However, a range of entities could potentially claim to serve as guardians or trustees for nature, raising questions of definition. For example, requiring guardians to hold certain forms of expertise could limit representation, while broadly permitting citizens to bring claims through a public trust approach could expand representation (e.g. Chapron, Epstein, & López-Bao 2019, 1393). Shelton (2015) acknowledges the challenges inherent in demarcating guardians and draws upon Ecuador's RoN experiences to note that enforcement or guardianship efforts bearing governmental approval have seemed to enjoy the greatest success (at para 32). Ultimately, while guardianship considerations will inevitably shape RoN claims, others note that these challenges are not unique to environmental issues and are resolved in other domains "every day" (see e.g. Houck 2018, 27).

Implementation

Securing access to court represents an initial, not final, challenge. Once inside the courtroom, further questions emerge regarding how to implement an RoN approach. For example, Shelton (2015) notes that a successful RoN claim would have to meet standards that apply in other legal domains, including demonstration of causation and satisfaction of a certain burden of proof (at para 29). Because rights of nature claims are expansive and invoke other considerations and legal doctrines, commentators have emphasized the challenges inherent in clarifying this complex milieu. For instance, researchers have noted that depending upon how they are framed, rights of nature obligations could either coexist or conflict with existing mineral and water rights regimes (Prior 2016; Healy 2019), which have historically emphasized privatization and human ownership of natural resources.

Similarly, researchers note that broader rights of nature protections within dominant legal systems could conflict with existing legal duties. Examples include the "duty to consult," which is enshrined in Canadian law (e.g. Lynes 2019; with whom would the government consult before undertaking relevant projects if natural objects were viewed as legal persons?), and the principle of "prior informed consent" (e.g. Humphreys 2015; how could actors secure consent from natural objects?). Finally, at an even broader level, researchers have emphasized challenges that can result as RoN interacts with other legal doctrines. For example, although RoN approaches can benefit from the existence of complementary social movements and legal frameworks, they can also be rendered vulnerable if those movements are themselves threatened. Borrás (2016) highlights this potential challenge by examining Ecuador. There, an executive decree permitting governmental oversight of non-governmental organizations was leveraged to dissolve human rights organizations that were also actively involved in promoting RoN (see Borràs 2016, 137). Likewise, researchers emphasize that cases concerning RoN will frequently require justices to balance and rank human and non-human interests (e.g. Chapron, Epstein, & López-Bao 2019, 1393). Collectively, these pieces remind us that the implementation of RoN will be intricately linked with other legal interests and challenges.

Outcome

Third, researchers have accompanied considerations of access and implementation with considerations of outcome, examining whether and how an RoN approach can meaningfully protect environmental and related rights. As noted above, some researchers have questioned whether RoN, which in the abstract bears expansive, revolutionary potential, would actually realize this effect if it must be operationalized within dominant legal frameworks (e.g. Akchurin 2015). For example, many of the ideas inherent in RoN contrast with the fundamental underpinnings of environmental law, which may be seen as closely aligned with growth, human interests, and property rights regimes (e.g. Garver 2019, 427, 432). Some initial accounts have borne out this concern, for instance noting that, even in the exemplar jurisdiction of Ecuador, "no lawsuits over Nature's Rights have been won by the communities affected in petroleum-producing provinces" (Valladares & Boelens 2017, 1028). Furthermore, indigenous communities have, at times, expressed concern that using rights of nature as a mechanism to exert legal control over domains previously falling outside legal frameworks "would grant the state another way of regulating and controlling communities' most intimate spaces" (id. at 1026). In sum, the emancipatory potential of rights of nature approaches are accompanied by concerns of access, implementation, and outcome that are deeply multiscalar: resonating both in highly place-based contexts and at the systems level.

The Rights of Nature in Relation to Philosophical, Religious, and Cultural Perspectives

As indicated above, existing scholarship has not viewed RoN in isolation. Instead, the rights of nature have been discussed by many authors in relation to broader legal, political, philosophical, cultural, and religious perspectives and practices. For example, legal scholarship on rights of nature considers the relationship to legal standing (building on Stone), legal personhood (Pecharroman 2018), and earth jurisprudence (Koons 2008; Cullinan 2011; Humphreys 2017), and also assesses RoN in comparison with other approaches to environmental and natural resources protection (Chaturvedi 2019). Social science researchers have explored the extent to which RoN is an effective political strategy for achieving environmental protection, advancing indigenous rights (Akchurin 2015), gathering together disparate interests (Stone 1972), and protecting the rights of future generations (Pecharroman 2018). Power and politics have been another focus: a number of researchers have examined the ways in which RoN discourses are politically contested, as leaders and various constituencies adapt rights of nature ideas to advance particular ends (Valladares & Boelens 2017; Tola 2018).

The incorporation of rights of nature into legal decisions and frameworks has also been considered from philosophical, cultural, and spiritual and religious perspectives. Stone's work (1972) offered a precedent for consideration of these dimensions, as he emphasized the importance of a philosophical as well as a legal shift in recognizing rights for natural objects. More recently, scholars have cited the RoN approach as a way of challenging anthropocentrism (Clark et al. 2018), recognizing nature's intrinsic value (Emmenegger & Tschentscher 1994), acknowledging nonhuman personhood (Pecharroman

2018), and integrating indigenous concepts—such as *sumak kawsay* (translated as *buen vivir* or *good living*), a central idea for Andean indigenous peoples—into environmental and natural resources law, even if the translations of these concepts into legal frameworks are imperfect[1] (Beitl 2016; Tola 2018). Scholars from multiple disciplines have actively explored the connections between RoN and associated cultural and religious perspectives, giving voice to both concerns and opportunities. Although there are exceptions, much of the legal scholarship has been sanguine about the institutionalization of the RoN, viewing this as a form of legal progress, as suggested in Stone's original work. Scholars in the social sciences have tended to take a somewhat more critical view, perhaps because their work has documented some of the complex social and political dynamics that accompany efforts to enact legal reforms.

Because of the limited contexts in which rights of nature have been implemented in practice, much of the literature exploring the relationship between RoN and cultural, religious, and philosophical perspectives focuses on New Zealand (Clark et al. 2018; Athens 2018; Prior 2016; Shelton 2015), Ecuador (Tănăsescu 2013; Akchurin 2015), and Bolivia (Tola 2018; Calzadilla & Kotzé 2018), where rights of nature have been enshrined in specific laws (New Zealand, Bolivia) or in the nation's constitution (Ecuador). However, a number of case studies and commentaries have focused on other locales, including India (Chaturvedi 2019), the Colorado River (Healy 2019), and the Columbia River basin (Athens 2018).

In many instances, the move to establish legal rights for nature is described as consonant with indigenous values and perspectives (e.g. in New Zealand, Bolivia, and Ecuador), connected to certain religious beliefs (such as Hinduism in India, see e.g. O'Donnell 2018; Alley 2019), or as enacting a shift from anthropocentrism to non-anthropocentrism. However, the relationships between rights of nature and various cultural, religious, and philosophical perspectives are complex and contested. For example, in establishing rights for the Ganges and Yamuna Rivers in India, the High Court of Uttarakhand cited the sacredness of rivers to Hindu people (O'Donnell 2018). Although the court acknowledged that not all Indians believe that rivers are sacred, O'Donnell (2018) and Alley (2019) note that this religiously based legal reasoning may damage religious tolerance in India or advance Hindu nationalism.

More generally, scholarship on the relationship between the rights of nature and religious, cultural, and philosophical views ranges from optimism to pessimism, with others remaining agnostic, or noting that the compatibility between RoN and non-anthropocentrism, indigenous knowledge systems, or particular religious views depends on the context as well as on the ways rights are implemented. The discussion below samples the range of positions in the literature and explores some of the synergies and tensions between RoN and religious and cultural perspectives, with a focus on the consonance or dissonance with indigenous knowledge and worldviews.

Optimism

Much of the optimism about the compatibility between rights of nature and various religious, cultural, and philosophical views focuses on 1) the resonance between rights of nature and a shift away from anthropocentrism, and/or 2) the compatibility of rights of nature approaches with the perspectives of indigenous peoples throughout the world. With respect to the shift to non-anthropocentrism, Clark et al. 2018 cite the early work of Stone (1972), and later, the contributions of theologian Thomas Berry (1988) and environmental lawyer Cormac Cullinan (2011), as advancing ecocentric philosophical and legal approaches. They further note that the Community Environmental Legal Defense Fund (CELDF) has engaged in significant efforts to promote these approaches domestically and globally. Similarly, Borràs (2016) argues that rights of nature initiatives represent a fundamental shift toward biocentrism, embracing a "holistic approach to all life and all ecosystems," which represents "a radical move away from the assumption that nature is property" (Borràs 2016, 118).

With respect to the relation between rights of nature and indigenous views, Pecharroman (2018, 6) asserts that "[t]he paradigm that embraces and understands nature as a being with rights has been part of many indigenous populations' worldviews for hundreds of years." Pecharroman presents indigenous views as unproblematically compatible with the rights of nature, citing consonance with the Andean indigenous concept of *sumak kawsay*, Asian indigenous perspectives, and African philosophies "of reciprocity and respect for nature" (6). Although Pecharroman may be right, her analysis operates at a high level of generality and does not explore in detail specific aspects of the compatibilities (as well as potential tensions) between rights of nature and the various perspectives she cites.

Can the rights of nature both respect indigenous worldviews and inaugurate a more sustainable relationship between humans and the broader world? Knauß (2018), too, is optimistic, suggesting that the rights of nature can serve as a "trans-cultural tool to justify Human Stewardship over the Earth in the Age of Anthropocene" (703). In Knauß's view, indigenous worldviews can be "translated into Rights of Nature" (703), and one of the strengths of the RoN approach is its "transcultural-applicability" (705). Knauß sees particular resonance between the rise of the Anthropocene concept—which he describes as holistic and systemic (though the concept of the Anthropocene is itself contested)—and indigenous views. Knauß draws on examples from New Zealand and Ecuador to support this argument; however, he provides little detail in analyzing these cases, and leaves open the question of "whether there is really no contradiction" (705) between rights of nature and the indigenous perspectives he cites. Nevertheless, Knauß holds that the rights of nature approach can draw thoughtfully and effectively on diverse perspectives and traditions, employing a kind of "border thinking" (715) to cross familiar dichotomies between science and religion, the local and the global, the modern and the traditional, and the holistic and the individualistic. Ultimately, Knauß argues that the Anthropocene narrative of planetary integrity finds voice in the rights of nature approach, which is compatible with indigenous cosmovisions and can ground an ethos of planetary stewardship (719).

Along similar lines, but with greater nuance, Borràs (2016) provides examples of how Ecuador and Bolivia have integrated indigenous concepts and perspectives into their legal frameworks, and Espinosa (2019) argues for "interpretive affinities" in Ecuador among various groups in the development of a rights of nature approach. More specifically, Espinosa focuses on three groups: 1) a U.S.-based NGO, the Community Environmental Legal Defense Fund (CELDF), which promotes the rights of nature internationally, 2) the indigenous movement in Ecuador, led by the Confederation of Indigenous Nationalities of Ecuador (CONAIE), and 3) the Ecuadorian environmental movement. Espinosa explores the narratives these groups employ, and how they each identify "problems" and "solutions" in relation to the rights of nature approach. For CELDF, the problem is that environmental laws are anthropocentric. Corporations are the "villains" and nature is the "victim," with rights of nature as the solution. For the indigenous movement, the problem is "the pervasiveness of outdated colonial structures, reproducing the exclusion and domination of non-Europeans" (Espinosa 2019, 613). Here, the narrative focuses on the role of indigenous peoples in "defending the common good" (Espinosa 2019, 613), drawing on the Kichwa concept of *sumak kawsay* (translated into Spanish as *vivir bien* or *buen vivir*, and into English as *living well* or *good living*) as a guiding principle. The indigenous movement shares with CELDF the view that nature is the victim of market exploitation; however, the solution is inflected slightly differently, focusing on plurinationality, recognition of indigenous rights, and *sumak kawsay*. The third group, the Ecuadorian environmental movement, identifies the problem as development patterns based on overexploitation of natural resources. Again, market actors are seen as villains, aided by the state's poor enforcement of environmental laws. The victims include indigenous people, local communities who experience the effects of environmental degradation, and nature. The environmental movement sees the solution as "deepen[ing] and institutionaliz[ing] individual and collective environmental rights," expanding public participation, and prioritizing environmental justice (Espinosa 2019, 615).

Despite these affinities, the rights of nature were controversial at Ecuador's 2005 national environmental assembly, with some expressing concern about how to operationalize such rights and others worrying that the rights of nature might impinge on local communities' abilities to access national resources (Espinosa 2019, 615, 616). At the later 2007–2008 constitutional assembly, indigenous communities argued successfully to embed *sumak kawsay* as a central principle in the new constitution, and for the compatibility of *sumak kawsay* with rights of nature. As Espinosa explains, "the contributions of indigenous CA [Constitutional Assembly] delegates were decisive in anchoring rights of nature within indigenous knowledge systems" (618). Nevertheless, these elements of the new constitution were not universally embraced. In particular, the inclusion of references to Pachamama led to concern about tensions with Catholic religious views regarding humans' dominion over nature (though this view, itself, was contested).

Agnosticism

Despite a general sense of optimism—particularly among legal scholars—regarding the rights of nature as a way of inaugurating a shift toward biocentrism and enabling greater incorporation of indigenous perspectives into environmental law, some scholars remain agnostic about the extent to which rights of nature approaches incorporate these views. Rather than celebrate the compatibility of rights of nature with non-anthropocentrism, various religious perspectives, or diverse indigenous views, some of these more cautious approaches focus on the descriptive task of characterizing the relationships between rights of nature and various perspectives, values, and interests or analyzing the potential fit between the generally non-anthropocentric orientation of RoN and existing legal structures.

Akchurin (2015), for example, offers a detailed case study of the development of rights of nature ideas in Ecuador, leading to the adoption of a new constitution in 2008, which incorporated not only rights of nature, but also recognition of Ecuador as a plurinational state and a commitment to the Kichwa principle of *sumak kawsay* (954). Using a sociological approach and drawing on archival documents, media reports, and secondary literature, as well as interviews with participants in the constitutional process, Akchurin provides a careful analysis of the way in which multiple environmental, indigenous, and other groups engaged in political action and negotiations that shaped the new constitution. Akchurin argues that there were commonalities and divergences not only between environmentalists and indigenous groups but within each of these constituencies as well. Nevertheless, various groups were able to come together "to combine radical Western ecological perspectives, politicized indigenous beliefs, and legal rights discourse to construct a hybrid concept that imagined and codified nature as a subject of constitutional rights" (Akchurin 2015, 961). Akchurin concludes:

> This story was not only an instance of an alternative philosophy becoming incorporated into a legal framework, but also an important case of how indigenous politics influenced nonindigenous systems of authority and created the space for a different understanding of nature/society relations to be conceptualized, described, and incorporated into the constitution, pushing the boundaries of existing ideas about rights, authority, and the state. This process also allowed for the legal materialization of broader ontological debates about the status of nature.
>
> (Akchurin 2015, 961)

Lynes (2019) takes a more prospective approach, exploring how rights of nature might influence future natural resources decisions in Canada. After briefly reviewing the evolution of rights of nature approaches around the world and discussing New Zealand's Whanganui River case in particular, Lynes argues that the rights of nature may come to influence Canadian policy through the existing duty of the federal government to consult with indigenous peoples of Canada on projects that affect their lands and resources. She concludes that "Canada is primed for Rights of Nature cases—with its commitment to reconciliation with First Nations, ongoing challenges with the interpretation of the duty to consult and increasing pressures from civil society to act on climate change" (361). However, the prospect raises numerous questions:

> [W]ith whom would industry consult on matters of development? Nature of course can't represent itself, so would the Crown consult with itself if it were on an advisory board representing nature along with First Nations, or recuse itself? And if nature really had a voice, what would it be?
>
> (361)

Akchurin (2015) and Lynes (2019) represent two examples of rights of nature research that takes a primarily descriptive and analytical approach while deemphasizing normative judgments. Other research in this vein includes Miller (2019) and Prior (2016). Miller (2019) examines in detail an unsuccessful 2017 lawsuit asserting that the state of Colorado had violated the rights of the Colorado River, offering a careful analysis of the legal arguments and why they failed, pointing to the plaintiffs' failure to establish standing as a key weakness. As he explains, "the plaintiffs dedicated most of their complaint to persuading the court that their cause was worthy of consideration, instead of satisfying technical justiciability requirements" (369). A more successful approach might have been to show "injury, traceability, and redressability" (369), as required by Article III of the U.S. Constitution. That is, the plaintiffs needed to prove that the river had in fact been harmed, show that the harm to the river was traceable to state actions, and identify practical means through which the harm could be redressed. The complaint failed to do this, and Miller concludes that

> [i]f the plaintiffs had drafted their pleadings in a way that met the requirements for standing and not as a Rights of Nature manifesto, they would have had a much better chance to litigate the case on the merits and make inroads toward the recognition of environmental personhood.
>
> (373)

Thus, while Miller acknowledges that a rights of nature approach has the potential to generate a shift toward non-anthropocentrism, he believes that such efforts will be more successful if they attend closely to the requirements of existing legal systems.

In an article focused on New Zealand, Prior (2016) suggests that the broadening of "legal personality"—or legal personhood—can be part of a shift toward Earth trusteeship and away from anthropocentric approaches to environmental governance, as well as a means of acknowledging and integrating indigenous views. Interestingly, and in a departure from many other scholars, Prior (2016, 34) suggests that the rights of nature have served primarily as an instrumental and anthropocentric tool, though the extension of legal personhood to animals and the environment may catalyze a deeper shift, incorporating non-anthropocentric and indigenous worldviews. Prior argues that "recent developments in New Zealand law and resource management appear to signal a willingness to consider, and adopt, trusteeship-based models and solutions for particular natural resources, and that there is a place within these for indigenous perspectives" (Prior 2016, 38). She observes that in granting legal personhood to the Whanganui River, the government acknowledged a spiritual connection between Whanganui Iwi[2] and the river (Prior 2016, 43). Thus, Prior is cautiously optimistic about the developments in New Zealand surrounding legal personhood for natural entities, arguing that

> in both the Whanganui River and Te Urewera Treaty settlements, the Crown has taken the opportunity to listen closely to iwi stories about the land, the river and other natural resources, and to understand the existential significance of these to the respective iwi.
>
> (45)

The government thus seems to "[acknowledge] that it sees a Māori worldview as one with a valuable contribution to make to New Zealand's legal system" (Prior 2016, 45). In this sense, the granting of legal personhood to the Whanganui River and Te Urewera protected area in New Zealand may represent not just a pragmatic or superficial effort by the government to address the concerns of the Whanganui and Tūhoe Iwi, but a more thoroughgoing philosophical shift. However, there remain tensions surrounding this approach within New Zealand, as some seek to protect economic and development opportunities, and accordingly, to limit the extension of legal personhood to nonhuman entities (Prior 2016, 47).

Concern

Not all researchers are sanguine about the prospects for a happy partnership between the rights of nature, non-anthropocentrism, and diverse religious, spiritual, and philosophical views, including indigenous views, and some doubt that the rights of nature will be an effective approach. For example, Chaturvedi (2019) worries that in the Indian context, the rights of nature approach addresses the wrong problem. Chaturvedi argues that the challenges to environmental protection in India stem from a lack of enforcement of existing environmental regulations, not a fundamental inadequacy in the laws themselves. On a different note, Shelton (2015) and Valladares and Boelens (2017) caution that granting rights to nature doesn't inherently or necessarily align with indigenous values. In support of this point, Shelton notes the controversy over rights of nature in Bolivia, and more specifically, tensions between some environmental and indigenous groups.

One of the challenges of finding compatibility between a rights of nature approach and diverse worldviews may lie in the conceptual presuppositions associated with rights. For example, Chaturvedi (2019) argues that "rights as a concept was born from the West's journey of attempting to bridge the inequities created by dualities that sprang from the history and philosophy endemic to the West" (Chaturvedi 2019, 722). Rights, in this view, are a Western solution for Western problems, and rights of nature, when applied in nations such as India, thus represent "a kind of Western interventionism" (Chaturvedi 2019, 723). Focusing on India's Ganges River, Chaturvedi asks whether a rights-based approach can address Ganges River pollution by filling gaps in existing Indian environmental law. He concludes that it cannot. First, standing is not an issue in India because public interest litigation allows citizen suits concerning broad issues of public concern, even if the suit-bringers themselves haven't been harmed much or at all. The real problem is implementation and enforcement, and granting rights of nature cannot solve this. Chaturvedi identifies other problems as well: nature's rights may create conflicts with cultural rights, and the grounds for granting rights to nature may diverge from the rationales central to environmental protection in religious traditions such as Hinduism (2019, 732). Chaturvedi explains,

> Older civilizations and philosophies have never viewed nature as man's property (at least in theory), so there is a danger that the Western understanding of rights to remedy this conceit will be thrust on cultures whose understanding of ecocentrism may be richer and deeper.
>
> (2019, 732)

Another concern regarding the rights of nature approach has to do with the mistranslation or cooptation of various traditions, values, and perspectives, particularly those of indigenous peoples. Tola (2018) argues that in both Ecuador and Bolivia, the indigenous concept of Pachamama is introduced into legal frameworks that meld "aspects of Western notions of rights with indigenous views of justice" (Tola 2018, 31), creating "juridical hybrids." This in itself may be unproblematic; however, she argues that Evo Morales (President of Bolivia from 2006–2019) "has turned the generativity of Pachamama/Mother Earth into an asset for bolstering economic growth and his own reputation in climate-change negotiations" (Tola 2018, 32). According to Tola's analysis, Morales uses a Western adaptation of Pachamama as a female-gendered "Mother Earth," and imports a gender binary absent from the indigenous view as well as colonial associations between Pachamama and the Virgin Mary. Moreover, Tola argues that Morales deploys the concept of Pachamama instrumentally. In the international arena, Morales plays up his role as protector of Pachamama; domestically, he argues that Pachamama is a generous provider of resources (e.g., cheap gas) and subject to the control of the state (Tola 2018,

34) Whereas Morales uses Pachamama strategically to justify development and resource extraction, indigenous and feminist groups understand Pachamama "as an entity that does not belong to anyone but affects everyone" (Tola 2018, 36). In cases like this, rights of nature frameworks may distort indigenous concepts and coopt them to support broader agendas, obscuring ongoing tensions between environmental protection and extractivist models of development (cf. Humphreys 2017).

In Ecuador, Beitl (2016) describes a related dynamic, where Western concepts are integrated with indigenous ones, at times in ways that undermine indigenous values. Beitl argues that the development of *custodias* (collective property rights and marine management agreements) in Ecuador provide rights to ancestral peoples (Beitl 2016, 318) but also integrate Western conceptions of property rights and sustainable development: "Through this ideological lens, stewardship takes the form of ownership and promotes competitive relationships over the cooperative relationships envisioned by the Buen Vivir philosophy, in which nature is revered with deep respect and appreciation as kin" (Beitl 2016, 332).

Lastly, some authors caution that RoN approaches may not only involve mistranslation or cooptation but can actively conflict with indigenous interests. For example, in Ecuador, the government has drawn on the concept of *sumak kawsay* to justify large-scale developments, such as mining, oil development, and hydroelectric projects (Valladares & Boelens 2017). After the passage of the new constitution—which was supposed to integrate the rights of nature as well as indigenous knowledge systems—Valladares and Boelens (2017, 1018) report that "the state began using the new constitutional guarantees to undermine existing [I]ndigenous rights."

Of course, rights of nature provisions could be enacted in ways that better support indigenous values and rights. Valladares and Boelens (2017) note that although indigenous and non-indigenous groups who favor the rights of nature approach (and not in the cynical, pro-development mode that the state has employed) draw on different starting points and conceptions of nature, an "epistemic pact" between these views may be possible, from which to challenge capitalist, extractivist views of nature. Thus, although they caution against viewing the RoN approach as a panacea, Valladares and Boelens (2017, 1026) see potential here for "re-politicizing the environmental debate by challenging the dominant mono-cultural, functionalist and extractivist notion of nature, defined by capitalism and science." More specifically, RoN could serve as a legal tool, a focal point for political organizing, and "an educational tool rooted in new narratives" (Valladares & Boelens 2017, 1029) that can support territorial defense for indigenous people. However, as in Bolivia, former Ecuadorian President Rafael Correa used RoN strategically, including to promote industrial development within Ecuador and to gain respect and prominence internationally. Valladares and Boelens (2017, 1029) thus argue that the Ecuadorian government dilutes nature's rights internally to fit its objectives but "[highlights them] to the outside world to show environmental concern."

Conclusion

Although the rights of nature idea is not new, the actualization of this idea in law—jurisprudence, statutes, and constitutions—has increased in recent decades, in conjunction with indigenous and environmental movements, new legal writings on Earth Jurisprudence, and the work of non-governmental organizations including the Community Environmental Legal Defense Fund (CELDF), which has provided guidance and legal templates for rights of nature initiatives around the world. There is widespread agreement that RoN approaches have the potential to produce a paradigm shift in the legal frameworks through which environment and natural resources are managed, as well as in the broader understanding of the value and significance of the natural world. However, because RoN approaches often mesh poorly with existing legal systems and political interests, institutional inertia and power dynamics create friction against this kind of paradigmatic change.

From a practical perspective, questions of access to the courts, implementation strategies, and outcomes all come into play. Access issues involve who has the standing to bring a case before the court, and on what grounds; how jurisdiction is established; how legal personhood should be conceptualized and defined; and how guardians for natural objects and ecosystems might be defined and identified. Issues of implementation involve how legal claims are handled once they arrive in court. What legal standards of causation or burden of proof should apply, how might the rights of nature be integrated with other legal requirements, and how should conflicts between (e.g.) rights of nature and human rights be resolved? Lastly, legal outcomes remain uncertain and will become clearer only as more RoN cases are litigated. Based on the limited cases thus far, it is difficult to know whether RoN provisions will translate into meaningful environmental protection on the ground.

Although linked by a common thread, the ways in which RoN have been incorporated into law and utilized in practice vary across locations and jurisdictions. For example, Ecuador has constitutional provisions; in Bolivia and New Zealand, rights of nature are incorporated into statutory law at the national level; in the U.S., various municipalities have passed laws protecting the rights of nature or specific natural objects; and India's rights of nature for rivers and glaciers were established (then later struck down) by judicial ruling. Additionally, the ways in which rights of nature have been articulated vary from place to place. Some jurisdictions have specified rights for nature generally, others have granted legal personhood to specific entities (such as the Ganges River in India or the Whanganui River in New Zealand), and still others, including Ecuador, Bolivia, and New Zealand, have explicitly attempted to integrate rights of nature approaches with indigenous values and worldviews. These context-dependent approaches provide opportunities for greater consonance between the rights of nature and locally and regionally specific cultural, religious, and philosophical perspectives,. and for the adaptation of rights of nature frameworks to address local needs. However, the adaptation of rights of nature in various contexts will always be subject to complex political and power dynamics, thus the compatibility between RoN and indigenous values, as well as the ability for RoN to limit the anthropocentrism of existing law, is likely to remain a site of intense contestation in the decades to come.

This chapter illustrates the diversity of existing scholarly approaches to RoN movements and implications, and our literature survey demonstrates several opportunities to extend and further enrich research on the rights of nature. First, this chapter repeatedly notes the robust attention that legal scholars have directed to RoN. In the years since Stone's initial analysis, the past decade in particular has brought new legal analyses offering expansive, epistemological assessments; descriptive, case-based analyses; and focused, procedural examinations. However, our review also highlights the emergence of valuable contributions from other disciplines, notably including philosophy and the social sciences. Given the complex normative questions that accompany efforts to extend legal rights to natural objects, as well as the interlinked social implications of those initiatives, we believe that these disciplines' insights can be highly complementary.

Additionally, we believe that existing accounts have proven particularly effective at examining three broad areas: the paradigmatic potential of rights of nature movements; the institutional and practical considerations that could emerge amidst these innovative legal processes; and the philosophical, religious, and cultural implications that accompany efforts to extend rights to nature. However, our review suggests fertile ground for additional scholarship, as multiple valuable questions have received only limited consideration. For example, existing case study accounts richly characterize the diverse understandings and operationalizations of RoN. However, future research might more explicitly consider the theoretical and practical implications of this diversity. For instance, diversity may foster innovation and support broader adoption of RoN in diverse domestic and socio-legal contexts, but it may also constrain efforts to generate common understandings or regulatory approaches. A second potential research opportunity might consider the increasingly diverse contributions to RoN literature from scholars of various disciplines. As legal insights are increasingly accompanied by perspectives from other disciplines, researchers may wish to further examine how these disciplinary distinctions inflect analyses, understandings, and recommendations. Ultimately, by highlighting the flourishing discourse surrounding rights of nature, we hope that this chapter may serve both as an assessment of what scholars have found and as a catalyst for what can be further explored.

Notes

1 The Quechua concept of *sumak kawsay* arises frequently in the literature on rights of nature in Bolivia and Ecuador. This term, which describes "a fullness of life in a community, together with other persons and Nature" (Gudynas 2011, 442) or harmonious living in the world, is often translated into Spanish as *buen vivir* or *vivir bien* (*good living* or *living well*). These latter terms arguably have different connotations than *sumak kawsay*,

in part because *buen vivir* and *vivir bien* have been explicitly integrated into the 2008 and 2009 Constitutions of Ecuador and Bolivia, respectively. *Buen vivir/vivir bien* have been explicitly articulated as representing alternatives to Western, Eurocentric models of development, though the terms and their applications are contested and evolving. *Buen vivir/vivir bien* have been informed by multiple indigenous concepts, including but not limited to *sumak kawsay*. For further discussion, see Gudynas 2011 and Vanhulst and Beling 2014.

2 The Māori word "*iwi*" is often translated as "people," "nation," or "tribe."

References

Akchurin, Maria. 2015. "Constructing the Rights of Nature: Constitutional Reform, Mobilization, and Environmental Protection in Ecuador." *Law and Social Inquiry* 40(4): 937–968.

Alley, Kelly D. 2019. "River Goddesses, Personhood, and the Rights of Nature: Implications for Spiritual Ecology." *Religions* 10(9): 502. doi: 10.3390/rel10090502

Athens, Allison Katherine. 2018. "An Indivisible and Living Whole: Do We Value Nature Enough to Grant it Personhood?" *Ecology Law Quarterly* 45(2): 187–226.

Babcock, Hope M. 2016. "A Brook with Legal Rights: The Rights of Nature in Court." *Ecology Law Quarterly* 43(1): 1–61.

Beitl, Christine M. 2016. "The Changing Legal and Institutional Context for Recognizing Nature's Rights in Ecuador: Mangroves, Fisheries, Farmed Shrimp, and Coastal Management since 1980." *Journal of International Wildlife Law & Policy* 19(4): 317–332.

Berry, Thomas. 1988. *The Dream of the Earth*. San Francisco: Sierra Club.

Borràs, Susana. 2016. "New Transitions from Human Rights to the Environment to the Rights of Nature." *Transnational Environmental Law* 5(1): 113–143.

Calzadilla, Paola Villavicencio, and Kotzé, Louis J. 2018. "Living in Harmony with Nature? A Critical Appraisal of the Rights of Mother Earth in Bolivia." *Transnational Environmental Law* 7(3): 397–424.

Chapron, Guillaume, Yaffa Epstein, and José Vicente López-Bao. 2019. "A Rights Revolution for Nature." *Science* 363(6434): 1392–1393.

Chaturvedi, Ipshita. 2019. "Why the Ganga Should not Claim a Right of the River." *Water International* 44(6–7): 719–735.

Clark, C., Emmanouil, N., Page, J., and Pelizzon, A. 2018. "Can You Hear the Rivers Sing: Legal Personhood, Ontology, and the Nitty-Gritty of Governance." *Ecology LQ* 45: 787.

Clark, Cristy, Nia Emmanouil, John Page, and Alessandro Pelizzon. 2018. "Can You Hear the Rivers Sing? Legal Personhood, Ontology, and the Nitty-Gritty of Governance." *Ecology Law Quarterly* 45(4): 787–844.

Cólon-Ríos, Joel. 2014. "Constituent Power, The Rights of Nature, and Universal Jurisdiction." *McGill Law Journal* 60: 127–172.

Cullinan, Cormac. 2011. *Wild Law: A Manifesto for Earth Justice* (2nd edition). Chelsea, VT: Chelsea Green.

Emmenegger, Susan, and Axel Tschentscher. 1994. "Taking Nature's Rights Seriously: The Long Way to Biocentrism in Environmental Law." *Georgetown International Environmental Law Review* 6(3): 545–592.

Espinosa, Cristina. 2019. "Interpretive Affinities: The Constitutionalization of Rights of Nature, Pacha Mama, in Ecuador." *Journal of Environmental Policy & Planning* 21(5): 608–622.

Garver, Geoffrey. 2019. "Confronting Remote Ownership Problems with Ecological Law." *Vermont Law Review* 43(3): 425–454.

Gordon, G. J. 2017. "Environmental Personhood." *Columbia Journal of Environmental Law* 43(1): 49–91.

Gordon, G. J. 2019. "Environmental Personhood." *Columbia Journal of Environmental Law* 43(1). doi: 10.7916/cjel.v43i1.3742

Gudynas, Eduardo. 2011. "Buen Vivir: Today's Tomorrow." *Development* 54(4): 441–447.

Healy, Meredith N. 2019. "Fluid Standing: Incorporating the Indigenous Rights of Nature Concept into Collaborative Management of the Colorado River Ecosystem." *Colorado Natural Resources, Energy, and Environmental Law Review* 30(2): 328–360.

Houck, Oliver A. 2018. "Noah's Second Voyage: The Rights of Nature as Law." *Tulane Environmental Law Journal* 31: 1–50.

Humphreys, David. 2015. "Know Your Rights: Earth Jurisprudence and Environmental Politics." *International Journal of Sustainability Policy and Practice* 10(3–4): 1–14.

Humphreys, David. 2017. "Rights of Pachamama: The Emergence of an Earth Jurisprudence in the Americas." *Journal of International Relations and Development* 20(3): 459–484.

Kauffman, C., and Sheehan, L. 2019. "The Rights of Nature: Guiding Our Responsibilities through Standards." In S. Turner, D. Shelton, J. Razzaque, O. McIntyre, and J. May (Eds.), *Environmental Rights: The Development of Standards* (pp. 342-366). Cambridge: Cambridge University Press.

Knauß, Stefan. 2018. "Conceptualizing Human Stewardship in the Anthropocene: The Rights of Nature in Ecuador, New Zealand and India." *Journal of Agricultural and Environmental Ethics* 31(6): 703–722.

Koons, Judith E. 2008. "Earth Jurisprudence: The Moral Value of Nature." *Pace Environmental Law Review* 25(2): 263–339.

Lynes, Laura S. 2019. "The Rights of Nature and the Duty to Consult in Canada." *Journal of Energy and Natural Resources Law* 37(3): 353–362.

Maloney, Michelle. 2016. "Building an Alternative Jurisprudence for the Earth: The International Rights of Nature Tribunal." *Vermont Law Review* 41: 129–142.

Miller, Matthew. 2019. "Environmental Personhood and Standing for Nature: Examining the Colorado River Case." *The University of New Hampshire Law Review* 17(2): 355–377.

O'Donnell, Erin L. 2018. "At the Intersection of the Sacred and the Legal: Rights for Nature in Uttarakhand, India." *Journal of Environmental Law* 30: 135–144.

Parenteau, Patrick. 2019. "Green Justice Revisited: Dick Brooks on the Laws of Nature and the Nature of Law." *Vermont Journal of Environmental Law* 20: 183–201.

Pecharroman, Lidia Cano. 2018. "Rights of Nature: Rivers that Can Stand in Court." *Resources* 7(13): 23–36. doi: 10.3390/resources7010013

Prior, Hannah. 2016. "Environmental Trusteeship of the Global Commons: Can New Zealand Take the Lead?" *New Zealand Journal of International Law* 203: 19–56.

Shelton, Dinah. 2015. "Nature as a Legal Person." *VertigO—la revue électronique en sciences de l'environnement.* Hors-série 22, septembre 2015, http://journals.openedition.org/vertigo/16188. doi: 10.4000/vertigo.16188

Stone, Christopher D. 1972. "Should Trees Have Standing? Toward Legal Rights for Natural Objects." *Southern California Law Review* 45: 450.

Tănăsescu, Mihnea. 2013. "The Rights of Nature in Ecuador: The Making of an Idea." *International Journal of Environmental Studies* 70(6): 846–861.

Tănăsescu, Mihnea. 2014. "Rethinking Representation: The Challenge of Non-humans." *Australian Journal of Political Science* 49(1): 40–53.

Tănăsescu, Mihnea. 2015. "Nature Advocacy and the Indigenous Symbol." *Environmental Values* 24: 105–122.

Taylor, Prudence E. 1998. "From Environmental to Ecological Human Rights: A New Dynamic in International Law?" *Georgetown International Environmental Law Review* 10(2): 309–397.

Tola, M. 2018. "Between Pachamama and Mother Earth: Gender, Political Ontology and the Rights of Nature in Contemporary Bolivia." *Feminist Review* 118(1): 25–40.

Valladares, Carolina, and Rutgerd Boelens. 2017. "Extractivism and the Rights of Nature: Governmentality, 'Convenient Communities' and Epistemic Pacts in Ecuador." *Environmental Politics* 26(6): 1015–1034.

Vanhulst, Julian, and Adrian E. Beling. 2014. "Buen Vivir: Emergent Discourse Within or Beyond Sustainable Development?" *Ecological Economics* 101: 54–63.

White, Hannah. 2018. "Indigenous Peoples, the International Trend toward Legal Personhood for Nature, and the United States." *American Indian Law Review* 43(1): 129–165.

3 Pachamama as a Legal Person?

Rights of Nature and Indigenous Thought in Ecuador

*Andreas Gutmann**

Introduction

The question of whether nature can or even should have rights has recently gained momentum. Fifty years after the publication of Christopher Stone's seminal article "Should Trees Have Standing?," several legal systems recognize the rights of nonhuman natural entities (Stone 1972; cf. Boyd 2018, 13). Giving rights to nature is therefore possible. However, these rights are still undetermined in practice and the question of what they might look like is still a subject of debate. This chapter will explore what is probably the most far-reaching guarantee of rights of nature (hereafter RoN), provided by Article 71 of the Ecuadorian Constitution (hereafter CRE). This might be considered the most innovative provision of the constitution and reads as follows:

> Nature, or Pacha Mama, where life is reproduced and occurs, has the right to integral respect for its existence and for the maintenance and regeneration of its life cycles, structure, functions and evolutionary processes.
>
> All persons, communities, peoples and nations can call upon public authorities to enforce the rights of nature. To enforce and interpret these rights, the principles set forth in the Constitution shall be observed, as appropriate.[1]

So far, Ecuador is the only country that explicitly guarantees RoN on a constitutional level. The country's 2008 constitution clearly refers to indigenous thinking by invoking the principle of *sumak kawsay*, a holistic philosophical concept based on Andean and Amazonian indigenous cosmovisions (Altmann 2017). It equates nature with Pachamama (often translated as Mother Earth). Nevertheless, it is arguable as to whether these RoN adequately reflect the local indigenous thinking. The constitution names three substantive RoN (cf. Simon Campaña 2013, 12): the right to integral respect (Art. 71 para 1), the

* This is an enhanced and updated translation of Andreas Gutmann, "Pachamama als Rechtssubjekt? Rechte der Natur und indigenes Denken in Ecuador," originally published in *Zeitschrift für Umweltrecht (ZUR)* 2019, 611–618.

right to respect for the maintenance and regeneration of its life cycles, structure, functions, and evolutionary processes (Art. 71.1), and the right to have its integrity restored (Art. 72). These rights have binding effects for both public and private actors.

The RoN can be enforced by any (human) person. No personal interest is required to be at stake when pursuing a right as a legal representative of nature (Ávila Santamaría 2008, 47). Anyone can bring a lawsuit regarding nearly every (potential) harm to the environment. Nevertheless, the number of RoN cases is still rather low (Chapron, Epstein, & López-Bao 2019, 1393; Nieto Sanabria 2018, 127). Both courts and activists may need some time to get used to this new legal concept. However, some of these lawsuits illustrate that the Ecuadorian RoN can be put into practice (see Kauffmann & Martin 2017).

The Ecuadorian RoN grant subjective rights to nature, i.e. rights that can be enforced directly and independently by the legal subject or person[2] "nature." This chapter aims to reconstruct and reconsider the subject of the Ecuadorian RoN. It is based on the assumption that RoN go further than creating a new legal subject. If they are really going to transform the way we (legally) treat our environment, then a reconstruction of the notion of subjective rights is needed (Fischer-Lescano 2018a, 393, 2018b, 213; Bosselmann 1992, 209). This paper will argue that indigenous thinking must be taken into consideration when interpreting the CRE. In particular, the RoN cannot be understood properly without taking these philosophies into account. Furthermore, taking seriously the indigenous influences that shaped the CRE will enrich the western view of legal personhood and subjective rights, and thereby could overcome some of the deficiencies of rights-based legal systems.

This thesis is elaborated in three steps. First, the concept of hybridity—a key element of postcolonial theories—is used to underline the necessity of taking indigenous thinking seriously for a true understanding of the Ecuadorian RoN and the unfolding of their transformative character. Second, the core elements of Andean indigenous thinking concerning Pachamama and what we call "human–nature relations" are presented. Finally, the RoN granted by the Ecuadorian constitution will be interpreted while considering their indigenous background and their postcolonial hybridity. This final section demonstrates how our understanding of RoN may be enhanced by viewing legal personhood and (subjective) rights from a non-western perspective.

Postcoloniality

In 2008, Ecuador adopted a new constitution (Constitución de la República del Ecuador), which aimed at far-reaching social, economic, and ecological transformations (Acosta 2009, 219). The CRE is a very innovative constitution due to numerous human and environmental rights that it grants, a new institutional framework, and its attempt at decolonization. It grants many individual and collective rights which can be enforced by strong judicial remedies. The

CRE is a hybrid document that connects different epistemologies. As with almost every constitution, it is shaped by inherent contradictions and areas of conflict (Yrigoyen Fajardo 2016, 159). While this may be criticized as a lack of coherence, I will use the hybridity concept of Homi K. Bhabhas and the Andean concept of *ch'ixi* to argue that these contradictions are an emancipatory element of a decolonial project.

Hybridity

The CRE, being the constitution of a formerly colonized country, is deeply shaped by coloniality.[3] On the one hand, it takes numerous elements from the legal orders of the colonializing countries (cf. Knauß 2018, 704). Even concepts such as rule of law and the nation-state have western origins and were brought to other regions by use of force. On the other hand, the CRE defines itself as an emancipatory and decolonizing document (Quijano Obregón 2010, 59). The preamble pays tribute to "social liberation struggles against all forms of domination and colonialism." This is also reflected in numerous references to indigenous thinking. The most visible expression of indigenous thinking is the *sumak kawsay* (*buen vivir*), which is considered a key element of Andean thinking and became a leading principle of the new constitutional order. The CRE therefore confirms Maximilian Pichl's finding that "every postcolonial constitution is at the same time a break and a continuity of colonial constitutional law" (Pichl 2012, 139).[4]

When interpreting the CRE, we must take this background into consideration. Important tools can be provided by postcolonial theories. According to one such theory, "the Other must be viewed as neither essentially exotic nor normal"; in other words, other (legal) cultures are to be seen as "split, hybrid, and embedded in contexts of power" (Berman 1997, 284).

Hybridity is a key concept of postcolonial theories, mainly attributed to Homi K. Bhabha (2007, 121 ff.). According to Bhabha, there are always "third spaces" between different cultures, a kind of in-between, where negotiation and translation take place and something new arises. Culture, Bhabha states, is always hybrid and a product of such third-space negotiations.

Ch'ixi

A similar concept, "*ch'ixi*," is found in Andean indigenous thinking. *Ch'ixi* is something that emanates from the confrontation of two elements. Such confrontations create something new, which at the same time preserves the former elements. According to Silvia Rivera Cusicanqui, *ch'ixi* rests upon:

> the Aymara understanding, that something is and is not at the same time, it follows the logic of the included Third. The color Ch'ixi-grey is at the same time white and not-white, as well as black, its exact opposition.
> (Rivera Cusicanqui 2018, 91)

We might conceive the CRE as a hybrid or *ch'ixi* document. The constituent assembly that drafted the constitution in 2007 and 2008 was a kind of third space, a space of in-between (cf. Melo, Greene, & Puente 2010, 4). Civil society participated in this process (Carter Center 2008, 12), and indigenous, environmental, and other social movements had a notable influence on the drafting (Melo, Greene, & Puente 2010, 4). There was a fruitful dialogue between different epistemologies that were articulated by a wide variety of very heterogeneous parties (Melo, Greene, & Puente 2010, 4). It was this variety of intellectual sources that created the hybrid character of the CRE. Hybridity is expressly recognized by the CRE when it invokes the concept of interculturality (*interculturalidad*).

Interculturalidad was an important demand of the indigenous movement (Andrade 2009, 13). It means dialogue and mutual appreciation between different cultural backgrounds, as well as reciprocal teaching and learning (cf. Walsh 2009, 41). *Interculturalidad* and *ch'ixi*, therefore, find a common ground. Intercultural processes should both create something new and preserve the epistemologies which are involved in the intercultural dialogue (Andrade 2009, 46 f.). *Interculturalidad* aims to uncover marginalized epistemes, such as Andean indigenous thinking (Walsh 2009, 46). It therefore embodies a pronounced attempt at decolonization, which pays attention to international power structures shaped by coloniality. Even the Ecuadorian Constitutional Court demands an intercultural interpretation of every legal document, and this includes consideration of indigenous thinking (Corte Constitucional 2010, 43 f.).

Human–Nature Relations

Considering the theoretical background outlined above, this section will analyze the CRE's understanding of human–nature relations. The *ch'ixi* character of the CRE becomes obvious when we take a closer look at Article 71 paragraph 1. This clause uses western terms such as "nature" or "rights" and links them to indigenous ideas such as Pachamama. Both concepts are interrelated by the Constitution, and therefore become drastically modified (cf. Knauß 2018, 704).

Nature as Pachamama

If we take *interculturalidad* seriously, we cannot simply translate "Pachamama" as "nature," like some authors do (see Acosta 2013, 302). There is no exact equivalent of the term "nature" in Andean indigenous languages such as Kichwa or Aymara (Estermann 2015, 202; Llasag Fernández 2011, 57, 78). Therefore, we need to understand what is behind the term "Pachamama."

Pachamama has no uniform meaning, as different communities have different conceptions of it (Prieto Méndez 2013, 61 ff.). For this reason, every attempt to define Pachamama brings the risk of essentializing indigenous concepts. An intercultural interpretation of the CRE must bear this in mind and abstain from rashly assigning one single meaning to the constitutionalized term "Pachamama." Nevertheless, there are some commonalities that allow for a tentative approximation.

Pachamama is both a Kichwa and an Aymara term (Estermann 2015, 165) and is often translated into English as "mother earth" (Valladares & Boelens 2019, 70). However, this oversimplifies its meaning, since "Pacha" is a very broad term. Its meaning comes close to "cosmos" (Estermann 2015, 166), where the Andean sense of cosmos includes both time and space (Silva Portero 2008, 111 ff.). As this demonstrates, Pacha is a very complex term and its translation into other languages will be imperfect (Huanacuni Mamami 2010, 21 f.; Bouysse-Cassagne & Harris 1987, 18).

Andean cosmovisions conceive Pachamama as a benevolent fertility goddess (Gregor Barié 2014, 16; Bouyse-Cassagne & Harris 1987, 18) who gives life and provides everything needed for human existence (Moreno 1983, 128). Since Christianity was imposed on the Andean region, a fusion[5] of the Catholic cult of Mary and indigenous adoration of Pachamama has been observed (van Kessel 1993, 3 f.). Pachamama is not a transcendent deity, but rather, is ubiquitous. As Fernando Huanacuni states, "Pachamama are all beings (the mountain, the river, the tree, the insect etc.)" (Huanacuni 2015, 997).

According to Andean cosmovision, the cosmos is a living entity (Estermann 2015, 205). There is no separation between nature and culture (Oviedo Freire 2014, 148). Humans are part of the Pacha (Llasag Fernández 2011, 78). The preamble of the CRE refers to this idea, paying tribute to "the Pacha Mama (Mother Earth), of which we are a part and which is vital to our existence."

Relationality

Numerous relations and interdependences exist between human and non-human entities within the living totality of Pacha (Claverías Huerse 1990, 143). This principle of relationality is therefore crucial for Andean indigenous thinking (Estermann 2015, 143). According to this idea, the whole world is a complex living network, consisting of different forms of life. Single entities, such as humans or members of other species, can only exist within this network. Every entity performs a specific role and has specific tasks that sustain the totality (Llasag Fernández 2009, 115).

Andean thinking does not focus on the individual subject but takes multiple relationships as the point of origin for its worldview (Macas 2010, 30; Medina 2006, 113). Relations produce subjects, which form intersections of a complex web (Estermann 2015, 114). No one can exist individually (Estermann 2015, 134). Therefore, the daily Andean praxis consists of taking care of relationships. In particular, the links between humans and Pachamama need to be established and cultivated steadily, requiring communication, which is undertaken through agriculture and rituals (Estermann 2015, 202). Human relationships within the family or the *ayllu* (community) also need constant attention. A state of equilibrium and harmony is the primary objective of every activity (Lalander & Cuestas Caza 2017, 34). Therefore, the impact of every (human) practice on the cosmic web must be taken into consideration. Since the relational network is fluid and agile, a fixed state of equilibrium can never be reached. For this reason, taking care of the cosmic web is a continuous process.

The Ecosystem Approach and Indigenous Thinking

The CRE acknowledges this cosmovision, which is most apparent in the section concerning RoN. These rights focus on the protection of ecosystems. Numerous constitutional provisions refer to ecosystems, e.g. by defining their protection as a national interest (Art. 14 para 2) or demanding integral restoration of ecosystems that have been affected by environmental damage (Art. 396 para 2). The indigenous notion of Pachamama and the ecosystem-oriented approach of western science are able to in some way converge (Yánez Cossío 2012, 55). Article 2 of the Convention on Biological Diversity (CBD) defines an ecosystem as "a dynamic complex of plant, animal and micro-organism communities and their non-living environment interacting as a functional unit." Ecosystems are thus shaped by relationships between numerous entities and rely on their mutual interactions (Kauffman & Sheehan 2019, 360). Thus, the western understanding of nature as the totality of existing ecosystems and the Andean notion of a cosmological web called Pacha are able to find common ground. Ambitious RoN aim to protect this relational network.

This broad understanding of nature helps to avoid the problem of RoN supporting claims against natural entities. Natural interests are manifold and may conflict (cf. Leimbacher 1988, 103 f.). For example, the construction of a hydroelectric power station could be favorable for the climate, but lethal for some species (Rühs & Jones 2016, 185; Fish 2013, 9). If RoN aim at the protection of natural relationality, they must preserve the systemic equilibrium of ecosystems. The protection of single natural entities against natural processes will privilege some components of nature over others, and in turn, destroy this natural equilibrium. In somewhat polemic terms: RoN will not entitle mice to sue cats.

Animal Rights?

Nevertheless, Ecuadorian courts have in some cases permitted rights-claims of single entities, primarily animals. Animals are held to somehow represent the ecosystem of which they are part. Paradigmatically, an ombudsperson ruled in favor of some endangered birds that are frequently hit by cars exceeding the speed-limit (Defensoría del Pueblo 2016, 2). There are also criminal judgments condemning illegal shark fishing and trafficking, which hold that sharks are protected by RoN because they form a vital part of the marine ecosystem (Unidad Judicial Mulicompetente con Sede en el Cantón San Cristobal 2017, 27). Domestic animals that are mistreated by humans can also have rights-claims. Since these animals are to some extent placed outside of their systemic connections to other natural beings, they are particularly vulnerable. For example, bull- or cockfights have been found to violate the CRE, because RoN prohibit killing animals for fun (Corte Constitucional 2011, 4; Unidad Judicial Penal Parroquia Iñaquito 2019).

However, the Ecuadorian RoN do not ban every human use of environmental services. After all, humans form a part of certain ecosystems, or broadly speaking, the cosmic web. Andean communities, often described as agrocentric (Rivera Palomino 1994, 31), conceive of agriculture as a form of communication between humans and the Pachamama (de la Torre Sandoval & Sandoval Peralta 2004, 20). Pachamama does not represent a romanticized untouched wilderness. Rather, Pachamama is formed and vitalized through human interaction. Consequently, Article 71 of the CRE does not prohibit all human use of nature but instead safeguards the reproduction of the ecosystem (Bedón Garzón 2016, 137).

Can Legal Rights be Granted to Pachamama?

How can RoN—or generally speaking, the law as such—reflect Andean philosophy? The CRE translates the Andean notion of human–nature relationships into the constitutional setting. It goes without saying that such translation gives rise to certain frictions and mutual irritations. On the one hand, nature's interests as conceived by an Andean cosmovision must be translated into a legal language, which implies a reconstruction of these concepts. On the other hand, the law itself must undergo some transformations in order to be capable of dealing with the claims of nature. A formalistic approach to RoN, which only creates a new legal subject and does not question the concept of legal personhood, will produce numerous contradictions that can undermine the potential of RoN (Bosselmann 1992, 205). From the perspective of German environmental law doctrine, Ulrich Ramsauer has criticized RoN as very limited and unable to substantially improve environmental protection (Ramsauer 2019). Holistic RoN must be introduced through legislation, which according to Ramsauer, substantially limits them. This is because RoN merely permit a claim to be made on behalf of the environment (Ramsauer 2019, 473). However, this requires scales for weighing human rights and rights of nature, which could deepen the anthropocentrism found in the law (Ramsauer 2019, 471). For example, RoN might consolidate the status quo in favor of human interests, rather than produce substantial change.

If RoN are understood in the way Ramsauer suggests, they will obviously not increase the level of environmental protection. Furthermore, in the case of Ecuador, they will not be compatible with the indigenous thinking outlined above.

The CRE's Notion of "Rights"

The CRE, and in particular the provisions concerning RoN, are quite open to an understanding of rights that embraces the Andean relationality. First, there is no hierarchy between the numerous rights granted by the constitution (Noguera Fernández 2009, 121). For example, unlike in traditional constitutionalism, liberty rights do not prevail over social and economic rights. So-called "diffuse rights" (see Kommer 2012), in particular collective and environmental rights, have the same weight as individual rights. The adjudication of these rights must be done on a case-by-case basis. Even human interests do not necessarily prevail over the interests of non-human entities. The CRE repeatedly stresses the importance of harmony between humans and nature. The document does not prescribe a fixed status of rights, but instead aims at a steady process of searching the *sumak kawsay*. In the words of Article 11 Number 8 of the CRE: "The contents of rights shall be developed progressively."

Second, the rights enshrined in the CRE create mandatory obligations for both the state and private persons (Noguera Fernández 2009, 121). This is crucial in the case of RoN, since environmental damage is primarily caused by non-state actors, in particular corporations (Leimbacher 1988, 151). Therefore, all citizens have "[t]o respect the rights of nature, preserve a healthy environment and use natural resources rationally, sustainably and durably" (Art. 83 No. 6 CRE). There are positive obligations concerning the protection of nature binding the state (Art. 396 para 1 CRE) and private persons (Art. 399 CRE). This approach distinguishes so-called Latin American Neo-Constitutionalism (Velázquez Velázquez 2018, 102), and it helps to ensure the effectiveness of the constitution in a world where many (human) rights violations are caused by non-state actors.

Personhood of Pachamama

Article 10 paragraph 2 of the CRE calls nature the "subject" of constitutional rights. At first glance, there is a contradiction between indigenous cosmovisions and a western-oriented legal order that is based on subjective rights. Granting legal rights to Pachamama seems paradoxical since autonomous subjects do not exist in the Andean worldview.

Criticizing Rights

Fernando Huanacuni and other indigenous scholars criticize western jurisprudence for its focus on individual rights. There are always conflicts between individual rights that must be resolved. Therefore, individual rights foster disputes between individuals and lead to disharmony within society (Huanacuni Mamami 2015, 2734).

At this point, we can see striking similarities between indigenous and western critiques of rights. The latter is most prominently articulated within the German context by Christoph Menke and Daniel Loick (Menke 2018; Loick 2017). The legal subject, they argue, perceives its freedom as opposed to the freedom of other legal subjects. These ideas can be traced back to Marx, who argued that the legal subject is permanently inclined to extend its legally protected sphere as far as possible and does not pay attention to the rights and interests of other community members (Marx 1976, 364 ff.).

The legal subject does not experience society (i.e. the totality of the legal subjects surrounding it) as a condition or part of its own freedom and legal subjectivity but as their limit. Human rights, Loick states, misunderstand mutual dependencies between humans (Loick 2013, 306).

Shortcomings of RoN

Some scholars also apply this critique to RoN (Nieto Sanabria 2018, 132). While proponents of RoN argue that granting legal rights to nature will radically transform the way we treat the environment and therefore foster environmental protection (Gudynas 2011, 100), others fear that RoN will deepen the rifts between nature and culture (Sánchez Parga 2011, 38 ff.; Nieto Sanabria 2018, 132). As nature becomes a legal subject just like humans, legal conflicts between human rights and rights of nature will arise. This creates the necessity to establish a separation between human rights and rights of nature and to ponder their conflicting legal positions.

Ecuadorian courts have applied this idea in some cases. In the most famous RoN case, a court in the city of Loja stated that the rights of a river prevailed over human interests in an infrastructure project, which involved building a road and dumping sewage into the riverbed (Corte Provincial de Loja 2011). In the opinion of the court, it was possible to construct the road without affecting the river. Furthermore, the interests of nature generally prevail over the interests of a particular human, since environmental damages frequently affect large numbers of humans (Corte Provincial de Loja 2011, 5). At this point, the contradictions within the judgment become obvious: the court reformulates environmental interests as human interests in order to be able to undertake a consideration based on the number of affected (human) persons. The substantial result of the Lojaen judgment favors environmental protection, but at the same time stipulates a strong dichotomy between humans and nature. It applies traditional (western) legal techniques by defining the scope of different legal positions and invoking a legal consideration. It is very doubtful whether this lives up to the expectations of the CRE.

Rights Based on Relationality

What might a system of rights that includes the indigenous concepts of Pachamama and relationality look like? A legal system based on rights that grant legal spheres of autonomy to individuals is hardly compatible with Andean cosmovisions. As mentioned previously, these cosmovisions cannot imagine an autonomous subject. It is also impossible to define the scope of the legal subject "nature" or "Pachamama." Since Pachamama embraces almost everything, including humans, it is virtually impossible to distinguish human and natural legal subjects. Rather than a static and well-defined entity, nature is a fluid network consisting of human and non-human beings.

If relationality is to be taken seriously, every legal process must aim at establishing harmony, and therefore balancing the relationships within the cosmic network. Harmony and equilibrium are often identified as the main goals of indigenous justice (Brandt 2017, 108). In Fernando Huanacuni's words, indigenous legal systems "do not confront particular individual rights with other rights but harmonize relationships and equilibrate them" (Huanacuni Mamami 2015, 2872).

This might sound esoteric to readers socialized in the western world but, in a nutshell, maybe it only widens the focus of legal decisions. Every legal decision must therefore consider its possible impacts on the complex web of relationships or the Pachamama. This approach has been implemented by some Ecuadorian courts. A Galapagos court stated that jurisprudence must "apply these new principles that overcome positivism [...] and therefore consider the specific norms in question as well as the entire legal system as touchstones of deliberation" (Juzgado de lo Civil y Mercantíl de Galápagos 2012, 5). Balancing constitutional rights must therefore be based on the principles of harmony and equilibrium. In doing this, they must develop the rights that are at stake at far as possible and refrain from restricting them, as Article 11 Number 4 of the CRE states.

Applying these principles, rights would not protect individual spheres of freedom that inevitably collide with the freedoms of others, but instead facilitate a well-balanced society of humans and non-humans. Legal trials will have to acknowledge the mutual dependencies between humans and so-called nature.

Thus, RoN must be considered *ex officio* in any legal proceeding that might have implications for the environment, even if nature does not actively take part (Bustamante Romo Leroux 2016). RoN imply the right to be heard, not only before courts but also in administrative procedures. For this reason, the constitutional court ruled that a mining license issued without prior assessment of environmental impacts violates Article 71 paragraph 1 of the CRE (Corte Constitucional 2015, 13 f.).

Conclusion

Taking the Ecuadorian RoN seriously may generate a system of rights that overcomes some of the deficiencies of the traditional interpretation of subjective rights outlined above. Of course, this newly conceived system of rights does not provide a panacea that instantly creates an ideal world and a clean environment, but is rather, under "permanent construction" (Maldonado 2014, 209).

There is no fixed status of "cosmic justice" (Estermann 2015, 168) or harmony encompassing the entire society, which can be reached by balancing the rights of all community members and will last forever. The *sumak kawsay* is an ongoing process rather than a utopia (Estermann 2015, 272). It implies the permanent construction and reconstruction of numerous relationships. In essence, this can be considered the original human duty.

The Ecuadorian RoN therefore require an ongoing (re-)adjustment of human–nature relations, through the establishment of a holistic discourse that gives a voice to nature. Justice or harmony is always yet to come (Derrida 1990, 1029), and can never be reached and maintained entirely. It is an ongoing task for the entire society, a society of which nature is a part and where non-human entities will be heard, as Bruno Latour has proposed (Latour 2004).

Notes

1 English translation of the CRE available at http://pdba.georgetown.edu/Constitutions/Ecuador/english08.html
2 Although there a huge philosophical debates on the terms of "person" and "subject" they are often used synonymously in the context of the Ecuadorian RoN (cf.Viciano Pastor 2019). The concepts are interchangeable at the Ecuadorian civil law (Larrea Holguín 2008, 149).
3 The term "coloniality" (*colonialidad*) was shaped by A.E. Quijano Obregón and describes how colonial power structures still form part of todays politicial, economic, and epistemological systems. See Quijano Obregón 1992.
4 German and Spanish quotes are translated by the author.
5 The coexistence of different religious or spiritual concepts is also visible at the preamble of the CRE that is "celebrating nature, the Pacha Mama (Mother Earth), of which we are a part and which is vital to our Existence [and] invoking the name of God and recognizing our diverse forms of religion and spirituality."

References

Acosta, A., 'Das "Buen Vivir": Die Schaffung einer Utopie', *Juridikum* (2009), 219–223.

Acosta, A., 'Die Rechte der Natur - Für eine zivilisatorische Wende', in C. v. Barloewen, M. Rivera and K. Töpfer (eds.), *Nachhaltige Entwicklung in einer pluralen Moderne: Lateinamerikanische Perspektiven* (Berlin: Matthes & Seitz, 2013), pp. 286–317.

Altmann, P., 'Sumak Kawsay as an Element of Local Decolonization in Ecuador', *Latin American Research Review* 52 (2017), 749–759.

Andrade, S., 'El reto de la interculturalidad: Interculturalidad, plurinacionalidad y ciencias sociales en el Ecuador', *Antropología. Cuadernos de Investigación* 8 (2009), 13–23.

Ávila Santamaría, R., 'Los principios de aplicación de los derechos', in R. Ávila Santamaría (ed.), *La Constitución del 2008 en el contexto andino: Análisis desde la doctrina y el derecho comparado* (Quito: Ministerio de Justicia y Derechos Humanos, 2008), pp. 39–72.

Bedón Garzón, R., 'Contenido y aplicación de los derechos de la naturaleza', *Ius Humani: Revista de Derecho* 5 (2016), 133–148.

Berman, N., 'Aftershocks: Exoticization, Normalization, and the Hermeneutic Co', *Utah Law Review* 281 (1997), 281–286.

Bhabha, H. K., *The Location of Culture*, Reprint (London: Routledge, 2007).

Bosselmann, K., *Im Namen der Natur: Der Weg zum ökologischen Rechtsstaat*, 1st ed. (Bern: Scherz, 1992).

Bouysse-Cassagne, T. and Harris, O., 'Pacha: En Torno al pensamiento aymara', in T. Bouysse-Cassagne, O. Harris, T. Platt and V. Cereceda (eds.), *Trés reflexiones sobre el pensamiento andino* (La Paz: Hisbol, 1987), pp. 11–59.

Boyd, D. R., 'Recognizing the Rights of Nature: Lofty Rhetoric or Legal Revolution', *NR&E* (2018), 13–17.

Brandt, H.-J., *"Justice Is Achieved if Peace Is Restored": Indigenous Justice, Legal Pluralism, and Change in Peru and Ecuador*, Working Paper (2017).

Bustamente Romo Leroux, Francisco J., *Los derechos de la naturaleza en la jurisprudencia constitucional ecuatoriana* (2016). http://www.ijeditores.com.ar/pop.php?option=articulo &Hash=75cf7b0a41ed880b224414921b4f956c.

Carter Center, *Report on the Constituent Assembly of the Republic of Ecuador* (Quito: Carter Center, 2008).

Chapron, G., Epstein, Y. and López-Bao, J. V., 'A Rights Revolution for Nature', *Science (New York, N.Y.)* 363 (2019), 1392–1393.

Claverías Huerse, R., *Cosmovisión y planifiacación en las comunidades andinas* (Lima: Dugrafis, 1990).

Corte Constitucional, *Constitucionalidad de la Ley de la Minería, 001–10-SIN-CC* (18 March 2010).

Corte Constitucional, *Proyecto de enmienda de la Constitución, N.° 0001-11-CP* (15 February 2011).

Corte Constitucional, *Minería Artesanal, N.° 1281-12-EP* (9 July 2015).

Corte Provincial de Loja, *Rio Vilcabamba, 11121-2011-0010* (30 March 2011).

Defensoría del Pueblo de Ecuador, *Resolución No. C-2013-200100068* (12 September 2016).

Derrida, J., 'Force de Loi: Le "Fondement mystique de l'autorité"', *Cardozo Law Review* 11 (1990), 920–1045.

Estermann, J., *Filosofía andina: Estudio intercultural de la sabiduría autóctona andina, 2da. edición* (Quito: Ediciones Abya-Yala, 2015).

Fischer-Lescano, A., 'Natur als Rechtsperson: Konstellationen der Stellvertretung im Recht', *ZUR* 29 (2018), 205–217.

Fischer-Lescano, A., 'Subjektlose Rechte', in A. Fischer-Lescano, H. Franzki and J. Horst (eds.), *Gegenrechte: Recht jenseits des Subjekts*, 1st ed. (Tübingen: Mohr Siebeck, 2018), pp. 377–420.

Fish, L., 'Homogenizing Community, Homogenizing Nature: An Analysis of Conflicting Rights in the Rights of Nature Debate', *Standford Undergraduate Resarch Journal* 12 (2013), 6–11.

Gregor Barié, C., 'Nuevas narrativas constitucionales en Bolivia y Ecuador: el buen vivir y los derechos de la naturaleza', *Revista de Estudios Latinoamericanos* 59 (2014), 9–40.

Gudynas, E., 'Los derechos de la naturaleza y la construcción de una justicia ambiental y ecológica en Ecuador', in C. Espinosa Gallegos-Anda and C. Pérez Fernández (eds.), *Los Derechos de la Naturaleza y la Naturaleza de sus Derechos* (Quito: Ministerio de Justicia, Derechos Humanos y Cultos, 2011), pp. 95–122.

Huanacuni Mamami, F., 'Paradigma Occidental y Paradigma Indígena Originario', *ALAI America Latino en movimiento* 452 (2010), 17–22.

Huanacuni Mamami, F., *Vivir bien/Buen Vivir*, 6th ed. (La Paz: Instituto Internacional de Integración (III-CAB), 2015).

Juzgado de lo Civil y Mercantil de Galápagos, *Avenida Charles Darwin*, p. 269 (28 June 2012).

Kauffman, C. M. and Martin, P. L., 'Can Rights of Nature Make Development More Sustainable? Why Some Ecuadorian lawsuits Succeed and Others Fail', *World Development* 92 (2017), 130–142.

Kauffman, C. M. and Sheehan, L., 'The Rights of Nature: Guiding Our Responsibilities through Standards', in S. J. Turner, D. Shelton, J. Razzaque, O. McIntyre and J. R.

May (eds.), *Environmental Rights: The Development of Standards* (Cambridge: Cambridge University Press, 2019), pp. 342–366.

van Kessel, J., 'Pachamama, la Virginia: La que creó el mundo y fundó el pueblo', *Cuadernos de investigacion en cultura y tecnologías andinas* 6 (1993), pp. 3–43.

Knauß, S., 'Conceptualizing Human Stewardship in the Anthropocene: The Rights of Nature in Ecuador, New Zealand and India', *Journal of Agricultural and Environmental Ethics* 31 (2018), 703–722.

Kommer, S., 'Diffuse Umweltrechte in Brasilien: am Beispiel von Kollektivklagen gegen ökologische Schäden durch queimadas', *Zeitschrift für Umweltrecht* 23(2012), 459–468.

Lalander, R. and Cuestas-Caza, J., 'Sumak Kawsay y Buen-Vivir en Ecuador', in A. D. Verdú Delgado (ed.), *Conocimientos ancestrales y procesos de desarrollo: Nacionalidades indígenas del Ecuador* (Loja: Ediloja, 2017), pp. 30–64.

Larrea Holguín, J., *Manual elemental de derecho civil del Ecuador: Tomo I* (Quito: Corporación de estudios y publicaciones, 2008).

Latour, B., *Politics of Nature: How to Bring the Sciences into Democracy* (Cambridge, MA: Harvard University Press, 2004).

Leimbacher, J., *Die Rechte der Natur, Zugl.: Bern, Univ., Diss., 1988, Neue Literatur zum Recht* (Basel: Helbing & Lichtenhahn, 1988).

Llasag Fernández, R., 'El sumak kawsay y sus restricciones constitucionales', *Foro: Revista de Derecho* 12 (2009), 113–125.

Llasag Fernández, R., 'Derechos de la naturaleza: una mirada desde la filosofía indígena y la Constitución', in C. Espinosa Gallegos-Anda and C. Pérez Fernández (eds.), *Los Derechos de la Naturaleza y la Naturaleza de sus Derechos* (Quito: Ministerio de Justicia, Derechos Humanos y Cultos, 2011), pp. 57–92.

Loick, D., 'Abhängigkeitserklärung: Recht und Subjektivität', in R. Jaeggi and D. Loick (eds.), *Nach Marx: Philosophie, Kritik, Praxis, Suhrkamp-Taschenbuch Wissenschaft*, 1st ed. (Berlin: Suhrkamp, 2013), pp. 296–318.

Loick, D., *Juridismus: Konturen einer kritischen Theorie des Rechts, Suhrkamp Taschenbuch Wissenschaft, Erste Auflage, Originalausgabe*, vol. 2212 (Berlin: Suhrkamp, 2017).

Macas, L., 'El Sumak Kawsay', *Yachaykuna* 13 (2010), 13–39.

Maldonado, L., 'El Sumak Kawsay / Buen Vivir / Vivir Bien: La experiencia de la República del Ecuador', in A. L. Hidalgo Capitán, A. Guillén García and N. Deleg Guazha (eds.), *Sumak Kawsay Yuyay: Antología del pensamiento indigenista ecuatoriano sobre Sumak Kawsay* (Huelva: Centro de Investigación en Migraciones, Universidad de Huelva, D.L., 2014), pp. 195–210.

Marx, K., 'Zur Judenfrage', in K. Marx and F. Engels (eds.) *Werke* (Berlin[-Ost]: Dietz Verlag, 1976), pp. 347–377.

Medina, J., *Suma Qamaña: Por una convivialidad postindustrial* (La Paz: Editorial Garza Azul, 2006).

Melo, M., Greene, N. and Puente, F., *Experiencia: Reconocimiento de los Derechos de la Naturaleza en la Constitución Ecuatoriana, Iniciativa ciudanizando la política ambiental* (Quito: Fundación Pachamama, 2010).

Menke, C., *Kritik der Rechte, Suhrkamp-Taschenbuch Wissenschaft*, 1st ed., vol. 2241 (Berlin: Suhrkamp, 2018).

Moreno R. H. O., *Introducción a la filosofia indigena: Desde la perspectiva de chimborazo* (Riobamba: Pontificia Universidad Catolica del Ecuador, 1983).

Nieto Sanabria, L., 'The Subalternization of a Progressive Legal Project: The Rights of Nature in Ecuador', *Mexican Law Review* X (2018), 117–138.

Noguera Fernández, A., 'El constitucionalismo de los derechos: apuntes sobre la nueva Constitución ecuatoriana de 2008', *R.V.A.P.* 83 (2009), 117–147.

Oviedo Freire, A., 'Ruptura de dos Paradigmas: Una lectura de la Izquierda desde la Filosofía Tetrádica Andina', in A. Oviedo Freire (ed.), *Bifurcación del buen vivir y el sumak kawsay, 1ra edición* (Quito: Ediciones Sumak, 2014), pp. 139–225.

Pichl, M., 'Die Verrechtlichung der Welt – Ansätze einer postkolonialen Rechtstheorie', *KJ* 45 (2012), 131–143.

Prieto Méndez, J. M., *Derechos de la naturaleza: Fundamentos, contenido y exigibilidad jurisdiccional, 1a; ed.* (Quito: CEDEC: Corte Constitucional del Ecuador, 2013).

Quijano Obregón, A. E., 'Colonialidad y modernidad/racionalidad', *Perú Indígena* 13 (1992), 11–20.

Quijano Obregón, A. E., '"Bien Vivir" para REDISTRIBUIR el poder: Los pueblos indígenas y su propuesta alternativa en tiempos de dominación global', *Yachaykuna* 13 (2010), 47–63.

Ramsauer, U., 'Vom Umweltrecht zu Eigenrechten der Natur?', in S. Schlacke, G. Beaucamp and M. Schubert (eds.), *Infrastruktur-Recht: Festschrift für Wilfried Erbguth zum 70. Geburtstag, Schriften zum öffentlichen Recht* (Berlin: Duncker et Humblot, 2019), pp. 465–477.

Rivera Cusicanqui, S., *Ch'ixinakas utxiwa: Eine Reflexion über Praktiken und Diskurse der Dekolonisierung*, 1st ed. (Münster: Unrast-Verlag, 2018).

Rivera Palomino, J., 'Concepción de la naturaleza en el mundo occidental y den el mundo adino-amazónico', *Logos Latinoamericano* (1994), 26–37.

Rühs, N. and Jones, A., 'The Implementation of Earth Jurisprudence through Substantive Constitutional Rights of Nature', *Sustainability* 8 (2016), 174–193.

Sánchez Parga, J., 'Discursos retrovolucionarios: Sumak Kausay, derechos de la naturaleza y otros pachamamismos', *Ecuador Debate* 84 (2011), 31–50.

Silva Portero, C., '¿Qué es el buen vivir en la Constitución?', in R. Ávila Santamaría (ed.), *La Constitución del 2008 en el contexto andino: Análisis desde la doctrina y el derecho comparado* (Quito: Ministerio de Justicia y Derechos Humanos, 2008), pp. 111–154.

Simon Campaña, F., 'Derechos de la naturaleza: ¿innovación trascendental, retórica jurídica o proyecto político?', *Iuris Dictio* 13 (2013), 9–38.

Stone, C. D., 'Should Trees Have Standing?: Towards Legal Rights for Natural Objects', *Southern California Law Review* 45 (1972), 450–501.

Torre Sandoval, L. M. *de la and Sandoval Peralta, C., La Reciprocidad en el Mundo Andino: El caso de Otavalo* (Quito: Abya Yala, 2004).

Unidad Judicial Multicompetente Con Sede En El Cantón San Cristobal, *Tráfico de Tiburónes, 20331-2017-00179* (04 September 2017).

Unidad Judicial Penal Parroquia Iñanquito, Distrito Metropolitano de Quito, *Pelea de Gallos, Juicio No: 17294201901759* (05 December 2019).

Valladares, C. and Boelens, R., 'Mining for Mother Earth. Governmentalities, Sacred Waters and Nature's Rights in Ecuador', *Geoforum* 100 (2019), 68–79.

Velázquez Velázquez, S., *La Corte Constitucional de Ecuador y el estado constitucional de derechos y justicia, Processus iudicii*, vol. 56 (Barcelona: Atelier, 2018).

Viciano Pastor, R., 'La problemática constitucional del reconocimiento de la naturaleza como sujeto de derechos en la constitución del Ecuador', in L. Estupiñan Achury, C. Storini, R. Martínez Dalmau and de Carvahlho Dantas, F. A. (eds.), *La naturaleza como sujeto de Derechos en el Constitucionalismo Democrático* (Bogotá: Universidad Libre, 2019), pp. 137–154.

Walsh, C. E., *Interculturalidad, estado, sociedad: Luchas (de) coloniales de nuestra época*, 1. ed. (Quito: Univ. Andina Simón Bolívar, 2009).

Yánez Cossío, C., *Pachamama, Sumac causai y Derechos de la naturaleza* (Quito: Macac, 2012).
Yrigoyen Fajarado, R., 'The panorama of pluralist constitutionalism: From multiculturalism to decolonization', in C. A. Rodríguez Garavito (ed.), *Law and society in Latin America: A new map, Law, Development and Globalization, 1st issued in paperback* (London: Routledge, 2016), pp. 157–174.

4 "Rights of Nature" in a Water Market

Francine Rochford

Introduction

> It is a characteristic element of that primitive interpretation of nature we call animism to imagine a soul, spirit or deity within or behind the phenomena, in order to explain their existence or function…The progress of natural science consists to a great extent in its emancipation from animism.
>
> (Kelsen 1948, 377)

This chapter interrogates the notion of rights subsisting in nature, and the consequences of vesting legal personhood on the natural entity to enable enforcement of those rights. It will consider the idea of legal personhood in non-humans, including some historical context. It will then consider the extent to which legal personhood remedies problems arising from lack of legal standing or the capacity of a natural entity to bring legal action on its own behalf. It will focus on rivers and riverine ecosystems as legal persons and will review attempts in legislation and in case law to recognize these entities in law. It will then consider the nature of rights, and whether the conceptualization of rivers as juristic persons capable of deploying rights may have adverse outcomes. It will finally consider the approach taken by the Victorian legislature through the Yarra River Act, comparing it with the project of marketization of water resources in the agreement between the Australian States and the Federal government to manage the waters of the Murray-Darling Basin in Australia. It will compare the environmental outcomes sought to be achieved by the assignment of rights and will consider whether current techniques in Australian legislation are capable of achieving the same or better outcomes for rivers. The management approach to delivering water to the environment, in particular, allows a range of diverse management strategies accounting for environmental values aside from river flow, whereas the "market" allocation of water to various consumptive and non-consumptive uses can have unplanned and potentially undesirable outcomes.

The Legal Personhood of Non-Humans

Personhood as a legal construct conveys specific sets of meaning in common law systems. Immediately it enables the attachment of rights—so for the natural legal person the fullest set of rights adheres and the law will avenge an infringement of those rights. Artificial legal persons, such as corporations, can be holders of rights to a lesser extent. The rights are specifically enunciated in law to enable an entity taking the corporate form to realize the benefits (and undertake the responsibilities) of legal transactions. Other collectives or things have been afforded more nuanced or particularized sets of rights. Whether that results in legal personhood is largely outside the scope of this chapter, but recent commentary suggests the "emplacement and constitution of personality in a techne-mediated world…in new, more virtual, registers" (Parry 2020, 23). Collective ownership of copyright in "culturally specific properties" (Carpenter 2004) extends the aspect of legal personality (ownership) to an unspecified class (potentially temporally undefinable):

> authorship may reside in pre-human creator ancestors...Authorship is replaced by a concept of interpretation through initiation. Ownership yields to a concept of custodianship of dreamings, or legends. Alienation, is contradicted by the concept of immutable communal property. Exploitation, is subject to cultural restraints and taboos. Incentivization also has to yield to concerns about spiritual adulteration.
>
> (Blakeney 1999)

Typically, the possessor of rights also owes to others the corollary duty.

> The idea of rights implies universal rights—since every one, for the purposes of this discussion, at least, must be taken, not only to protect his [sic] own rights, but to observe those of others. Hence, in the possession of rights is involved the negative idea of duties. The holder of rights is likewise a debtor to duties.
>
> (Deiser 1908, 217)

The capacity of non-human persons to be repositories of rights and duties is not a new discussion. Indeed, contemplation of whether nature can have legal personality is not new; modern commentators typically trace the argument to Christopher Stone's work (Stone 1972) but the debate is far older. Personification of non-humans in order to vest them with rights and responsibilities at law characterized many—perhaps most—legal systems at one point. In 1916 Hyde wrote about accounts by Plato and Aristotle of the ceremonial prosecution of non-humans at the Prytaneum at Athens, where "inanimate things—such as stones, beams, pieces of iron, etc., which had caused the death of a man by falling upon him—were put on trial at the Prytaneum; and lastly animals, which had similarly been the cause of death" (Hyde 1916, 696). Hyde notes that

> [i]t is not strange that a people like the Greeks, who saw something divine in every river, fountain and tree, should have endowed unfeeling objects

> with life. The strange thing is...that such ideas...should have clung to the Greek imagination...and have been countenanced by their greatest thinker.
>
> (Hyde 1916, 699)

The "interaction between the Semitic and Greco-Roman traditions" (Jackson 2011, 273) can be seen in the categorization of animals which has continued in some jurisdictions to the present day. In Roman law, the *action de pauperie*, a strict liability action applying to domesticated animals, rendered the owner of an animal liable for its actions, with the alternative remedy of noxal surrender (Jackson 2011, 269–270; Jackson 1978). Echoes remain in the *scienter* action which imposes liability on the owner of an animal for the damage caused by that animal, based on whether the animal is classified as *farae naturare* (wild) or *mansuetae naturarae* (domesticated). There are accounts of ancient Persians and Hebrews treating animals as responsible beings (Hyde 1916, 700). Karl von Amira (1891), Carlo d'Addosio (1892), and Gustav Tobler (1893) demonstrate a strong interest in the subject in the late 19th century. Evans (1906) relied and expanded upon these sources and recounted in depth the common law and ecclesiastic approach to animal malefactors. Accounts of medieval trials of animals exist, and from the 13th to the 16th centuries were reasonably commonplace. Pastoureau enumerated "a hundred cases between 1266 and 1586" (Pastoureau 2004), although Dinzelbacher notes that "animal trials took place only under extremely unusual circumstances...to create the impression that authorities were assiduously maintaining law and order" (Dinzelbacher 2002, 406). Historical records include reports of trials brought against individuals or groups of animals of the same species (such as a swarm of bees) in both civil and criminal proceedings. Criminal prosecutions of wild animals persisted in the ecclesiastical courts in the middle ages, while domestic animals were tried in ordinary criminal courts. In either case, an advocate would be appointed to defend the animal party (Hyde 1916, 704). Thus, the weevils of Mont Cenis, the rats of Autun, and the grasshoppers of Arles were afforded the same legal protections as human defendants in the courts. In America, rats were served writs of ejectment smeared with grease by pushing them into the rat hole (Hyde 1916, 714). Under Germanic law, animals were considered competent as witnesses in court (Hyde 1916, 719). In India in some regions, the tree spirit was punished where a person died by falling from the tree. In China, a ship that had sailed badly could be put into a pillory (Hyde 1916, 724–725).

In earlier moral systems there was nothing inconsistent with the trial and punishment of an animal. Pastoureau notes that the Book of Exodus 21:28 was authority for the proposition that some species of animal could be responsible for their actions because of the presence of souls, and Aristotle is the basis for arguments that "higher" animals "dream, recognize, deduce, remember, can acquire new habits" (Pastoureau 2016; Jackson 1978). Aquinas, however, differentiated the "brute animal" from the beings vested with free will, also inclined by intellect (Aquinas 2017, 1.83).

The practice of trying domestic or wild animals as rational beings was not consistent with later developing philosophies of law; Edouard Osenbrüggen argued that for law to be consistent, animals would have to have been vested with the rights and responsibilities of a human (Hyde 1916, 719). Teubner commences by saying that "today, under the influence of rationalizing science, the number of actors in the legal world has been drastically diminished…the only remaining plausible actor is the human individual. The rest is superstition" (Teubner 2006, 499). He then avers that increasingly strong movements to (re)introduce legal agency to non-humans raise provocative questions for the modern legal system. Theorists such as Luhmann would avoid Aristotle's requirement of rationality and argue that "a closed and autonomous ensemble of recursive communications which encounters [an] entity, constructs this entity via the semantic artefact of an 'actor'" (Teubner 2006, 501). It is the "surrounding social system—and not the entity itself—that constitutes identity, capacity for action and communication, responsibility, rights and duties: in short, it attributes the subjectivity of its artefacts" (Teubner 2006, 501). Latour enables a further step to take in the personality of collectives (Latour 1998) and that "legal personification empowers non-human entities, formal organizations, associations, corporations, and states to enter into fully-fledged political negotiations and intricate economic transactions" (Teubner 2006, 505). Thus, the law "stabilizes social expectations about collective actors by constructing them as juridical persons, granting them rights and imposing upon them duties and responsibilities" (Teubner 2006, 505).

The conceptualization of the proper subject of law has (in effect, rather than in cause) traveled full circle. In a secularized legal system the pressure to vest rights in nature or elements of nature has the general aim of preservation of the elements of nature considered to have contemporary value, but there are at least four discrete forms of reasoning justifying the legal form. Not all of this reasoning supports the full suite of rights afforded by creating legal personhood, and some of this reasoning risks adverse consequences.

Why Recognize Legal Rights in Ecosystem Elements?

The primary driver for acknowledgment of the legal personality of nature, either as individual components or as collectives, is the perception that this is the best way to protect and preserve these ecosystems. In part, there is a symbolic component: "it is not until nature is recognized as holding certain rights that we will realize that nature is deserving of a chance to speak for itself" (Pecharroman 2018). The movement also raises awareness and creates a potent political statement. O'Donnell attributes to eco-centrism the desire "to elevate the river to equal status in the law with human beings" (Eckstein et al. 2019, 811). Other related motivations are to acknowledge the spiritual dimension of an aspect of the environment, particularly from the perspective of indigenous or First Nation laws or cultural values (Eckstein et al. 2019, 811), "to enable the river to advocate for its own interests in policy debates (private interest regulatory theory)" (Eckstein et al. 2019, 811), and "to enable the river to participate in water and ecosystem services markets (market environmentalism)" (Eckstein et al. 2019, 811). It is important to distinguish these various motivations and their outcomes since legal personhood in western legal systems assigns a particular set of characteristics, powers, and duties.

Legal personality creates a legal subject capable of holding rights and enables legal standing. The apparent importance of the capacity to protect ecosystem interests in judicial proceedings seems to motivate the eco-centric approach. The privileging of the inherent interests of an ecosystem (rather than its value in human applications) is potentially enabled if the environment can enforce its own values. This section considers the concept of standing in law and the way in which lack of standing has affected the capacity of proponents of environmental claims to use litigation to support those claims. Of course, this presupposes that human agents for the environment can correctly interpret those values and effectuate them through legal remedies. There are cogent arguments for the protection of the environment and its elements by regulation. However, frustration with "ineffective" or "piecemeal" regulation (Peel 2007, 96) has made litigation an attractive alternative or additional response. "Courts, with their independence from government and capacity to develop legal principles of broad application, can offer an attractive mechanism for spurring legal change where political processes are deadlocked" (Peel 2007, 96).

Standing is the "right to make a legal claim or seek judicial enforcement of a duty or right" (Angstadt 2016, 346) or, in basic terms, the right to bring an action in court. Lack of standing in court is a significant barrier to the protection of the environment by environmental groups (Craig 2009, 1). Meyer notes pithily, "[i]f you do not have standing, you do not get through the door. You may have a cause of action and a door may exist, but if you do not have standing, you cannot get through it" (Cassuto et al. 2006, 66). Where "neither trees nor animals have standing" (*Robinson v. Waitakere City Council* 2010, 23) the legislature has to find other mechanisms, including creating specific courts or tribunals for the protection of the environment. Administrative processes such as environmental impact assessments relating to approvals of planning developments, for instance, may invite submissions from any objectors (*Re Australian Conservation Foundation v. Latrobe City Council (Hazelwood)* 2004; *Gray v. Minister for Planning (Anvil Hill)* 2006). This form of procedural protection characterizes the approach of the Yarra River Act.

The causes of action are also significant in this sense. Indeed, standing and the requirement of a reasonable cause of action are closely related. The rules on standing depend on the relief sought and it would be misleading to say that there was a "law" of standing. In common law actions relating to damage to the environment, the appropriate cause of action might, for instance, be nuisance. For damage to the environment that is generalized, public nuisance would apply, so the Attorney General would generally have standing: *Attorney General v. PYA Quarries Ltd* (1957). These rules of standing were transplanted from nuisance to administrative law. In an action in administrative law in

Australia, the general rule set out in *Boyce v. Paddington Borough Council* (1903) long governed *locus standi* of a public individual seeking injunctive relief or a declaration:

> A plaintiff can sue without joining the Attorney-General in two cases: first, where the interference with the public right is such as that some private right of his is at the same time interfered with…and secondly, where no private right is interfered with, but the plaintiff, in respect of his public right, suffers special damage peculiar to himself from the interference with the public right.
>
> (*Boyce v. Paddington Borough Council* 1903)

Legal standing, however, is dependent on the action or constitutional or legislative context: "generalizations about standing to sue are…worthless" (*Association of Data Processing Service Organisations Inc v. Camp* 1970).

Legal standing historically has been a major inhibitor of litigation by environmental groups, particularly in common law jurisdictions. Until litigation arising around the 1980s, "technical" rules had prevented applications by those without the special interest required to create standing. However, there are reasons for rules of standing. Bogart notes that there are four general justifications for *locus standi*: courts respond to disputes and are not intended to resolve all legal norms; just because an interest should be recognized does not mean that all interests should be recognized; rules of legal standing will develop incrementally according to normal curial process; and finally, "there are no bright lines to determine recognition of non-traditional legal interests" (Bogart 1989, 198). Rules on standing at least expose the value systems espoused:

> [w]hen a court or the legal system does decide to recognize and hear a person in a case, that decision may be taken (and criticized) as an announcement that the values he is pursuing, the purposes of the role he is assuming, have a legal value.
>
> (Vining 1978, 62)

In the context of a legal dispute in which it is claimed that environmental damage had occurred *and there was otherwise no damage to the interests of a legal person*, "the environment," or an element of it such as a river or forest, would be the damaged "party." If "the environment" had legal personality, it would be the legally appropriate person to bring an action according to the rules of standing. In the absence of legal personality, the Attorney General, as the guardian of the public interest, is the appropriate person to sue. In cases that give rise to constitutional issues, standing is afforded to the relevant states—as can be seen in Australian environmental cases such as *Commonwealth v. Tas* (Tasmanian Dam case) (1983) and *Queensland v. Clth* (Tropical Rainforests case) (1989). Of course, legitimate questions can arise as to the motivation of these potential applicants to protect environmental assets for their inherent value; and this is typically the background to agitation for alternatives.

In more inventive approaches, proxies can be created. It is notable that the Ganga Pollution cases did not suffer the issues of standing, since Indian laws allow "any public-spirited citizen to bring suit against regulatory authorities in matters of public concern" (Chaturvedi 2019, 724). In the European Union, environmental non-governmental organizations have standing (Wilk et al. 2019, 687), and legal standing, environmental information, and public participation are recognized by the Aarhus Convention (United Nations 1998). In *Oposa v. Department of the Environment and Natural Resources* (1994) the Supreme Court of the Philippines granted a group of children standing to sue to uphold the environmental rights of themselves and future generations (Allen 1994). Jurisdictions allowing class actions may also loosen traditional rules of standing. Broadening of standing rules themselves would enable litigation by parties with other than pecuniary or proprietary interests, so departing "from a regime absorbed with the protection of individual proprietary, economic and pecuniary values and [and recognizing] other values, many of which may be more collective than individualistic, and more inspired by altruism than self-interest" (Bogart 1989, 207).

The use of human agency is necessary in all cases. Even supposing an element of the environment with legal personhood, its interests are nevertheless, *sans* testimony from itself, not always clear. Defining the interests of the environment, or parts of it, is likely to become a significant issue in determining the success of the approach of legislatures and courts vesting rivers with legal personhood. Cases such as *Wildlife Preservation Society of Queensland Proserpine/Whitsunday Branch Inc v. Minister for the Environment and Heritage* (2006) demonstrate the difficulty of specifying the interests of an environmental area (in this case the Great Barrier Reef). The Federal Court of Australia was ruling on an administrative decision not to require an Environmental Impact Assessment under the federal Environment Protection and Biodiversity Conservation Act 1999 (Cth) (the EPBC Act). In the course of his judgment, Justice Dowsett noted that the applicant was acting out of the concern for the impact of climate change in the future—a "change of unidentified magnitude, such climate change having been caused by levels of greenhouse gases (derived from all sources) in the atmosphere" (*Wildlife Preservation Society of Queensland Proserpine/Whitsunday Branch Inc v. Minister for the Environment and Heritage* 2006).

Even absenting the speculative impact of climate change at some period in the future on a particular segment of the environment, the impact of actions on parts of the environment now can be difficult to trace. The inability of the environment, or its parts, to speak on their own behalf in defining the range of potential harms and their impact requires speculation, reduced to a verbal formula, in regulation. Even if placed at the same level of legal personhood as an adult, traditional redress would not necessarily afford the levels of protection sought, particularly where the harm is as a result of government action. For instance, common-law action after compulsory acquisition or expropriation, although it may require payment of compensation, will "not give redress to one seeking recovery for grief, pain and suffering, mental anguish, loss of comfort, or any other legalism describing...emotional and psychological injuries" (Klein 1968, 3).

The Legal Personality of Rivers

Despite the alternatives to affording legal personhood, including standing, in environmental disputes, in recent years several jurisdictions have created legislation or handed down judicial decisions which, in their various forms, grant legal rights to nature, and in particular rivers. In Ecuador, a court found that the rights "to exist" of the Vilcabamba River had been violated by damage due to road widening (*Wheeler et al. v. Director de la Procuraduria General del Estado en Loja, Corte Provincial de Justicia de Loja* 2011; Pecharroman 2018). The Ganges and Yamuna Rivers and tributaries were granted legal personhood in *Mohd Salim v. State of Uttarakhand* (2017), as were lakes, glaciers, air, jungles, wetlands, and other ecological sites in *Lalit Miglani v. State of Uttarakhand* (2017)—although the Supreme Court of India issued a stay of the High Court's order pending appeal. In Colombia a court found the Atrato River and its tributaries and the river basin to have the right to be protected (Pecharroman 2018). A river was recognized as a valid party to a suit in New York (Byram River 1975), as were a marsh and brook (*Sun Enterprises Ltd v. Train* 1975). Litigation in the Colorado Federal Court claimed that the Colorado River ecosystem was a legal person (*Colorado River Ecosystem v. State* 2017), although applicants voluntarily withdrew their complaint as a result of threatened sanctions for submission of pleadings with improper purpose or frivolous arguments, and a motion to dismiss was granted (Fendt 2017).

Other avenues have utilized customary or indigenous laws as the basis for the claim: Te Urewera, land in Aotearoa New Zealand, was declared a legal entity in 2014 (Te Urewera Act 2014 s3[3]), and the Whanganui river declared a legal person in 2017 (Te Awa Tupua [Whanganui River Claims Settlement] Act 2017 s12) as part of a compromise between indigenous groups and the state (Sanders 2018). In the United States, the rights of Manoomin (wild rice) have been recognized (LaDuke 2019) and the Klamath River has been granted legal personhood in tribal frameworks (Smith 2019). Some of these cases appear to be an attempt to resolve competing views about the relationship between man and nature: "Native American religions and ethnic systems did not recognize a duality between man and nature" (Chatuvedi 2019, 723, citing Nash 1989). Some recognize spirits or power inhabiting certain places (Ward 1992, 797; White 2018, 131).

Other successful actions have been based on Constitutional provisions or other overarching legal principles. The Universal Declaration of the Rights of Mother Earth (ICUN 2010), although not binding in itself, has been implemented in Ecuador and Bolivia. The success of *Wheeler v. The Director of Attorney General's Office in the State of Loja* (2008) in Ecuador was premised on Article

71 of the Ecuadorian Constitution, "which states that Nature, or Pachamama, where life is reproduced and occurs, has the right to integral respect for its existence and for the maintenance and regeneration of its life cycles, structure, functions and evolutionary processes" (Chaturvedi 2019, 720). Reposing rights in the environment was an attempt to bridge the gap between western dualism and (some) indigenous worldviews. The draft Universal Declaration of River Rights, prepared by the Earth Law Center, set out specific rights of rivers: flow, performance of ecosystem functions, freedom from pollution, to feed and be fed by sustainable aquifers, native biodiversity, and restoration (Global Alliance for the Rights of Nature 2018).

Three general strategies emerge—claiming legal personhood in customary legal frameworks, litigation, and legislative change. The difficulties inherent in the litigation strategy are evident from *Colorado River Ecosystem v. State* 2017, where the applicants were threatened with sanctions, *Mohd Salim v. State of Uttarakhand* (2017), and *Lalit Miglani v. State of Uttarakhand* (2017). In the latter two cases, a fundamental issue relating to legal personhood arose. It was argued that reposing legal personality on the river for the purposes of asserting rights would also give rise to responsibilities. The Ganga Management Board, which was in the action said to be acting *in loco parentis* for the river, was the regulatory authority which, in effect, should have been enforcing the environmental rules already in effect for the river. Since the rivers flow through multiple jurisdictions, any applicable court order would have to have central authority. These issues are central to the nature of legal personality as a jurisdictionally defined construct and are pivotal to the larger application of legal personhood to rivers.

The jurisdictional question arises because rivers are not contained. For that reason, also, water in rivers was not traditionally capable of being property: "water is a moveable, wandering thing, and must of necessity continue common by the law of nature" (Blackstone 1787, 18), although there are multiple legal categories of water depending on their state—lying haphazardly over land, in an identifiable channel or underground (Fisher 2000, 64), navigable or non-navigable (MacGrady 1975). Transboundary water issues are typically resolved through political rather than legal avenues. In federations with multiple jurisdictions, such as Australia or the United States of America, strong intergovernmental agreements might enable something close to workability. The capacity of a river to sue as a person when it flows through multiple nation-states is nominal. International water law is governed by conventions (the UN Watercourses Convention 1997 and the UNECE Water Convention) and a large number of basin-level or bilateral water treaties. In the absence of jurisdictionally specific mechanisms for the enforcement of law, "[i]mplementation of international law depends entirely on the consent of state actors to be bound by it" (Zeitoun, Cascão, and Warner 2017). Whilst cooperative water management using these tools is a feature of modern transboundary arrangements (Baranyai 2019), interactions resulting in conflict are a feature of some river basins. The Amu Darya and Nile rivers, which traverse states with power asymmetries (Zeitoun, Cascão, and Warner 2017), illustrate that the use of jurisdictionally based legal forms such as ascription of personality is unlikely to yield useful results. The second issue arises because legal personhood, although varying according to jurisdiction, typically involves the attribution of responsibilities as well as rights. In *Mohd Salim v. State of Uttarakhand* (2017) and *Lalit Miglani v. State of Uttarakhand* (2017), a question arose, as yet unanswered, whether legal personhood would make the river liable for damage due to flood events (Alley 2019). This eventuality corresponds with O'Donnell's view that conferring rights on rivers means that it must "promote its own interests ahead of those who rely on the river, which emphasizes conflict and competition… it entrenches humanity in an adversarial relationship with the environment" (Eckstein et al. 2019, 812).

The Yarra River Act

The Australian response to calls for the rights of rivers has not, so far, been to provide legal personhood to rivers or their environs. However, a novel legislative approach has been deployed in the case of the Yarra River in Victoria. The Yarra River rises on the southern Great Dividing Range at Mount Baw Baw, traverses the Yarra Ranges, and after 250 kilometers flows through Melbourne, the capital city of the State of Victoria, to exit to Port Phillip Bay. The river is significant to the Wurundjeri people and has iconic status to Melbourne inhabitants both unironically and as "the river that flows upside down" due to turbidity. The Yarra River Protection (*Wilip-gin Birrarung murron*) Act 2017 (Vic) ("Yarra River Act") recognizes the river and associated ecosystem as valuable and sets up principles of management for the river, but neither enables it as a holder of rights nor asserts inherent rights of nature. The legislative response recognizes the Yarra River and surrounds as a living and integrated natural entity and creates a suite of principles to manage the river whilst acknowledging the economic and social (human) dependents upon water and the river landscape. In this way, it avoids specifically asserting legal personality on the river but assigns it a value, but that value is defined in circumspect terms by the Act itself. The objects of the Act (s5) are, in part, to assert that the river and its surroundings are "one living and integrated natural entity." This falls short of assigning legal personhood. The Act also recognizes the value of the river and its surroundings in terms of "the economic prosperity, vitality and liveability" of the city and surrounds, including "ecological health, and the cultural, social, environmental and amenity values of the Yarra River and the landscape" and "the environmental significance of the biodiversity corridor along the Yarra River" (Yarra River Act s5). The Act defines "environment" in specific terms to mean "the physical factors of the surroundings of human beings including the land, waters, atmosphere, climate, sound, odours, tastes, the biological factors of animals and plants and the social factor of aesthetics" (s3). This does not include inherent personhood characteristics, but a range of value assignations according to both human and biological referents. This does not represent an eco-centric or indigenous spiritual approach, as O'Donnell notes, but recognizes the value of the river and its ecosystem as "encompassing not just Aboriginal cultural values but also post-settlement cultural diversity and heritage, and values embodied in environmental, social, recreational, management and general protection principles" (Eckstein et al. 2019, 819).

The values assigned to the river are to be taken into account in the development of a strategic plan for the river itself, and Yarra protection principles are to be considered in statutory decision-making. The five general principles (s8) apply to the development of and decision-making related to the Yarra River and Yarra River land. Again, these principles are anthropo- rather than eco-centric. These principles are that:

> (1) Proposed development and decision-making should be based on the effective integration of environmental, social and cultural considerations in order to improve public health and wellbeing and environmental benefit.
> (2) Decision-makers should take into account the best practicably available information about the potential impacts of climate change so as to avoid, so far as possible, serious or irreversible damage resulting from climate change.
> (3) Decision-makers should take into account the impact of any individual action or policy on public health and wellbeing and seek to ensure that public health and wellbeing is enhanced by the action or policy.
> (4) Each generation should ensure that the environmental, social and cultural benefits that have been acquired are maintained or enhanced for the benefit of future generations.
> (5) Protection of the environment and delivery of sustainable development is a responsibility shared by all levels of government, industry, business, communities and the people of Victoria.
>
> (Yarra River Act s8)

Significantly, the Yarra River Act does not give the river independent legal standing, and the Birrarung Council, although charged with the obligation to advocate for the protection and preservation of the river, is not its legal guardian. The Council cannot bring proceedings on behalf of the river itself. By contrast, the Te Awa Tupua Act 2017 in New Zealand gives legal personhood to the Whanganui River, which enables the Te Pou Tupua (the river system) to bring an action in the name of the river itself. O'Bryan notes that

> the Te Awa Tupua Act 'specifically provides for the Whanganui River' to have 'all the rights, powers, duties, and liabilities of a legal person' which are exercised on behalf of the river by Te Pou Tupua, the human face of the Whanganui River.
>
> (Eckstein et al. 2019, 819)

Personhood and the Market

The approach of the Yarra River Act is to provide a set of bureaucratic procedural protections, rather than substantive rights (Oksanen et al. 2017). It establishes a set of agencies and avenues through the river and its environs that can contribute to planning and policy. O'Donnell equates this with "private interest regulatory theory" (Eckstein et al. 2019, 811). This approach is significantly different from rights approaches based on legal personhood because the leverage afforded to the river is based on external valuations. It echoes the commodification of nature and its private value as an asset.

The management of other Australian rivers also adopts elements of the private interest regulatory theory but with strong elements of market environmentalism. This approach would not be necessary for the Yarra River Act because of the limited options for trade in the small catchment, which rises in the Yarra Ranges and runs through Melbourne to the sea. By comparison, the Water Act 2007 (Cth) applies a regulatory framework to the rivers and waters of the Murray-Darling Basin, which crosses four Australian states and a territory. The application of private-interest regulatory theory in this river system operates in the context of a water market. The market paradigm has been an accepted principle in the management of water resources in Australia since the mid-1990s (CoAG 1995; CoAG 2004; NWC 2010) and is inherent in assumptions underlying the Water Act 2007 (Cth) and the associated plans. Private water users (for instance, irrigators) compete in the market against federal and state agencies such as the Commonwealth Environmental Water Office, which at the end of February 2020 held 2,861 gigaliters of registered entitlements. State Environmental Water Holders also "own" water—the New South Wales RiverBank/Office of Environment and Heritage, the Victorian Environmental Water Holder, and the South Australian Department of Environment, Water, and Natural Resources are either statutory entities or operate within government departments. There is also a range of non-governmental not-for-profit organizations that hold water for the environment (O'Donnell 2013, 511). In many cases, the water portfolios are managed according to the needs of the environment or sold back into the water market, but management of water is largely an optimization of environmental, economic, and social needs. Environmental water carries the same obligations as privately held water in terms of contribution to infrastructure.

The status of Australian rivers as "working" rivers is well-established in Australian water policy. Given that even the greatest rivers in the Murray-Darling Basin would, in their natural states, periodically flood or run dry, the basic needs of a settled community will often be adverse to ecosystem requirements. The compromise, in the form of environmental "watering" that partly mirrors but does not replicate natural flows, follows anthropocentric priorities, and in all cases, the Water Act 2007 (Cth) requires the prioritization of "critical human needs" in the creation of a plan in relation to the Murray-Darling Basin waters. "Critical human water needs" are defined in s86A(2) as

> the needs for a minimum amount of water, that can only reasonably be provided from Basin water resources, required to meet:
>
> (a) Core human consumption requirements in urban and rural areas; and
> (b) Those non-human consumption requirements that a failure to meet would cause prohibitively high social, economic or national security costs.

Section 86A(1) specifies that "critical human water needs are the highest priority water use for communities who are dependent on Basin water resources."

The anthropocentric approach aligns with international recognition of the human right to water and to the use of rivers. In particular, the United Nations Convention on the Non-Navigational Uses of International Watercourses (1997), although oriented towards the sustainable use of water, was premised on the need for extraction for human needs and makes it clear that there are legitimate claims to water from rivers. Other international instruments provide specific human rights to water: the United Nations Committee on Economic, Social, and Cultural Rights General Comment No 15 (United Nations 2002); the United Nations International Covenant on Economic, Social and Cultural Rights (United Nations 1966); and the United Nations Universal Declaration of Human Rights (United Nations 1948, art 25).

From an ecocentric perspective, however, the commodification of the environment is problematic. Ecocentrism has as a central tenet that the environment is the focus of obligation in itself, rather than as an incident to human needs (Fieser 1992). The "thought experiment on the river Rhine" by Wilk et al. (2019) is a more appropriate analogy to Australian rivers, at least in the south, than the Whanganui River or the Yarra River. The authors note that

> [g]ranting procedural and material rights to the river implies that an ecocentric, normative stance is taken. In this moral position, humans are not above or separate from nature, but are on par with…rivers. This implies that the existing set of rights held by humans will need to be restricted and that humans will have to take on certain additional duties.

Should the representative of a river such as the Murray River have standing to assert one of the material rights specified in ecocentric thinking, and could that assertion be that the ecosystem be returned to some specified, "pre-damage state" (Wilk et al. 2019, 694)? In the case of a working river with naturally highly variable flows, such as the Murray River, what would such a state entail? Given the massive dams reversing the flow of the river to enable an irrigation network and to smooth domestic demand between years, the return of the river to its original state is unviable without the abandonment of settlements in the Murray-Darling Basin. The ecocentric view cannot align with, for instance, optimization of social, economic, and environmental interests, or with the privileging of critical human needs. Should the normative claims of the river be recognized, the hard decision would be to determine how to simultaneously recognize the equivalence of the rights of the river against acknowledged human rights. An analysis such as this would naturally feel threatening to those dependent on river systems.

Conclusions

Bell notes that the "problem of *modernity* is the problem of belief. To use an unfashionable term, it is a spiritual crisis, since the new anchorages have proved illusory and the old ones have become submerged" (Bell 1996, 28, original emphasis). The pursuit of a rights agenda in a denormatized legal system, the legitimacy of which rests on procedural mechanisms, has resulted in new value claims, alongside the more commonly cited procedural and market-based processes supporting modern claims to justice. Citing the claims of a river to legal personhood based on spiritual or religious systems in the face of a more generalized "uncoupling of positive legal norms from the body of private morality" (Cohen & Arato 1992, 353) raises questions of legitimacy. Protection of the spiritual beliefs of one set of people in a form of religious relativism is a risky strategy in communities with many belief systems, particularly in relation to water availability, which is critical to species survival.

Perhaps a more central issue is that utilizing the concept of personhood to pursue a rights agenda will not necessarily forward the ecological goals sought by proponents of this course of action. Provision of rights can, counterintuitively, deliver adverse landowner attitudes to the environment by de-emphasizing the connectedness between environmental components (including humans) and by responsibilizing the environment for the protection of its own rights.

In Australia, the Yarra River Act provides a set of bureaucratic procedural protections to the river and its environs, but value propositions clearly take an anthropocentric view of water use and diversion. Similarly, the network of procedural mechanisms supplementing the market allocation of resources accommodates anthropocentric uses alongside managed environmental programs. These approaches do not have the evocative symbolism of attribution of legal personhood, but also avoid many of the risks associated with attribution of legal responsibility.

References

d'Addosio C. (1892) *Bestie Delinquenti*. L. Pierro, Napoli.

Albertus Magnus (1258) *Quaestiones super animalibus,* published in Geyer B. et al. (eds) (1955) *Alberti Magni opera omnia, editio coloniensis*. tome XII, Aschendorff, Munster, 281–309.

Allen T. (1994) "The Philippine Children's Case: Recognizing Legal Standing for Future Generations" *Georgetown International Environmental Law Review*, 6, 713–742.

Alley K.D. (2019) "River Goddesses, Personhood and Rights of Nature: Implications for Spiritual Ecology" *Religions*, 10, 502, https://doi.org/10.3390/rel10090502; doi:10.3390/rel10090502 von Amira K. (1891) "Thierstrafen und Thierprocesse" *Mitteilungen des Instituts für Oesterreichische Geschichtsforschung*, XII, 546–606.

Angstadt M. (2016) "Securing Access to Justice Through Environmental Courts and Tribunals: A Case in Diversity" *Vermont Journal of Environmental Law*, 17, 345–371.

Aquinas T. (2017) *Summa Theologica*. 2nd, rev. ed., trans. Fathers of the English Dominican Province 1920, New Advent, 2017, https://www.newadvent.org/summa/1075.htm#article3

Baranyai G. (2019) *European Water Law and Hydropolitics*. Springer, Cham.

Bell D. (1996) *The Cultural Contradictions of Capitalism*. BasicBooks. New York.

Blackstone. (1787) *Commentaries*. 10th ed. ii, cap 2.

Blakeney M. (1999) "Intellectual Property in the Dreamtime – Protecting the Cultural Creativity of Indigenous Peoples" Oxford Intellectual Property Research Centre, Research Seminar (November 9).

Bogart W. (1989) "Book Review: The Lessons of Liberalized Standing?—Locus Standi: A Commentary on the Law of Standing in Canada, by T.A. Cromwell" *Osgoode Hall Law Journal*, 27, 195–209.

Carpenter M.M. (2004) "Intellectual Property Law and Indigenous Peoples: Adapting Copyright Law to the Needs of a Global Community" *Yale Human Rights and Development Law Journal*, 7, 51–78.

Cassuto D., Lovvorn J., Meyer, K. and Tischler J. (2006) "Legal Standing for Animals and Advocates" *Animal Law*, 13, 61–86.

Chaturvedi I. (2019) "Why the Ganga Should Not Claim a Right of the River" *Water International*, 44, 719–735.

Cohen J. and Arato A. (1992) *Civil Society and Political Theory*. MIT Press, Massachusetts.

Council of Australian Governments (CoAG) (1995) *Intergovernmental Agreement on a National Water Initiative between the Commonwealth of Australia and the Governments of New South Wales, Victoria, Queensland, South Australia, the Australian Capital Territory and the Northern Territory*.

Council of Australian Governments (CoAG) (2004) *Intergovernmental Agreement on a National Water Initiative between the Commonwealth of Australia and the Governments of New South Wales, Victoria, Queensland, South Australia, the Australian Capital Territory and the Northern Territory*.

Craig R.K. (2009) "Standing and Environmental Law: An Overview" Public Law Research Paper No. 425, Florida State University College of Law, http://dx.doi.org/10.2139/ssrn.1536583

Deiser G.F. (1908) "Juristic Person" *University of Pennsylvania Law Review and American Law Register*, 57, 216–235.

Dinzelbacher P. (2002) "Animal Trials: A Multidisciplinary Approach" *Journal of Interdisciplinary History*, 32, 405–421.

Eckstein G, D'Andrea A, Marshall V, O'Donnell E, Talbot-Jones J, Curran D and O'Bryan K. (2019) "Conferring Legal Personality on the World's Rivers: A Brief Intellectual Assessment" *Water International*, 44, 804–829.

Evans E.P. (1906) *The Criminal Prosecution and Capital Punishment of Animals*. Heinemann, London.

Fendt L. (2017) "Colorado River 'Personhood' Case Pulled by Proponents" *Aspen Journalism*, December 5.

Fieser J. (1992) "The Compatibility of Eco-Centric Morality" *International Journal of Applied Philosophy*, 7, 37–40, https://doi.org/10.5840/ijap1992714

Fisher D.E. (2000) *Water Law*. LBC Information Services, North Ryde.

Global Alliance for the Rights of Nature (2018) *Universal Declaration of the Rights of Rivers*, https://www.earthlawcenter.org/river-rights/

Hyde W.W. (1916) "The Prosecution and Punishment of Animals and Lifeless Things in Modern Times" *University of Pennsylvania Law Review*, 64, 696–730.

IUCN (2010) *Universal Declaration of the Rights of Mother Earth*, Plurinational Legislative Assembly, Act of the Rights of Mother Earth (December 7), http://f.cl.ly/items/212y0r1R0W2k2F1M021G/Mother_Earth_Law.pdf

Jackson B.S. (1978) "Liability for Animals in Roman Law: An Historical Sketch" *Cambridge Law Journal*, 37, 122–143.

Jackson B.S. (2011) "Liability for Animals: An Historico-Structural Comparison" *International Journal of Semiotics in Law*, 24, 259–289.

Kelsen H. (1948) "Law, State and Justice in the Pure Theory of Law" *Yale Law Journal*, 57, 377–390.

Klein M.R. (1968) "Judicial Response to the Human Disruption" *Journal of Urban Law*, 46, 1–40.

LaDuke, Winona (2019) "The White Earth band of Ojibwe legally recognized the rights of wild rice. Here's why" *Nation of Change*. https://www.nationofchange.org/2019/02/04/the-white-earth-band-of-ojibwe-legally-recognized-the-rights-of-wild-rice-heres-why/

Latour B. (1998) "To Modernise or to Ecologise? That is the Question", in Braun B. and Castree N. eds., *Remaking Reality: Nature at the Millenium*, London: Routledge, 221–242.

MacGrady G.J. (1975) "The Navigability Concept in the Civil and Common Law: Historical Development, Current Importance, and Some Doctrines That Don't Hold Water" *Florida State University Law Review*, 3, 513–615.

Nash R.F. (1989) *The Rights of Nature: A History of Environmental Ethics*. University of Wisconsin Press, Maddison.

National Water Commission (NWC) (2010) *The Impacts of Water Trading in the Southern Murray–Darling Basin: An Economic, Social and Environmental Assessment*. Canberra.

O'Donnell E.L. (2013) "Australia's Environmental Water Holders: Who is Managing our Environmental Water" *Australian Environment Review*, 28, 508–513.

O'Donnell E.L. (2018) "At the Intersection of the Sacred and the Legal: Rights for Nature in Uttarakhand, India" *Journal of Environmental Law*, 30, 135–144.

Oksanen M., Dodsworth A. and O'Doherty, S. eds. (2017) *Environmental Human Rights: A Political Theory Perspective*. Routledge, Abingdon.

Osenbruggen E. (1868) *Studien zur Deutschen und Schweizerischen Rechtsgeschichte*. Fr. Hurter, Schaffhausen.

Parry B. (2020) "Spectral Personas: Exploring the Constitution and Legal Standing of 'Virtual Personhood'", in de Leeuw M and van Wichelen S eds., *Personhood in the Age of Biolegality*. Cham, Springer, 21–38.

Pastoureau M. (2004) *A Symbolic History of the Middle Ages*. Le Seuil, Paris, 29–48.

Pastoureau, M. (2016) "Classes of Animals: The Example of the Western Middle Ages", in Jeudy-Ballini M. ed., *Le Monde en Melanges: Textes offerts à Maurice Godelier*. CNRS Éditions, Paris, 403–424, http://books.openedition.org/editionscnrs/29625; ISBN:9782271130372; doi:10.4000/books.editionscnrs.29625

Pecharroman L.C. (2018) "Rights of Nature: Rivers That Can Stand in Court" *Resources*, 7, 13, doi:10.3390/resources7010013

Peel J. (2007) "The Role of Climate Change Litigation in Australia's Response to Global Warming" *Environmental and Planning Law Journal*, 24, 90–105.

Sanders K. (2018) "'Beyond Human Ownership'? Property, Power and Legal Personality for Nature in Aotearoa New Zealand" *Journal of Environmental Law*, 30, 207–234.

Smith A.V. (2019) "The Klamath River Now Has the Legal Rights of a Person" *High Country News*, September 24, https://www.hcn.org/issues/51.18/tribal-affairs-the-klamath-river-now-has-the-legal-rights-of-a-personClick here to enter text.

Stone C.D. (1972) "Should Trees Have Standing? - Towards *Legal* Rights for Natural Objects" *Southern California Law Review*, 45, 450–501.

Teubner G. (2006) "Rights of Non-humans? Electronic Agents and Animals as New Actors in Politics and Law" *Journal of Law and Society*, 33, 497–521.

Tobler G. (1893) *Thierprocesse in der Schweiz*. Berne.

United Nations (1948) *Universal Declaration of Human Rights*, adopted 10 Dec. 1948, G.A. Res. 217 A (Ill), U.N. GAOR, 3d Sess. (Resolutions, pt. 1), at 71, U.N. Doc. N81 0.

United Nations (1966) *International Covenant on Economic, Social and Cultural Rights*, opened for signature 16 December 1966, 993 UNTS 3 (entered into force 3 January 1976) ('ICESCR').

United Nations (1997) *Convention on the Law of the Non-Navigational Uses of International Watercourses. ('Watercources Convention')*. United Nations, New York.

United Nations (1998) *UNECE Convention on Access to Information, Public Participation in Decision-making and Access to Justice in Environmental Matters ('Aarhus Convention')*. United Nations, Aarhus.

United Nations Committee on Economic, Social and Cultural Rights (2002) *General Comment No. 15*. United Nations, New York.

Vining J. (1978) *Legal Identity, The Coming of Age of Public Law*. Yale University Press, New Haven.

Ward R.C. (1992) "The Spirits Will Leave: Preventing the Desecration and Destruction of Native American Sacred Sites on Federal Land" *Ecology Law Quarterly*, 19, 795–846.

White H. (2018) "Indigenous Peoples, the International Trend Toward Legal Personhood for Nature, and the United States" *American Indian Law Review*, 43, 129–165.

Wilk B., Hegger D.L.T., Dieperink C., Kim R.E. and Driessen P.P.J. (2019) "The Potential Limitations on its Basin Decision-Making Processes of Granting Self-Defence Rights to Father Rhine" *Water International*, 44, 684–700.

Zeitoun, M., Cascão, A.E., Warner, J. et al. (2017) "Transboundary Water Interaction III: Contest and Compliance" *International Environmental Agreements*, 17, 271–294.

Legislation

Environment Protection and Biodiversity Conservation Act 1999 (Cth).

Te Awa Tupua (Whanganui River Claims Settlement) Act 2017 (NZ).

Te Urewera Act 2014 (NZ).

Water Act 2007 (Cth).

Yarra River Protection (*Wilip-gin Birrarung murron*) Act 2017 (Vic).

Cases

Association of Data Processing Service Organisations Inc. v. Camp, 397 U.S. 150 (1970).

Attorney General v. P.Y.A. Quarries Ltd [1957] 2 W.L.R. 770.

Re Australian Conservation Foundation v. Latrobe City Council [2004] V.C.A.T. 2029, [2004] 140 L.G.E.R.A. 100.

Boyce v. Paddington Borough Council [1903] 1 Ch. 109.
Colorado River Ecosystem v. State (2017) 17-cv–02316-NYW.
The Commonwealth of Australia v. State of Tasmania (1983) 158 C.L.R. 1.
Gray v. Minister for Planning [2006] NSWLEC 720, [2006] 152 L.G.E.R.A. 258.
Lalit Miglani v. State of Uttarakhand & others (2017, March 30). Writ Petition (PIL) No.140 of 2015. High Court of Uttarakhand at Nainital.
Mohd. Salim v. State of Uttarakhand & others (2017, March 20). Writ Petition (PIL) No.126 of 2014. High Court of Uttarakhand at Nainital.
Oposa v. Department of the Environment and Natural Resources 33 ILM 173 (1994).
Queensland v. Commonwealth ("Tropical Rainforest Case") (1989) 167 C.L.R. 232.
Robinson v. Waitakere City Council [2010] N.Z.Env.C. 314.
Sun Enterprises Ltd. v. Train, 394 F. Supp. 211 (S.D.N.Y. 1975).
Wheeler et al. v. Director de la Procuraduria General del Estado en Loja, Corte Provincial de Justicia de Loja, 31 marzo 2011, Judgment 11121-2011-0010.
Wildlife Preservation Society of Queensland Proserpine/Whitsunday Branch Inc v. Minister for the Environment and Heritage [2006] F.C.A. 736.

5 The Rights of Nature as Politics

Mihnea Tănăsescu

Introduction

I want to begin with my cards on the table: the rights of nature are not about nature, but rather about the political relations between different groups of people (some of whom might understand themselves as people of particular lands). My answer as to why nature should have rights will therefore center on the particularities of the political processes that led to them. Said differently, I will argue that there is no necessity for granting rights to nature; we are always dealing with contingent political processes that choose rights for reasons that can only be understood by paying attention to particularities. Contrary to those who view rights as on an inevitable course of expansion that is now due to incorporate nature[1] (Stone 1972; Cullinan 2011; Burdon 2011), I will argue that any examination of the legal status of natural entities must be conducted and understood in the particular context of a particular political struggle. In light of this, it may or may not make sense to appeal to rights for nature. When it does or does not make sense will become clearer throughout this chapter. Furthermore, the form that rights for nature will take is entirely dependent on the context of local political contestation.

The rights of nature have so far had two different histories: a theoretical one, grounded in Christopher Stone's pioneering work (1972, 2010), and a practical one, beginning in earnest with Ecuador's 2008 constitution (Tănăsescu 2013, 2016). Though these two strands of rights of nature (hereafter, RoN) have been in dialogue with each other, lately practice has outrun theory. The theoretical orientation in RoN scholarship has underlined these rights' potential to undermine notions of property and personhood (Margil 2014, 2017), to deliver environmental results (Gudynas 2009; Acosta 2011; Knauß 2018), and to promote "harmony with nature" (Cullinan 2011). In contrast, RoN in practice have begun to complicate all of these notions: RoN might themselves be a way to settle property disputes (Sanders 2018), while environmental results are not always the motivation behind actual legislation (Tănăsescu 2020). In other words, we are witnessing a veritable fanning out of RoN practice and, consequently, scholarship. Far from being a monolith, these rights turn out to be an ever-diversifying toolbox for achieving a growing number of goals. This chapter will attempt to take stock of this phenomenon of diversification in several different ways.

First, it will elaborate on Kauffman's and Martin's (2018) typology of RoN, based on its extant cases. There are already too many cases to do justice to in a single publication. Instead, this chapter will build on previous work to propose a categorization of RoN that have been developed so far. Second, it will argue that it is misleading to speak of a *movement* for RoN, as we are instead confronted with a growing number of different struggles adapting the mechanism of rights to their own particular purposes.[2] Third, even though RoN have often been presented as intrinsically tied to indigenous struggles, the argument presented here will show that the heterogeneity of indigenous views does not allow us to speak of one intrinsic connection between "indigenous cosmologies" and "rights of nature," something often expressed through the concept of harmony.[3]

Finally, the chapter will focus in particular on the case of Te Urewera, Aotearoa New Zealand. By looking more closely at this particular case, I will argue that the most radical meaning of RoN doesn't have to do with nature at all, or with guardianship over nature, but rather with a complex negotiation over relations between people, and between people and the lands they are allowed to develop complex relationships with. In developing this argument, I hope to contribute to a theory of RoN that accurately reflects the plurality of relations between people and lands, which is a precious aspect of our many worlds.

Kinds of Rights

The history of RoN, both intellectual and case-based, has been quite amply developed, both in this volume and elsewhere. In this sense, there is no need to recount it here. Instead, I want to first focus on how we can begin to understand the various extant cases of RoN, taken together. In other words, I am interested in developing a typology of RoN that might make it easier to understand the diversity of present and, surely, future cases.

The first systematic typology of RoN was proposed by Kauffman and Martin (2018) in an article drawing on the cases in Ecuador, New Zealand, and one Unites States municipal ordinance (the first such one, in the borough of Tamaqua, Pennsylvania, 2006). Their concern there was to understand how what they see as RoN meta-norms have ended up being expressed so differently in different cases. In other words, given that, for them, "RoN norms are expressed internationally," they wonder "why [...] the world's early RoN laws look so different" (2018, 48). They conclude that the diffusion of RoN norms has not only happened unidirectionally, from the international to the domestic level, but rather "occurs simultaneously at the domestic and international levels, with influence moving in multiple directions" (2018, 60). In other words, the idea of instituting legal personality for nature is refracted through local political struggles and therefore ends up producing what could be significant variations in RoN norms themselves.

Given the variability produced at the intersection of theory and practice, Kauffman and Martin offer a conceptual framework for dividing up the cases that they investigate according to their *scope* and *strength*. Scope refers to two interrelated issues, namely "how expansively [laws] define rights-bearing Nature" (2018, 48) and which particular rights are granted. Strength refers to four different aspects: the type of law and therefore the kind of legal standing granted; the hierarchy of rights; who are the representatives of nature; and whether or not the law mandates responsibility for nature. Together, these elements can plot the differences in RoN laws over and beyond the ones that the authors relied on specifically for their analysis.

Conceptualizing the differences in RoN laws according to their scope and strength is able to accommodate a great deal of variation between different cases. This is especially true if we are interested in understanding different cases according to a legal interpretation. In other words, focusing on scope and strength seems to tell us what the law attempts to do, and how it attempts to do it, but it cannot tell us why the law was adopted to begin with. In other words, this categorization cannot tap into the normative foundations of the law that are fundamental when we are considering legal moves that are unprecedented. To do that, we need further categories that can be used to examine the properly normative foundations of the rights of nature, over and beyond an analysis of positive law strictly speaking. This kind of normative foray would also allow for potentially important connections to be drawn between the normative foundations of law and politics, respectively.

Giving rights to natural entities necessarily leads toward the concept of political representation. As I have argued at length in Tănăsescu (2016), RoN involve the concept of political representation because, under any imaginable circumstance, the subject of rights would have to be spoken for. Not all kinds of representation are political, to be sure. In court, the lawyer represents the client without this needing to mean that the lawyer is the client's political representative. However, the concept of nature will not allow for a kind of representation that does not also involve its political variant. The lawyer who represents nature in court cannot simply perceive the client's interests without a previous effort to determine what these interests are, and thus without a previous engagement with political representation, especially inasmuch as the interests of nature-as-client cannot simply and unproblematically be read off by the lawyer. Whatever it is that lawyers will juridically represent will have to have been previously decided in a political fashion, that is, in a discursive competition to determine what nature's interests are.[4]

Furthermore, in the case of a natural entity with rights, these rights are inconceivable outside of a particular *institutionalization* of their representation. That is to say, RoN can never be an end in themselves, but rather the beginning of a political process of representation. The way in which the legal text itself interacts with the necessity for building infrastructures of representation is important because it gives fundamental clues as to how RoN might be implemented. It also indicates how the normative foundations of the law were (or were not) stretched in order to accommodate new legal and political practices.

Rights of nature can only ever be as good as this process of representation allows them to be. From this perspective, the most important category in Kauffman's and Martin's conceptualization is who the representatives of nature are (on the side of strength). But this cannot be the whole story. Instead, we also need to ask *why* the representatives of nature are the ones that the law mandates. This question, which is a variation on the why question asked earlier, points toward important parts of a new category that can cover more of the variation of RoN and, crucially, can begin to account for their political and normative importance. This category is *purpose*.[5]

Unlike scope and strength, and precisely because of its political nature, purpose cannot be easily determined. An inherently normative investigation, framed by the idea of political representation, will not be amenable to the kind of study that can confidently and uncontroversially determine what the purpose of each RoN law so far has been. But this is precisely the point: by complementing Kauffman's and Martin's legalistic categorization, I mean to put front and center the political ambiguity at the heart of all and every RoN law. In other words, this examination focuses on the normative dimensions of the category of purpose, which can complement more positivist accounts as well as unsettle received wisdom. Contrary to the claim that the purpose of RoN is always already that of increasing harmony with nature,[6] closer empirical examination reveals that purposes vary and, what is even more important, there are often cross-purposes within a single case.

In order to begin examining the category of purpose and illustrate its importance, we should pay attention to the language of the laws themselves, including but not limited to the portrayal of nature (as person or as entity, for example; see Tănăsescu 2020), the framing of representation (as guardianship, trusteeship, "human face," and so on), and the underlining problems that these rights are supposed to solve. When we look at it that way, we begin to see that nature is often but a conceptual proxy for other struggles, significantly, ones about the meaning of ownership in situations of political contestation of sovereignty and authority.[7] In order to establish the validity of this interpretive stance, I want to briefly turn to the case of Te Urewera.

However, before doing so, a caveat is in order. The arguments presented in this chapter draw heavily on the analysis of one particular case. I do not mean to imply that, through this analysis, anything has been proven that applies to all possible RoN cases. Instead, I want to suggest that looking at RoN cases through the lens championed here can be fruitful, and the application to Te Urewera is meant to lend credibility to the general method of investigation by demonstrating what it can accomplish. As I will argue, by examining the political processes and the purposes of granting legal entity status to (parts of) nature, we end up also complicating our view of the inherent normative commitments of RoN. While I can only show this in one case, I suspect that it can be shown in many others as well.

Te Urewera Act 2014

The first case of granting legal personality to a natural entity in New Zealand involved Te Urewera, the ancestral home of Tūhoe people, a Māori descent group of Aotearoa New Zealand.[8] The most important contextual clarification for understanding the legal personality of Te Urewera is placing it within the background of treaty negotiations between Māori groups in general and the New Zealand government. As Sanders (2018, 213) explains, "the grant of legal personality to Te Urewera and the Whanganui river took place as part of the Treaty of Waitangi settlement process, through which the Crown acknowledges breaches of its obligations to Māori under the 1840 agreement."

Seventy years after the first European landing in Aotearoa (James Cook's *Endeavour*), and many missionaries and settlers later, the British Crown and many (but not all) Māori chiefs signed the Treaty of Waitangi (1840), the most important document in New Zealand's history (Jones 2016). After the signing, in Waitangi, the treaty was taken across the island for additional signatures. While Tūhoe have never signed,[9] this does not mean that they were exempt from the effects of this monumental event. Starting in the 1860s, a period of aggressive colonization began, with land purchases and confiscations greatly expanding the settler populations. Demography shifted from Māori majority to Māori minority in little more than 50 years.

In this context, Te Urewera remained the last bastion of Māori *tikanga*,[10] since by 1865 the Crown "confiscated much of [Tūhoe's] most productive land."[11] Between 1865 and 1871 there was a war between the Crown and Tūhoe in Te Urewera which, by the Crown's own admission, devasted Māori groups through starvation, executions, and further appropriation of lands (O'Malley 2014). Tūhoe autonomy was officially recognized in law when, in 1896,

> the Urewera District Native Reserve Act provided for local Tūhoe self-government over a 656,000-acre Reserve, and for decisions about the use of land to be made collectively and according to Tūhoe custom. The Act guaranteed the protection of Tūhoe lands, which could not be sold without Tūhoe consent and then only to the Crown.[12]

The Act was never implemented, though it set a unique precedent in recognizing Tūhoe's authority in Te Urewera. "Perhaps the most remarkable aspect of [the Act] was its intention to give effect to tino rangatiratanga or mana motuhake"[13] (Jones 2014). Despite this intention, the early 20th century was marked by widespread disregard for the act, with "the government simply [...] buying land interests directly from individuals, in direct contravention of its own laws" (O'Malley 2014). As if to catch up with the reality on the ground, in 1922 the government repealed the Urewera District Native Reserve Act, putting an end to this early period of experimentation in plural sovereignty. In 1954 Te Urewera became a national park.

This lengthy period of colonization and denial of sovereign authority over traditional lands began to change with a new generation of Māori activism and politics. As a result of changing political conditions, the Treaty of Waitangi Act of 1975 inaugurated the Waitangi Tribunal, "a standing commission of inquiry established to inquire into Māori claims that laws, policies, acts or omissions of the Crown are or were inconsistent with the principles of the Treaty of Waitangi" (Sanders 2018, 208). Recent scholarship on the Treaty, as well as recent judicial decisions by the tribunal, have more or less settled on the opinion that, at the time of signing, Māori chiefs did not cede their sovereign ability to direct the life of the community or their ownership of their lands.

For the first decade of its functioning the tribunal, though it only had powers of recommendation, began to have a decisive influence on Māori–Crown relations. As Belgrave (2013) explains, "it was partly in recognition of this success that in 1985 the fourth Labour Government extended the tribunal's jurisdiction back to 1840, with far-reaching consequences that were only dimly understood at the time." This set in motion the contemporary era of negotiations between the government and Māori *iwi* and *hapū*[14] regarding breaches of the treaty, an ongoing period known as one of "treaty settlement."

The grant of legal personality to several landscapes in New Zealand can therefore only be understood in the post-1985 context of treaty settlements. In the case of Tūhoe and Te Urewera in particular, we cannot understand the purpose of the legal entity framework without attending to the longstanding disputes between Māori descent groups and the government. Importantly, these disputes are, and have consistently been, about authority, sovereignty, and ownership. In other words, Tūhoe have consistently claimed that the Crown has breached its treaty obligations by not respecting Tūhoe authority over Te Urewera. Another way of framing this issue, is to say that what was at stake in Te Urewera was the question of who, ultimately, owns the land.

The issue of ownership evidently arises out of the settler legal framework that has come to dominate New Zealand. This issue has not traditionally been important for Māori *iwi* or *hapū*, because use of the land was not tied, strictly speaking, to ownership. Similarly, authority and sovereignty are understood in Māori philosophy as being tied to the kinds of relationships to the land and to other people that a particular chief is able to maintain (Jackson 1992; Salmond 2017). Carwyn Jones explains that "relationships are central to Maori society [...] and Maori legal traditions. [...] How relationships are formed, maintained, changed, and dissolved are all key concerns of Maori legal traditions" (2016, 66). The question of the chief owning land has never been, from this perspective, a pertinent one. Rather, the question is about the kinds of relationships that a particular community is able to nurture.

As Jones argues, treaty settlement claims impose the official legal framework onto Māori descent groups, and the issue of ownership is part of this imposition. Despite its being foreign to Māori philosophical conceptions, it has nonetheless become important in defining the official, sanctioned relationship between *iwi* and particular lands. This means that many settlement claims are in fact about who has authority over, and by extension, who owns particular lands. As Sanders explains in relation to Te Urewera and Te Awa Tupua Act 2017,[15] "the grant of legal personality is an example of a compromise between the state and an indigenous descent group, each of which claim political authority in that space" (2018, 209).

Sidestepping Ownership

The dispute between Tūhoe and the Crown over the ownership of Te Urewera took the form of a treaty settlement claim, as shown by the history briefly described above. Within the current political context in New Zealand, the open negotiation for breaches of the treaty focused on fundamental issues of authority. The relevant political climate would not afford the possibility of actually transferring ownership of Te Urewera to Tūhoe. Sanders (2018) argues that "legal personality was recognized because the government would not transfer ownership to Māori." In other words, the legal personality arrangement is a compromise that chooses to sidestep the question of ownership by granting it to the land itself. Te Urewera owns itself,[16] and through this innovation the parties were able to avoid the currently insurmountable issue of choosing between one or another human owner.

As far as the Crown is concerned, settlements reached with *iwi* are final, and they are supposed to resolve *all* historical breaches of the treaty. However, there is no reason to suppose that this is in fact so. Inasmuch as the legal personality of Te Urewera is a compromise in the granting of authority, it is reasonable to suppose that the claim settlement process is, in fact, reframing "the terms under which this conflict [over authority] continues" (Sanders 2018, 209). One way to see this is by focusing on the issue of who is granted authority, under the Te Urewera Act 2014, to represent the legal entity. Here we are starting to get closer to the issue of purpose that I introduced earlier, and to see why it is important to focus on it when examining rights of nature cases.

The Te Urewera Act 2014 opts for the construction of a board that would be the de facto and de jure governor of Te Urewera, while the owner is Te Urewera itself. This means that the political authority of Te Urewera is not given to Tūhoe as such, but rather to a representative organ (the board) that is itself mandated by the law. Indeed, section 17 states that the board was "created in order to act on behalf of, and to 'provide governance'" to Te Urewera. Subsequent sections[17] explicitly allow the board to govern according to Tūhoe principles. Whatever that might look like in practice (for this issue, also see Tănăsescu 2020), it is clear that the link between political representation and the legal personality of nature[18] is central to the post-settlement status of Te Urewera.

It is too early to say just how the governance by the board will unfold over time, but it seems clear that whatever future conflicts might exist with the Crown will play out within this radically altered context. Te Urewera Act 2014 makes it possible to challenge the state from the point of view of Te

Urewera itself, which now speaks through its board. What, exactly, it will say remains to be seen. It also remains to be seen what rights Te Urewera might have. As a legal entity, it comes under the jurisdiction of the NZ Bill of Rights (Macpherson 2019, 117) and will therefore be able to enter contracts, hold property (it already owns itself), incur debts, and sue on its own behalf. But the precise nexus of rights and responsibilities that Te Urewera will have is, at this point, unclear.

This lack of clarity is important in itself. In the case of Te Urewera, the tendency of RoN literature to settle on a number of "fundamental rights" (see Berry 1999; Cullinan 2011) is challenged by a different approach. The minimalist grant of legal entity status[19] is used in order to facilitate a certain representative arrangement that privileges the relations between Tūhoe (organized in a board[20]) and Te Urewera. The fact that the exact rights that Te Urewera might enjoy are not specified indicates the central role of representation, and it also offers a conceptualization of nature that departs from the universal categories present in much RoN literature, instead favoring localized (Te Urewera is a specific place) environments.[21]

One of the closest precedents in common law to the legal form of Te Urewera is, perhaps strikingly, the corporation. David Ciepley (2013) proposed a theory of the corporation that recognizes its special status as a kind of "constitutional republic—a shareholder republic" (140). The basic rights of a corporation, on his account, do not have to do primarily with business, but rather with its specific form of government. These are

> the rights to own property, make contracts, and sue and be sued, as a unitary entity (a legal 'person'); the right to centralized management of this property; and the right to establish and enforce rules within its jurisdiction *beyond* those of the laws of the land.
>
> (2013, 141)

In other words, the corporation is a kind of entity that owns itself and its assets, despite the fact that it enjoys a certain privileged relationship with a particular group of people (its shareholders on the one hand, and its managers on the other). However, these groups are neither liable for the corporation's acts, nor are they the owners of its assets. In other words, shareholders and managers are in no way identical to the corporate form.

Similarly, Te Urewera owns itself and is governed by an appointed board that is not identical to it. The only obvious difference between the Te Urewera arrangement and a corporation is that financially and for tax purposes, Te Urewera and the board are the same person (Te Urewera Act 2014, 40). In all other respects, the new legal entity designating Tūhoe land seems to accord precisely with Ciepley's corporation, including in the board's ability to impose rules that are not those of the land. Article 18 points 2 and 3 explicitly allow the board to govern according to Tūhoe principles. And the legal entity of Te Urewera can own property, enter into contracts, and sue on its own behalf, which are all legal entitlements identical to those held by corporations.

This similarity makes sense if we consider that the idea of legal personality, and by extension rights of nature, is much friendlier to established legal custom than might initially be thought. Jones (2016) argues that "[legal personality] does not, in itself, recognize the value of Maori legal traditions." He continues:

> In fact, it confirms that Maori legal traditions will not be recognized on their own terms but instead only through the closest equivalent from the Western legal tradition. In effect, this mechanism enables lawmakers to avoid trying to source laws for the regulation of rivers and other landscape features in Maori legal traditions, instead deploying a mechanism from the common law that is deemed by the Crown to be a close enough match.
> (2016, 98)

Similarly, neither is the idea of legal personality for nature inherently friendly to nature.

The Te Urewera approach is markedly different from other RoN approaches, such as in Ecuador, where particular rights are granted (notably the right to respect, regeneration, and restoration), but no governing body is set up to represent the newly created legal entity. However, this does not mean that Te Urewera is not a RoN case, while Ecuador is such a case. In the case of Te Urewera, rights are reached by default, through the creation of a legal entity resembling a corporation; in the case of Ecuador, legal personality is reached by default, through the granting of particular (although particularly hard to interpret) rights. The differences between the two, which are both rightly considered to be RoN cases, have to do with the representative arrangements that accompany the creation of a new legal entity. But in order to understand why RoN look the way they do in the case of Ecuador, we would similarly need to attend to the political process that led to their creation in that country (see Tănăsescu 2013, 2016 for an analysis). As scholarship that has begun to do this has shown, it is not the meta-norm of "harmony with nature" that obviously leads to Ecuador-style RoN, but rather the particularities of the Ecuadorian case, not least of which is the involvement of an international network of policy entrepreneurs[22] devoted to the idea of "harmony with nature."

Relationality and Cross Purposes

Unlike the claims, related especially to the cases of Ecuador and Bolivia, that there is an intrinsic relation between the rights of nature and indigenous conceptual systems, Te Urewera provides an example of deep indigenous involvement that nonetheless ends up without a universal figure of nature, nor with specific rights, nor with a legal form that could in good faith be identified with *tikanga*. This should alert us to the multiplicity of indigenous positions. The rights of nature are often presented as ecocentric, as are indigenous philosophies. As I have argued in Tănăsescu (2015, 2016, 2020), this is an assimilation of indigenous thinking into western philosophical centrism and is not, in fact, reflective of either the multiplicity or the radical difference of indigenous worlds. Instead, indigenous philosophies could be understood as relational, and many do not possess a figure of "nature" as the external pole of "humanity," either to be protected for its own sake (ecocentrism) or for instrumental reasons (anthropocentrism).

Relational philosophies are localized ones, ways of being in the world that are rooted in paying attention to the particularities of places. In contrast, the rights of nature are often presented as an international movement to save the Earth. This tendency is well exemplified by the Universal Declaration of the Rights of Mother Earth, sponsored and formulated by the same transnational policy network that was instrumental in drafting Ecuador's rights of nature constitutional provisions. Rawson and Mansfield (2018) identified this network as being composed of environmental activists and lawyers, centered around the work of the Community Environmental Legal Defence Fund (CELDF) in the United States, which present a framework for RoN that risks naturalizing them as the sole instrument of emancipation in two related senses. First, rights are presented as the only way of reversing environmental policies that treat nature as a mere object. Second, the rights of nature are presented as inherently friendly towards indigenous communities. Both of these assumptions about RoN are included in the concept of "harmony with nature."

As this chapter has already begun to argue, the assumptions behind the ideal of harmony with nature are neither universally applicable to all RoN cases, nor the most logical ones given the legal history of the concept of rights. As I have argued in Tănăsescu (2020), because of the uneasy relationship between the concept of rights and Māori philosophy, Te Kawa o Te Urewera (hereafter Te Kawa), the management plan drafted by the board for the governance of Te Urewera, explicitly avoids the issue of rights. Instead, it focuses on the concept of responsibility and on the duty of Tūhoe to relearn ways of being in the world that are inspired by the specificity of the land itself. Tūhoe are not presented as guardians, but rather as subordinate to the power of Te Urewera's being. This should not be confused with ecocentrism, because the whole point is to learn new ways of common life, not to fetishize a generic nature that is intrinsically valuable, over and beyond the relationships that it makes possible and that it enters into. However, the fact that Te Kawa is deeply connected to Tūhoe philosophy is only incidentally related to the grant of legal personality. In other words, it is that grant that allows for a management plan, but this plan could have looked like the quarterly plan of a corporation while still falling within the letter of the law.

This specifically Māori way of looking at the world is present in the management plan that the Tūhoe majority board has drafted but, as Jones (2016) points out, the legal text itself relies heavily on Māori conceptions in the preamble and introduction, while sticking to western legal ontology throughout the rest. The idea of a board, just like the idea of an *iwi* that can negotiate on behalf of Tūhoe, is a particular way of continuing the imposition of the state's legal framework, despite the novelty of legal entity status for Te Urewera. By this, I do not mean to argue that there is nothing valuable here. Instead, I mean to point out how the idea of RoN cannot help but participate in the nexus of local political relations in ways that are neither intrinsically friendly to indigenous worlds (or to natural assemblages), nor free of sticky associations with colonial histories.

Based on the analysis presented above, it can be appreciated how the case of Te Urewera illustrates the coexistence of only partially aligning purposes in a RoN case. For the Crown, the legal entity status of Te Urewera was both a way of permanently settling historical claims of breaches of the treaty and of avoiding the politically impossible step of granting ownership of the land to Tūhoe. For Tūhoe, the purpose of granting legal entity status was principally in support of the return of authority over Te Urewera. This authority, crucially, has not been returned in the same form it had in the 1860s when it was first usurped. Instead, the mechanism of a board institutes a representative arrangement that in itself incorporates the different purposes of the negotiating parties. For the Crown, the board embodies the finality of the treaty settlement, while for Tūhoe it makes possible autonomous political intervention, which might as well be used to challenge the state again, but through a different mechanism.

The case of Te Urewera complicates the idea that the purpose of RoN is environmental protection. It further complicates the idea that the rights of nature are a set of meta-norms (chief among which is "harmony with nature"), a claim that implies the existence of a single movement for the diffusion of these norms.[23] The argument developed here has only relied, in empirical terms, on the case of Te Urewera. However, the concept of purpose and the normative investigation of legal constructs can be used for other cases as well, as was briefly indicated by reference to the case of the Ecuadorian constitution.

Kauffman and Martin (2018), despite being careful to recognize the multiple directions of exchange when it comes to norms, also imply that the rights of nature are a unified body of ideas that the exchange of norms is about. Te Urewera does not seem to bear this out. The policy entrepreneurs who were instrumental in the development of RoN laws elsewhere were not instrumental in New Zealand, and the purposes for which laws in Ecuador, Bolivia, India, the United States, Colombia, and New Zealand were passed cannot be assumed to be either similar or inherently complementary. In the case of Te Urewera, legal entity status was used as a compromise over authority, and whether and what environmental results it may deliver remains to be seen. In fact, the legal entity status of Te Urewera comes to replace the status of a national park, which had obviously been connected to environmental considerations. The Te Urewera Act 2014 removes the land from the authority of the Department of Conservation.

This case also presents the possibility of RoN norms also being local. A better conceptual description might then be to characterize the international aspect of rights for nature as having to do with the bare mechanism of rights (and legal personality) and not with particularly hard norms (such as harmony with nature). As Rawson and Mansfield argued, the internationalization of rights of nature fits seamlessly into the internationalization of rights as such, and into the hegemonic domination that rights enjoy over all manner of emancipatory discourse (also see Campbell 2011). What is internationally diffused is the idea of using the mechanism of legal personality for natural entities. That this can be done is now beyond dispute. Why it might be done remains a matter of local political struggle.

Conclusions

The analysis presented in this chapter has used the case of Te Urewera as an anchor, for several reasons. First, it is severely understudied, even though it offers striking new directions in RoN scholarship.[24] Second, it illustrates very well the idea of purpose and the messy and complex ways in which the issue of legal personality interacts with local political dynamics. But this does not also mean that the analysis presented here is limited to this one case. Though space does not allow for a fuller elaboration, I want to briefly indicate how other RoN cases are amenable to a similar analysis.

In the case of Ecuador, for example, I have argued (Tănăsescu 2013, 2016, 2020) that there were several different purposes for the constitutional provisions granting RoN. What is more, different actors had different goals (as in the case of New Zealand). It is no secret that the government of then-president Rafael Correa did not support the rights of nature and was committed to undermining them in the long run. The indigenous communities of Ecuador, organized through CONAIE,[25] lent their strategic support for Articles 71 and 72, as part of a comprehensive package of rights that was intended to strengthen their own territorial authority. Finally, the transnational policy network, which was comprised of several Ecuadorian and American NGOs (see Rawson and Mansfield 2018), had as their main goal the popularization of the idea of RoN itself (in their preferred form).[26]

This latter purpose is very important, precisely because it has been quite successful. Legal implementation of the rights of nature in Ecuador has been quite problematic, to say the least (Kauffman and Martin 2017), but the idea that rights for nature can solve environmental problems has become much more widespread. The success of the particular way of framing the idea in the Ecuadorian casecan be seen in how other RoN laws have mimicked the scope and strength of the approach taken in Ecuador, at the expense of taking local conditions seriously.

The goal of internationalizing the rights of nature, as a particular recipe centered around the issue of rights, does not adequately take into account the colonial histories that have often made rights an instrument of power and oppression. Even if we accept the existence of meta-norms such as "harmony with nature," the realization of such norms would depend on taking into account local struggles and therefore the relationship of local histories with concepts such as rights. In much RoN advocacy to date, the promotion of meta-norms has gone hand in hand with the assumption that indigenous peoples have a privileged relation to the concept of RoN, precisely because they are assumed to have a privileged relation to the norm of harmony. In other words, the meta-norms that policy entrepreneurs have promoted as intrinsic to RoN have also been largely understood as intrinsically friendly to indigenous struggles. The arguments presented here offer reasons to doubt both of these assumptions.

Viewed from this perspective, the supposed existence of RoN meta-norms is a *political* gesture on the part of RoN policy entrepreneurs, one that has the potential to undermine indigenous struggles for authority in lands that they claim as their own. The experience of New Zealand, juxtaposed with the other cases of RoN (Tănăsescu 2020), makes it possible to see how the idea of RoN meta-norms itself is a product of the goals of a particular policy network. The extent to which the mechanism of rights is able to accommodate local political struggles and to work on the side of emancipatory projects is hobbled by the hegemonic view promoted by organizations such as CELDF.

Returning to the initial concern of this chapter, which involves the kinds of rights and the reasons for granting them, we can revisit Kauffman's and Martin's categorization in terms of scope and strength, and see that it is not merely neutral and descriptive. Instead, we can employ that matrix as a way into the often-hidden politics of rights of nature, by insisting on ascertaining the purposes and processes that lay behind the scope and strength of a particular legal formulation. In other words, we treat the phenomenon of RoN as politics.

Why should nature have rights? This question cannot be answered in the abstract. This is because there is no convincing way of tying the concept of rights to a universal category of nature, in the form of an abstract proposition. Instead, we can see in a variety of cases how the mechanism of rights is used for political purposes, and how its association with the concept of nature works to both solidify the hegemonic power of rights discourses and to potentially benefit certain political configurations over others. Importantly, the framework of RoN has an internal multiplicity that frustrates the seemingly simple goal of bringing about harmony with nature. In the case of Te Urewera, I have argued that nature as such, and especially as a western concept, had very little to do with the political negotiation that eventually led to the Te Urewera Act 2014.

Based on the argument presented here, the legal recognition of RoN can be an important tool in political negotiations over authority, sovereignty, and the representation and governance of particular lands. But the question of why we should adopt rights of nature should not be merely assumed (for environmental protection, or for indigenous empowerment), but actively asked. In cases of rights of nature to come, the goal of granting such rights should be interrogated not simply as an analytic scholarly device for commenting after the fact, but as part and parcel of political strategy. This is one of the most important lessons that Te Urewera has to teach, namely the importance of thinking about the instrument of legal personality in political terms, and therefore seeing its potential for solving problems that were not initially understood as part of its jurisdiction.

Notes

1 This claim is often implied in rights of nature scholarship. It is also explicitly part of many advocacy efforts (see Margil 2014, 2017). The idea of an expanding circle of moral concern was most famously formulated by Peter Singer (1981) in the context of animal rights. For how this idea has traveled from animal to nature rights, see Tănăsescu (2016).

2 The claim that the rights of nature constitute a movement is too widespread to be pinpointed to any particular author; it has become an unreflective and fairly automatic way of describing rights of nature cases. For early indications away from the assumption of a movement, see Rawson and Mansfield (2018).

3 For a detailed overview (as well as a detailed critique) of the often-claimed relationship between rights of nature, ecocentrism, and indigenous philosophies, see Tănăsescu (2020). In short, the assumption of many authors (see, among others, Knauß 2018; Acosta 2011; Gudynas 2009; Kotzé & Villavicencio Calzadilla 2017; Borras 2016) is that the rights of nature are ecocentric, and that indigenous philosophies are also ecocentric. This leads them to suppose that the rights of nature share an intrinsic affinity with indigenous philosophies. This idea is often expressed through the norm of harmony with nature, a norm that is claimed to exist in ecocentric ways of conceiving of the natural environment.

4 For a detailed example of how this has worked in practice, see Tănăsescu (2013).

5 I don't mean to imply that this chapter will explore the category of purpose in its totality. Rather, and via the discussion of political representation, I mean to draw attention to (potentially conflicting) purposes in rights of nature scholarship and practice.

6 The idea that harmony is the end goal of RoN is also ubiquitous in the literature. It has its clearest expression in Cullinan (2011).

7 This way of looking at the rights of nature raises another important issue, namely the relationship between indigenous struggles and legal arrangements that grant rights, in one form or another, to territories that indigenous communities call home. I have dealt with this issue specifically in Tănăsescu (2020). Here, it is relevant to recall that it is by no means obvious that rights for nature advance indigenous interests.

8 Aotearoa is the original Māori name for the North Island, now widely used for the entire country; see Salmond (2017). Tūhoe are a Māori group that inhabit the lands of Te Urewera, currently having around 10,000 registered members; see Binney (2009).

9 Ngai Tūhoe Deed of Settlement Summary (June 4, 2013); also see Binney (2009).

10 This term refers to law, way, or custom. In legal discussions, the term is used to denote Māori law, that is to say legal custom of Māori origins and application. Much in the discussion of legal personality for nature centers around the idea that this construct represents a hybridization of *tikanga* Māori and Crown law.

11 Deed of Settlement Summary, note 9 above.

12 Finlayson, C. *Address to Tūhoe–Crown Settlement Day in Taneatua*, 23 August 2014. Available at https://www.beehive.govt.nz/speech/address-tuhoe-crown-settlement-day-taneatua

13 These two terms are very close in meaning and pivot around ideas of authority and sovereignty. Both terms also directly tie the history of Crown–Tūhoe conflict to the eventual Te Urewera Act 2014.

14 These are names for indigenous Māori descent groups. *Iwi* denotes a larger group than *hapū*.

15 This is the act that inaugurated legal personality for Whanganui river. This case, those coming three years after Te Urewera, is much better known internationally.

16 The idea of self-ownership, modelled on Te Urewera, has also been proposed for other planets. See Tepper and Whitehead (2018).
17 18.2 and 18.3.
18 For a more complete theorization of this link, see Tănăsescu (2016).
19 For the important difference between a legal entity and a legal person, see Naffine (2003), Grear (2013), Tănăsescu (2020).
20 The idea of a board is a form of organization that is acceptable to the Crown but bears no relation to *tikanga*. We should therefore also pay attention to the influence that the Crown settlement process is likely to have on Tūhoe politics.
21 For more on this, and the relation between Māori philosophy and the conceptualization of Te Urewera, see Tănăsescu (2020).
22 This term has roots in the public policy literature. It is explained in Cairney 2019 (271–272) with reference to Kingdon's (1984) influential model of policy windows of opportunity. In essence, a policy entrepreneur is someone (elected or unelected) who has a preferred policy solution and is waiting for the right problem to advance it. They are generally people well placed to influence political processes and have the access and ability to take advantage of opportunities in order to offer their preferred solution. This describes quite well much of RoN advocacy to date, as I document in Tănăsescu (2013) and as Rawson and Mansfield (2018) have also shown.
23 The international RoN advocacy network has been quick to appropriate New Zealand cases to a supposed international RoN movement, as media coverage of the New Zealand cases immediately exemplifies.
24 One of the reasons for the little attention it has received might even be the way in which it obviously complicates the idea that the rights of nature are a seamless international movement driven by internationalized norms.
25 This is the largest umbrella organization of indigenous nationalities in Ecuador.
26 Namely, a form that is supposedly inherently friendly to both nature and indigenous populations, through the embodiment of a norm of harmony with nature.

References

Acosta A. (2011) "El Buen (con) Vivir, una utopía por (re) construir: Alcances de la Constitución de Montecristi" *Otra Economía*, 4(6), 8–31.

Belgrave M. (2013) *Historical Frictions: Māori Claims and Reinvented Histories*. Auckland University Press, Auckland.

Berry T. (1999) *The Great Work: Our Way Into the Future*. Crown Publishing Group, New York.

Binney J. (2009) *Encircled Lands: Te Urewera, 1820–1921*. Bridget Williams Books, Wellington.

Borràs S. (2016) "New Transitions from Human Rights to the Environment to the Rights of Nature" *Transnational Environmental Law*, 5, 113–143.

Burdon P. (Ed.) (2011) *Exploring Wild Law: The Philosophy of Earth Jurisprudence*. Wakefield Press, Kent Town.

Cairney P. (2019) *Understanding Public Policy*. Red Globe Press, London.

Campbell T. (2011) *Rights: A Critical Introduction*. Taylor & Francis, London.

Ciepley, D. (2013) "Beyond Public and Private: Toward a Political Theory of the Corporation." *American Political Science Review*, 139–158.

Cullinan C. (2011). *Wild Law*. Siber Ink, Cape Town.

Grear A. (2013) "Law's Entities: Complexity, Plasticity, and Justice" *Jurisprudence*, 4(1), 76–101.

Gudynas E. (2009) "La dimensión ecológica del buen vivir: entre el fantasma de la modernidad y el desafío biocéntrico" *OBETS: Revista de Ciencias Sociales*, 4, 49–54.

Jackson M. (1992) "The Treaty and the Word: The Colonization of Māori Philosophy", In Graham O. and Roy W.P. eds., *Justice Ethics, and New Zealand Society*. Oxford University Press, Oxford, 1–10.

Jones C. (2014) "Tūhoe – Crown Settlement – Tūhoe Claims Settlement Act 2014; Te Urewera Report of the Waitangi Tribunal" *Māori Law Review*, October.

Jones C. (2016) *New Treaty, New Tradition: Reconciling New Zealand and Māori Law*. UBC Press, Vancouver.

Kauffman C.M. and Martin P.L. (2017) "Can Rights of Nature Make Development More Sustainable? Why Some Ecuadorian Lawsuits Succeed and Others Fail" *World Development*, 92, 130–142.

Kauffman C.M. and Martin P.L. (2018) "Constructing Rights of Nature Norms in the US, Ecuador, and New Zealand" *Global Environmental Politics*, 18(4), 43–62.

Kingdon J.W. (1984) *Agendas, Alternatives, and Public Policies*. Little, Brown, Boston.

Knauß S. (2018) "Conceptualizing Human Stewardship in the Anthropocene: The Rights of Nature in Ecuador, New Zealand and India" *Journal of Agricultural and Environmental Ethics*, 31(6), 703–722.

Kotzé, L. and Villavicencio Calzadilla, P. (2017) "Somewhere between Rhetoric and Reality: Environmental Constitutionalism and the Rights of Nature in Ecuador." *Transnational Environmental Law*, 6(3), 401–433. doi:10.1017/S2047102517000061

Macpherson E. (2019). *Indigenous Water Rights in Law and Regulation: Lessons from Comparative Experience*. Cambridge University Press, Cambridge.

Margil M. (2014) "Building an International Movement for Rights of Nature", In Maloney M. and Burdon P. eds., *Wild Law: In Practice*, Routledge, New York, 149–160.

Margil M. (2017) "The Standing of Trees: Why Nature Needs Legal Rights" *World Policy Journal*, 34(2), 8–11.

Naffine N. (2003) "Who Are Law's Persons? From Cheshire Cats to Responsible Subjects" *Modern Law Review*, 66, 346–367.

O'Malley V. (2014) "Tūhoe – Crown Settlement – Historical Background" *Māori Law Review*, October.

Rawson A. and Mansfield B. (2018) "Producing Juridical Knowledge:'Rights of Nature' or the Naturalization of Rights?" *Environment and Planning E: Nature and Space*, 1(1–2), 99–119.

Salmond A. (2017) *Tears of Rangi: Experiments Across Worlds*. Auckland University Press, Auckland.

Sanders K. (2018) "'Beyond Human Ownership'? Property, Power and Legal Personality for Nature in Aotearoa New Zealand" *Journal of Environmental Law*, 30(2), 207–234.

Singer P. (1981) *The Expanding Circle*. Clarendon Press, Oxford.

Stone C.D. (1972) "Should Trees Have Standing—Toward Legal Rights for Natural Objects" *Southern California Law Review*, 45, 450.

Stone C.D. (2010) *Should Trees Have Standing?: Law, Morality, and the Environment*. Oxford University Press, Oxford.

Tănăsescu M. (2013) "The Rights of Nature in Ecuador: The Making of an Idea" *International Journal of Environmental Studies*, 70(6), 846–861.

Tănăsescu M. (2015) "Nature Advocacy and the Indigenous Symbol" *Environmental Values*, 24(1), 105–122.

Tănăsescu M. (2016) *Environment, Political Representation and the Challenge of Rights: Speaking for Nature*. Springer, London.

Tănăsescu M. (2020) "Rights of Nature, Legal Personality, and Indigenous Philosophies" *Transnational Environmental Law*, first view, 1–25.

Tepper E. and Whitehead C. (2018) "Moon, Inc.: The New Zealand Model of Granting Legal Personality to Natural Resources Applied to Space" *New Space*, 6(4), 288–298.

6 Environmentally Conditioned Human Rights

A Good Idea?

Giulia Sajeva[1]

Introduction

The call for the protection of the environment is louder than it has ever been. The emergence of the idea (and, in certain countries, the legal reality) of the rights of nature is a clear response to this environmental plea. But this trend does not emerge in isolation: it is accompanied by many human rights issues that are equally in need of being addressed (Fisher & Lundberg 2015, 181).

However, combining the protection of the rights of nature and human rights[2] is not an easy task (see Francioni 2010). Greened human rights, procedural environmental rights, and the right to a healthy environment are great achievements in the common protection of human and nature's rights and well demonstrate the deep interdependence between human rights and the protection of the environment (see Taylor 2008). Nevertheless, they have different "underpinning rationalities" (Bosselmann 2015) and foundations, and within their structures the environment figures as one of the assets through which the protection of human interests may be achieved, or as an interest to be protected for the sake of human beings. Nature protection is hence limited within the short-term borders of human interests (see Sands 2012), which are "considered superior to the environment under the current international human rights regime" (Bosselmann 2015, 531). The anthropocentrism inherent in human rights approaches "deprive[s] the environment of direct and comprehensive protection" because their aims are and remain human life and wellbeing (Taylor 2008, 99).

The rights of nature, instead, place themselves *alongside* human rights, as an ecocentric instrument more powerful to protect nature (cf. O'Donnell & Talbot-Jones 2018). These rights allow for claims that focus on harms inflicted directly, and solely, on the environment, rather than on humans through environmental degradation. They place us in an alternative position, that of stewards of the Earth who elect the law as an instrument to protect it regardless of its human value (Daly 2018, 669, 671). From this *external* position, the rights of nature will interact with human rights, striving to reach equilibrium and a commonality of goals. This commonality is wide and deep, and the two sets of rights will often complement each other (the maintenance of a healthy ecosystem enhances children's rights; the conservation of a natural site may protect the religious rights of communities worshiping it; and so on). But the two sets of rights, as all rights, might also enter into conflict (cf. Gearty 2010, 9) because resources are limited, and different rights may require incompatible and contradictory demands (cf. Waldron 1993, 206)—such as when the halt of an environmentally detrimental industrial activity threatens the right to work of the employees of a company, or when the establishment of a strictly protected area leads to the eviction of indigenous peoples. In this latter case (which may vary depending on the national or regional legal framework), the harmony between humans' and nature's interests will mostly be delegated to courts that face the task of balancing competing rights.

This chapter looks at whether human rights and the rights of nature may be combined in a different, deeper, way. Can, as Taylor asked, "ecological limitations, expressed as responsibilities or duties, [...] be part of the human rights discourse"? She also elaborated a proposal that built on premises different from biocultural rights but that were somehow similar: *ecological human rights*. Taylor recommended the elaboration of human rights (in particular, property rights) whose limits were not only determined by other human rights or particularly important public interests (external limits) but also by ecological limitations founded on (internal limits such as) "the protection of intrinsic values and/or interpreted to include individual and state duties or responsibilities towards nature" (Taylor 2008, 103; also cf. Sajeva 2019 for a discussion on internal and external limits).

A few years ago, the Indian scholar Sanjay Kabir Bavikatte (see Bavikatte & Bennett 2015; Bavikatte 2014) argued that in international law there is a new set of rights emerging, a set of rights that is able to combine the protection of nature and human rights in a stronger and *sui generis* way: biocultural rights. They are grounded on a double foundation that incorporates environmental concerns as well as human ones (see Sajeva 2018). Biocultural rights combine the protection of nature and the protection of the interests of indigenous peoples and local communities, suggesting, amidst many challenges, a different way to conceive rights *vis à vis* the current environmental crisis.

This chapter will try to understand what the consequences might be of combining the protection of nature and human interests within the framework of biocultural rights. Do these rights make nature and indigenous peoples better or worse off? Does their *internal* interaction come with a price? Do biocultural rights make the rights of nature or of indigenous peoples redundant?

Let's Get Nature and People Together

One of the opportunities for bringing together nature and people derives from the special relationship that many indigenous peoples and local communities[3] have with their lands, waters, and natural resources: a relationship of stewardship.[4] In fact, biocultural rights place themselves within discussions concerning the protection of the environment through the implementation of community-based projects and attitudes, as opposed to older (though not yet extinct) *fences and fines* approaches (see Adams 2004; Brockington 2002). While the latter approaches were based on the idea that indigenous peoples and local communities are, by definition, detrimental to the protection of the environment, community-based conservation practices are grounded on the recognition that indigenous peoples and local communities are important allies in conservation (Garnett et al. 2018; see also Farvar et al. 2018; Martin et al. 2016; Gavin et al. 2015; Roe et al. 2010).

International environmental law is increasingly acknowledging the relevance of indigenous peoples' and local communities' traditional knowledge, practices, and ways of life for the conservation of the environment, and recognizing their rights to "fulfil their role as trustees of their cultures, lands, waters, and resources" (Bavikatte 2014, 21).[5] According to Bavikatte, such recognition is taking the new form of biocultural rights, which may be defined as the basket of rights that indigenous peoples and local communities need in order to preserve and enhance their role as environmental stewards.

The foundation of biocultural rights—*raisons d'être*, protected interests[6]—are the interests of indigenous peoples and local communities, and the conservation of nature. The former is the same interest that grounds indigenous peoples' rights, i.e. the recognition of the value of self-governance and cultural diversity of indigenous peoples and local communities. The latter, the conservation of nature, is also an interest of indigenous peoples and local communities (as they have often underlined in their revendications for rights), but it is framed so as to embrace the protection of nature itself.

Having a double foundation referring to the intrinsic value of indigenous peoples and of nature makes biocultural rights a *sui generis* form of human rights. Human rights usually have as their central focus—foundation—solely the protection of human interests (even in the broadest conceptions[7]). Up until now, the elevation of nature to the status of right-holder pertained only to the discussion of the rights of nature, not to human rights. Biocultural rights, by contrast, seem to welcome as their holders indigenous peoples and local communities, *as well as* nature. In fact, the aim of recognizing biocultural rights for indigenous peoples and local communities is to protect their role as environmental stewards. Precisely because they have such stewardship role, indigenous peoples and local communities may be recognized as holders of a basket of rights which is not recognized for other peoples and communities that lack this special stewardship relationship with nature grounded on traditional worldviews, practices, and identities.

A Price for Indigenous Peoples: Rights of Nature Through the Back Door?[8]

Indigenous peoples have a long history of conservation practices and sustainable lifestyles, and their human rights often go hand in hand with the protection of nature (such as, for example, when a community claims for the halt of environmentally harmful activities that are threatening its traditional livelihoods).

One may be tempted to think that biocultural rights are a simple specification of indigenous peoples' rights that further underlines their relationship with nature. It is in fact to be noted that indigenous peoples are recognized as holders of *indigenous peoples' rights* by international human rights law and the national laws of many countries. Indigenous peoples' rights evolved from general human rights, and, as such, are specially protected rights aimed at securing particularly important interests of indigenous peoples.

Biocultural rights' foundation, instead, hosts both indigenous peoples and nature as holders of interests that shall be protected. In fact, the basket of biocultural rights may contain only those rights that promote both the interests of indigenous peoples *and* nature (such as rights to lands and natural resources, rights to cultural identity related to nature, rights to self-government in matters concerning the management and governance of natural resources and lands).

Even though the protection of nature and the rights of indigenous peoples are strongly interlinked, they may also come into conflict with one another.[9] Not all indigenous peoples are sustainable, not all those that currently are sustainable will necessarily be so in the future,[10] and not all approaches to protecting nature will be compatible with the needs and interests of indigenous peoples.[11] This risk of conflict between the two protected interests grounding biocultural rights reveals the fact that they are—unlike indigenous peoples' rights—environmentally conditioned rights. Indigenous peoples' rights are not intrinsically limited by environmental considerations and do not impose any duty to protect nature. Moreover, indigenous peoples' rights are recognized for indigenous peoples because they are *indigenous*, without any reference to them being environmentally sustainable.

The difference between environmentally conditioned rights (that have a double foundation) and rights that shall be balanced with environmental considerations is a very complex and subtle one (cf. Sajeva 2019). All rights, one could say, are limited by other rights and important general interests (including the protection of nature) and shall be balanced with them. However, this statement is only partially true for the following reasons.

1) Biocultural rights leverage nature's interest and confer to it the status of an interest that is able to limit a set of indigenous peoples' human rights. Nature is elevated to the status of right-holder, but without this being fully explicit (the recognition of nature as a right-holder is not yet fully accepted and its entrance in the legal debate at the same level as human rights is not a settled issue). Indigenous peoples are offered a new set of rights, but they come with a price: *accept the elevation of nature to the status of co-right-holder*. Biocultural rights, in fact, emerge as part of a discourse that derives from environmental conventions, declarations, agreements, and court cases, where the environment is the dominant concern, and indigenous peoples figure as subjects whose rights are to be protected *because*

they preserve ways of life relevant for the protection of biodiversity.[12] Such protection becomes a duty to be respected through the implementation of biocultural rights, and the failure to respect it may, even, lead to the loss of biocultural rights.

2) In order to be holders of biocultural rights, it is necessary to be sustainable. It is equivalent to saying that, in order to hold a set of rights, *indigeneity is not enough*: it is necessary to have a further requirement, i.e. being sustainable. This idea was at the very root of their land eviction and marginalization through top-down *fences and fines* conservation practices. Hence, it should be no surprise that biocultural rights rhetoric is accused of bringing back old enemies, and that indigenous peoples' representatives fear that the idea of biocultural rights could pollute the understanding of indigenous peoples' rights, influencing the interpretation of indigenous peoples' rights by judges, politicians, and the like, and pushing towards environmental stewardship as a requirement to hold indigenous peoples' rights, as well.

Nature's Price

Recognition of the rights of nature is not a settled nor easy matter. Recognition of the intrinsic value of nature, as well as acceptance of nature as a subject and a right-holder, are issues of heated debate within legal theory, ethics, and positive law studies (as other chapters in this book demonstrate). Biocultural rights, as mentioned above, let the rights of nature enter through the back door: they do not involve an explicit discussion of nature's subjectivity but derive from environmental texts that states have agreed upon without considering how precisely nature should be valued or whether it has the capacity to hold rights. For example, the Preamble of the Convention on Biological Diversity affirms that:

> Conscious of the intrinsic value of biological diversity and of the ecological, genetic, social, economic, scientific, educational, cultural, recreational and aesthetic values of biological diversity and its components. [...] Affirming that the conservation of biological diversity is a common concern of humankind.

This mentions both the intrinsic and non-intrinsic value of nature, and hence does not take an explicitly anthropocentric or non-anthropocentric position. Thanks to this ethically ambiguous origin, biocultural rights offer leverage for the rights of nature: they can present nature as a right-holder to courts, governments, public servants, environmental NGOs, and the extractive industries.

However, sneaking in through the back door comes with a price. Protection of nature is one of the two foundations upon which biocultural rights are built. Nature's relevance is therefore restricted to matters of concern to biocultural rights, which involve indigenous peoples and local communities, and their lands, self-governance, and preservation of their cultural identity. Biocultural rights create environmental duties for indigenous peoples, states, corporations, and the like to bring about the implementation of these rights. However, these environmental duties arise only in relation to the implementation of biocultural rights. If a state recognized biocultural rights in its national law, the state would have duties to protect nature only in cases related to indigenous peoples and local communities. On the other hand, if nature itself is recognized as a right-holder, then the state, corporations, and the like will be bound to promote the protection of nature and to balance nature's rights with all other rights and important collective interests, regardless of whether indigenous peoples' and local communities' lands, resources, and identities are involved.

As with the interests of indigenous peoples, nature's status within biocultural rights is internally limited: it is bound—or limited by—the interests and needs of indigenous peoples. So, for example, if a community that was recognized as the holder of biocultural rights guarantees good conservation of the local ecosystem but not the best level of conservation possible—which could otherwise be reached through a strictly protected area—such an increase in environmental conservation would not justify the community's eviction and consequent decrease in the protection of the community's rights.[13] Hence, biocultural rights cannot be considered genuine substitutes for the rights of nature. They simply give recognition of nature a special place in matters concerning indigenous peoples.[14]

A Real Case: The Atrato River

As previously mentioned, biocultural rights have not yet been recognized in either international or national law. However, the Colombian Supreme Court—which operates under a constitution that combines classic anthropocentric approaches with more cosmocentric ones inspired by the cosmovisions of indigenous peoples, black communities descended from former slaves, and peasant communities (Melo Parra 2018)[15]—made reference to Bavikatte's work and acknowledged the biocultural rights of the peoples and communities living alongside the Atrato River. This occurs in the Court's opinion T-622 (cf. see Castillo Galvis, D'Janon Donado, & Ramírez Nárdiz 2019).

The Atrato River is 650 kilometers long and crosses Colombia from the Western Cordillera de los Andes to the Gulf of Urabá in the Caribbean Sea, passing through the Chocó *biogeográfico* region, one of the world's biodiversity hotspots. Along the river, indigenous peoples and local communities (mestizas and descendants of former slaves[16]) have thrived for centuries, making the area also rich in biocultural diversity (García & Varón 2018). Regardless of the fact that 90% of Chocó's region is a protected area (Kauffman & Martin 2018), mines and timber production, with the resulting pollution and habitat destruction, have made the region one of the poorest of Colombia, and are threatening the lives and health of its inhabitants, as well as depleting its natural resources. In 2015, this led the Centro de Estudios para la Justicia Social

Tierra Digna to take action on behalf of the local councils and peoples (the Consejo Comunitario Mayor de la Organización Popular Campesina del Alto Atrato, the Consejo Comunitario Mayor de la Asociación Campesina Integral del Atrato, the Asociación de Consejos Comunitarios del Bajo Atrato, the Foro Inter-étnico Solidaridad Chocó, and others) against the Presidencia de la República, the Ministerio de Ambiente y Desarrollo Sostenible, and others. In 2016, the Colombian Supreme Court issued opinion T-622 in response to this case.

Biocultural rights are mentioned in the "Considerations and Foundations" section of the opinion (which precedes the "Decision" section). Here the court recognizes the link between cultural and biological diversity and the special relationship of indigenous peoples and local communities with the environment (IV.5.11 ff.). Interestingly, the court pointed out that biocultural rights are evolving in international law, but should not be considered a new collective right in Colombia: rather, they are the unification of the collective rights to natural resources and to culture, which the constitution already recognizes indigenous peoples and local communities to have. Colombian politics, law, and jurisprudence are therefore invited by the court to tailor their actions towards the conservation of cultural diversity and the ways of life of indigenous peoples, black communities, and peasants, as a means to achieving the conservation of biological diversity (IV.5.18).

The court's opinion, after underlining the fact that the Chocó region historically involves humanitarian, socio-cultural, and environmental issues, recognizes that the exponential increase in illegal mining in the area has generated a humanitarian crisis (IV.9.4, IV.9.5, V.Tercer), and that, due to inaction, the accused state authorities are to be considered responsible for the violation of the human rights to life, health, water, food security, healthy environment, culture and land of the local communities and indigenous peoples of the region (IV.9.39, "Conclusion"). In order to overcome and halt these violations, the court recognized the Atrato River, as well as its water basin and tributaries, as a legal subject that holds rights to protection, conservation, sustenance, and restoration[17] (IV.10, V.Cuarto), and declared the state and the indigenous peoples and local communities of the region in charge of upholding these rights (IV.10). The court ordered the government (represented by the Ministry of Environment and Sustainable Development), together with the indigenous peoples and local communities of the region, to act as guardians of the river through the creation of the Comisión de Guardianes del Río Atrato (with the advice of the Humboldt Institute and WWF), which shall create and implement a plan for the decontamination of the river and the restoration of its ecosystems (see Roncucci 2019, 71). Furthermore, it ordered the government and the national police force, in cooperation with the indigenous peoples and local communities of the region, to create and implement a plan of action to halt local illegal mining. It also ordered the government to create and implement a plan, with the agreement of the indigenous peoples and local communities of the region, that aims to facilitate the restoration of their traditional means of subsistence and to *re-recognize* (*restablecer*) their rights to culture, participation, identity, land, ways of life, and food production (V.Septimo).

Biocultural rights are not mentioned in the decision section of the court's opinion; however, the rationale of biocultural rights permeates the entire opinion. The judges have, in fact, repeatedly underlined the importance of the preservation of the special relationship between culture and nature as reflected in indigenous peoples' cosmovisions. Moreover, the opinion explicitly recognizes the Atrato River as a right-holder, and orders the local government, *as well as* the indigenous peoples and local communities living in the region, to implement the rights of the river. They are elected, or rather *recognized*, in their role as guardians of nature. Similarly to Bavikatte's biocultural rights, which "denote all the rights required to secure the stewardship role of communities over their lands and waters" (Bavikatte 2014, 16), peoples and communities of the Atrato River are given recognition of their rights in order to be involved in decision-making procedures.[18] However, the indigenous peoples and local communities are also recognized as duty-holders toward the river: together with the government, they are called to prevent damages to the river and to actively act for its protection (Clark et al. 2018).

In the Atrato River decision, indigenous peoples and local communities are also *reiterated the recognition of* rights (the court emphasizes the fact that these are not new rights, but rights that should have already been protected) to culture, participation, identity, land, ways of life, and food production. These rights will then have to be balanced with the newly recognized rights of the Atrato River.

The Atrato River case embodies both the strengths and challenges of biocultural rights. They have helped the Colombian Constitutional Court to recognize the importance of the link between culture and nature, and to justify the need for actions aimed at their combined protection. Biocultural rights were used as a guide to bring indigenous peoples and local communities into the realm of actors whose existence and wellbeing is essential for nature to thrive and be conserved for future generations. However, the court also acknowledged the need to elevate the Atrato River, including its tributaries and water basin, to the status of right-holder, as the best available legal tool to create responsibilities and duties towards it, both in the case of indigenous peoples and local communities and in the case of the Colombian government. The call to act as guardians is a way of granting decision-making authority, surely welcomed by indigenous peoples and local communities. But it also creates duties and responsibilities which seem to be distributed evenly to peoples, communities, and government, without any explicit reference to their differences in funds, instruments, and power. Hopefully, the burden of restoring and protecting the Atrato River will not be shifted, disproportionally, from the state to indigenous peoples and local communities.

Moreover, if indigenous peoples and local communities continue to resemble the environmentally noble savage of myth, things should proceed smoothly. However, if their rights to culture, participation, identity, land, ways of life, or food production come into conflict with the rights of the Atrato River, which rights prevail and under which conditions remains an open question whose answer might not be fully welcomed by indigenous peoples.

A Cautious Move Ahead

While it is true that entering the Anthropocene requires radical changes in our way of interacting with nature, it is also true that human rights violations are still serious and widespread. This chapter began with the question of whether human rights and the rights of nature may be combined in a different and deeper way than through encounters as separate entities (a river's rights, a person's rights, a mountain's rights, a group's rights, and so forth). Biocultural rights were proposed as an emerging set of rights that could respond to both environmental and human needs, coalescing them as a double foundation. If fully recognized, biocultural rights present an important and powerful tool for protecting the interests of indigenous peoples struggling to have their indigenous rights accepted, as well as for local communities whose rights are still at a developmental stage. Furthermore, biocultural rights make nature a right-holder without having to overcome, explicitly, doubts and fears concerning its subjectivity and intrinsic value. Deriving from environmental conventions, declarations, and decisions, the viability of biocultural rights does not rest on determining whether nature is or is not worthy of being a right-holder, but rather on finding means (including legal ones) to guarantee its protection.

But the question that arises is: can biocultural rights be considered an acceptable and self-standing merger of the rights of indigenous peoples and the rights of nature? Unlike indigenous peoples' rights, biocultural rights involve indigenous peoples in a relationship of mutual care and protection with nature: a relationship that was preexisting, but that, within biocultural rights, ceases to be a choice of lifestyle, and instead becomes a legal duty and a requirement to be a right-holder. This makes among the most vulnerable and marginalized members of society bear the burden of protecting the environment, a burden that might be incorporated in their worldviews and practices but that could, at times, become unfair, especially if imposed by the state according to incompatible visions and understandings of environmental sustainability. Moreover, biocultural rights have been accused of compromising the fight for indigenous peoples' rights, providing states a more convenient alternative that is less costly and has positive environmental outcomes. Even worse, some have suggested that the rhetoric of environmental stewardship on behalf of indigenous peoples could endanger indigenous rights, leading judges, politicians, and the like to consider sustainability a requirement for indigenous peoples to hold rights.

On the other side, protection of nature may ground its own self-standing rights, which are also independent of and go beyond the interests of indigenous peoples. Instead, biocultural rights treat the relevance and protection of nature as restricted to circumstances that concern the interests of indigenous peoples.

Biocultural rights could, hence, offer a useful new way of framing problems related to the balance between human rights and the environment, but they should nevertheless be used *together with* indigenous peoples' rights and the rights of nature—the former are needed to provide full protection of indigenous peoples' interests (regardless of whether they are sustainable or not), while the latter are needed to hold not only indigenous peoples but also states, individuals, corporations, and the like accountable for full and all-encompassing protection of nature.

But how can the teachings of biocultural rights be brought to matter for the rest of humanity? Are we to engage in a worldwide de-growth exercise, adopt indigenous peoples' worldviews and practices, and become sustainable beings? While (maintaining a vigilant attitude toward environmentally noble savage myths) there would be a lot to say for the opportunity to learn from indigenous peoples' relationship with the Earth, the lessons that can be acquired from the study of biocultural rights are somehow more theoretical.

Firstly, they show that the structure of rights is not intrinsically, but only traditionally, anthropocentric and can accommodate nature's interests within their very foundation. This realization may appear obvious and superfluous *vis à vis* the recognition of rights to nature itself; however, as disagreement on whether nature can be considered a right-holder is still a reality, biocultural rights teach us that there are other ways to enter nature into the rhetoric of human rights.

Secondly—and linked to the reason why it would be unjust to substitute indigenous peoples' rights with biocultural rights—they warn us against conditioning (i.e. placing nature's interests and basic human interests at the same level) human rights to environmental considerations without adequately assessing its potential consequences. While it is true that if we recognize the intrinsic value of nature, we should strive to protect it as much as possible and to find a balance between nature and all other human needs, it is also true that human rights address needs and interests that can hardly bend to other considerations without the risk of very high trade-offs in terms of suffering, vanished identities, and lost lives. Moreover, even if it was accepted to limit all human rights to the respect of the rights of nature, biocultural rights would still share a burden heavier than that of other rights: the presence of nature in the very foundations of biocultural rights creates not only an obligation not to harm nature, but also the obligation to actively protect it, and the exclusion of unsustainable indigenous peoples as legitimate right-holders.

Thirdly, biocultural rights could be taken as a starting point for the creation of new rights that welcome nature into their foundations and concern a wider group of people, but do not qualify as human rights (understood as *fundamental rights* protecting special human needs and interests). A first step in this direction could be taken by recognizing *local communities*—rather than indigenous peoples—as their potential holders. Local communities may be both traditional and non-traditional communities, hence may also include newly established groups of people sharing sustainability-oriented goals and a certain level of self-governance (such as a community of peasants conserving traditional seed varieties, a well-organized ecovillage, or an association of urban dwellers taking care of a natural area). Reference to sustainable local communities enlarges the scope of action of these newly conceived rights and addresses the current lack of an alternative body of local communities' rights. Their enlargement could take the form of Rights for Ecosystem Services (RES),[19] which could be envisaged as rights granted by states to those communities willing to undertake activities for the protection of nature, which foster the same aims and values as the rights of nature.[20] Since they would not be a substitute for any existing human rights, RES would be a *new scheme* that a community could decide to engage with. They would have, in return for environmentally beneficial activities and the duty to maintain them, new rights—such as property rights (commons, civic usages of state lands), use rights (of resources placed within protected areas, for instance), and rights to a certain level of self-governance in matters relating to environmental issues. RES would have, of course, a limited impact on global pollution and environmental degradation; however, they would respond to Principle 19 of the Stockholm Declaration[21] calling on individuals and communities to protect and improve the environment in its full human dimension. It would also be an attempt to undertake environmental responsibilities not only in developing countries—as conservation practices mostly do—but also in rich, technology-advanced ones and to guide their citizens, including groups of urban residents, to change their impact on the Earth.

The further step of combining the rights of nature and human rights—not *simple* rights—as biocultural rights propose stands in need of further reflection (cf. Oksanen 2020). Maybe we are not ready to undertake such a change precisely in the instrument—human rights—aimed at protecting, still with limited success, the most vulnerable human beings against the power of unjust rulers and institutions.

Notes

1 This project has received funding from the European Union's Horizon 2020 research and innovation programme under the Marie Skłodowska-Curie grant agreement No 841546.

2 Human rights are here considered as tools to protect particularly important interests of individuals or groups, where at least one of such interest-holders is considered to have intrinsic value, and as being so important (from a moral or legal point on view) to "set the limits to the sovereignty of States" (Raz 2010, 328; Beitz 2003).

3 Rather than providing a definition, the 2007 UN Declaration on the Rights of Indigenous Peoples (UNDRIP) suggests a set of guiding characteristics to identify indigenous peoples:

> self-identification as indigenous nations and/or peoples; a shared history of suffering injustices, colonization and land dispossession; a complex web of place-based relationships; language, traditional practices, knowledge, and legal and cultural institutions distinct from those dominant in the national state where they reside; and knowledge, culture and practices that contribute to sustainable governance and management of human relationships with the natural world and beyond.
>
> (Sajeva, Borrini-Feyerabend, & Niederberberger 2019, 10)

Local communities, instead, may be defined as those communities that cannot be identified as indigenous but that, nevertheless, are usually small scale groups that "possess shared social and cultural elements, such as common history, traditions, language, values, life plans and/or sense of identity that bind them together and distinguish them from other sectors of society" (Sajeva, Borrini-Feyerabend, & Niederberberger 2019, 12).

4 Acting as steward, guard, or custodian means "conserving nature willingly, while living with it and from it, and holding it in trust for future generations" (Borrini-Feyerabend et al. 2010; see also Ruiz & Vernooy (eds.) 2012). The term *stewardship*—as well as *guardianship* and *custodianship*—is widely used in literature concerning the relationship of indigenous peoples with the environment. This relationship is described as one that is based not on private property claims and commodifiable and alienable lands and goods (Bavikatte 2014, 114, 128), but rather on fiduciary rights, care, and responsibilities that build on a genealogy of relatedness, affiliation, and non-separateness between the human and non-human (Whitt et al. 2001), and according to which the gods reside in the natural world and are part of it. This understanding of *stewardship* is not equivalent to the one deriving from certain interpretations of the Judeo-Christian tradition, according to which the world is not co-extensive with god, but is rather "an expression of God's creative purposes, and God is indwelling" in it (Attfield 2018, ch. 7). In this tradition, human beings are holders not only of special rights and privileges towards what god created, but also special responsibilities because they are given the Earth *in trust* and must, therefore, take good care of it (for a reconstruction of this interpretation of the Judeo-Christian traditions, see Callicot 1994). Indigenous peoples' stewardship is not equivalent, either, to the secularized version of the Judeo-Christian tradition, according to which human beings are to act as stewards of the environment because they hold a duty towards the wider human community and future generations (Attfield 2018). However, regardless of their different genealogies and rationales, these three understanding of stewardship share the common ground of recognizing intrinsic value to the natural world and holding humankind responsible for its conservation and sustainable use.

5 See, among the others: Principle 22 of the Rio Declaration on Environment and Development; sections 2.10 and 3.26 of Agenda 21; in particular Articles 8j and 10c of the UN Convention on Biological Diversity; Articles 6.2, 7, 12.1, and 16 of the Nagoya Protocol on Access to Genetic Resources and the Fair and Equitable Sharing of Benefits Arising from their Utilization to the Convention on Biological Diversity; Article 9 of the FAO Treaty on Plant Genetic Resources for Food and Agriculture; as well as the *Endorois Welfare Council v. Kenya* case of the African Commission on Human and People's Rights, the *Mayagna (Sumo) Awas Tingni Community v. Nicaragua*, the *Moiwana Village v. Suriname*, the *Saramaka People v. Suriname* of the Inter-American Court on Human Rights, the Niyamgiri case ruled by the Indian Supreme Court in 2013 (*Orissa Mining Corporation Ltd. v. Ministry of Environment & Forests & Others*), and the adoption of the 2017 Te Awa Tupua (Whanganui River Claims Settlement) Act in New Zealand.

6 The foundations of a right are here understood as the very reasons/interests/needs that a right was grounded upon or was recognized for (whether these are moral, legal, or political in nature).

7 Such as, for example, including the interest in enjoying the beauty of a well-conserved natural place.

8 This section concentrates on the comparison between indigenous peoples' rights and biocultural rights. It does not take into consideration local communities' rights because their condition is really different. Local communities are not, as yet, holders of specific rights in international law and, often, in national laws, unless they are linked to environmental considerations (food production, conservation of ecosystems, pastoralists' rights, breeders' rights, etc). Hence, the issues that this section evaluates for indigenous peoples *vis à vis* biocultural rights are not to be considered equivalent for local communities that do not enjoy their same protection on rights.

9 Denying such reality is equivalent to falling for the myth of the noble savage, according to a very rudimentary interpretation of which indigenous peoples have some inherent features that makes them not only unwilling, but also unable, to hurt the environment. Such a vision is at once false and offensive, as it negates the autonomy of thoughts and desires of indigenous peoples, as well as their capacity of altering and modifying the environment. On the noble savage myth, see Ellingson 2001; Redford 1991.

10 Halting sustainable practices may also backfire and lead, later on, to the fact that the rights of indigenous peoples that are dependent on a healthy environment could not be realized anymore.

11 For example, the realization of the right to self-government over local natural resources could lead to environmental harm if an indigenous people decided to license the use of a certain resource located in its traditional land to an extractive industry; or vice versa, the creation of a strict protected area could lead to the eviction of an indigenous people and the denial of its rights to land and natural resources.

12 They emerge from the interpretation of environmentally focused documents, such as the Convention on Biological Diversity, whose ultimate goal is the protection of biodiversity. Article 8j, considered one of the central tools in the debate on indigenous peoples and the environment, exemplifies this approach: "Each contracting Party shall, as far as possible and as appropriate: Subject to national legislation, respect, preserve and maintain knowledge, innovations and practices of indigenous and local communities embodying traditional lifestyles relevant for the conservation and sustainable use of biological diversity."

13 Moreover, it would be violation of the indigenous peoples rights of that community.

14 A place which is already recognized by indigenous peoples as well, as their rights' vindications are very often entrenched with nature's protection considerations.

15 The evolution of the combination of these approaches has followed the issue, since the 1991 adoption of the so-called Ecological Constitution, of numerous laws and constitutional court decisions (Melo Parra 2018). On the evolution of the decisions of the constitutional court on environmental issues, see Vargas, Albarracín, & Méndez Castillo 2019; Macpherson, Ventura, & Ospina 2020. On the 2018 case of the Colombian Supreme Court *Dejusticia y otros v Presidencia de la República y otros*, ruling STC4360, which recognizes the Colombian Amazon rainforest as a subject holder of rights, see Villavicencio Calzadilla 2019.

16 About 500,000 inhabitants, of which 87% are of African origins, 10% indigenous, 3% mestiza (Sentencia T-622/2016), and 48.7% of which live in poverty.

17 The rights of nature are not recognized in Colombian national law. The opinion justifies this decision by arguing that the rights of nature foster sustainable development as well as the protection of river ecosystems and the rights of communities and peoples. The opinion of the court falls under what has been called, often critically, *judicial activism* (Roncucci 2019, 64), i.e. the tendency of constitutional and supreme courts to make decisions that go beyond the letter of the law, regarding issues that usually compete with the legislative branch (cf. García & Varón 2018).

18 The opinion resembles the Whanganui river case, in which indigenous peoples are called to act as guardians, taking part in decision-making procedures concerning the river (for its origin and the history of the Treaty of Waitangi, see Iorns Magallanes 2015). On the comparison between the New Zealand, Colombia, and India cases (the latter recognizing legal personality to the Ganga and Yamuna Rivers), see Kauffman & Martin 2018.

19 Rights for Ecosystem Services is a name that echoes the complex debate about Payments for Ecosystem Services (PES). Ecosystem services were defined in the Millennium Ecosystem Assessment (2005) as the benefits people obtain from ecosystems, and payments for ecosystems services as schemes to provide, mostly, economic benefits to those groups that conserve, through their actions or inactions, the capacity of a certain ecosystem to provide benefits. For the main critiques against PES see Kosoy & Corbera 2010.

20 Rights for Ecosystem Services are being further explored as part of the Marie Curie project RES. For more info, visit: https://res-project.eu/

21 Principle 19:

> the younger generation as well as adults, giving due consideration to the underprivileged...[as] essential in order to broaden the basis for an enlightened opinion and responsible conduct by individuals, enterprises and communities in protecting and improving the environment in its full human dimension.

References

Adams W.M. (2004) *Against Extinction—The Story of Conservation*. Earthscan, London.

Attfield R. (2018) *Environmental Ethics. A Very Short Introduction*. Oxford University Press, Oxford.

Bavikatte S.K. (2014) *Stewarding the Earth. Rethinking Property and the Emergence of Biocultural Rights*. Oxford University Press, New Delhi.

Bavikatte S.K. and Bennett T. (2015) "Community Stewardship: The Foundation of Biocultural Rights" *Journal of Human Rights and the Environment*, 6(1), 7–29.

Beitz C.R. (2003) "What Human Rights Mean" *Daedalus*, 132(1), 36–46.

Borrini-Feyerabend G. with Lassen B., Stevens S., Martin G., Riascos de la Peña J.C., Ráez-Luna E.F. and Farvar M.T. (2010) (reprinted 2012) *Bio-cultural Diversity Conserved by Indigenous Peoples and Local Communities—Examples and Analysis*. IUCN/CEESP and CENESTA, Teheran.

Bosselmann K. (2015) "Environmental and Human Rights in Ethical Context" in Grear A. and Kotzé L.J. eds., *Research Handbook on Human Rights and the Environment*. Edward Elgar Publishing, Cheltenham – Northampton, 531–549.

Brockington D. (2002) *Fortress Conservation. The Preservation of the Mkomazi Game Reserve, Tanzania*. Oxford: James Currey.

Callicott J.B. (1994) *Earth's Insights. A Multicultural Survey of Ecological Ethics from the Mediterranean Basin to the Australian Outback*. University of California Press, Berkley, CA.

Castillo Galvis S.H., D'Janon Donado M.L. and Ramírez Nárdiz A. (2019) "El control de convencionalidad y el diálogo judicial frente al medio ambiente como sujeto de protección y reparación" *Revista Mexicana de Derecho Constitucionales*, 41, 397–428.

Clark C., Emmanouil N., Page J. and Pelizzon A. (2018) "Can You Hear the Rivers Sing? Legal Personhood, Ontology, and the Nitty-Gritty of Governance" *Ecology Law Quarterly*, 45(4), 787–844.

Daly E. (2018) "Environmental Constitutionalism in Defense of Nature" *Wake Forest Law Review*, 53(4), 667–690.

Ellingson T. (2001) *The Myth of the Noble Savage*. University of California Press, London.

Farvar M.T., Borrini-Feyerabend G., Campese J., Jaeger T., Jonas H. and Stevens S. (2018) "Whose 'Inclusive Conservation'?" Policy Brief of the ICCA Consortium no. 5. The ICCA Consortium and Cenesta, Tehran.

Fisher A.D. and Lundberg M. (2015) "Human Rights' Legitimacy in the Face of the Global Ecological Crisis—Indigenous Peoples, Ecological Rights Claims and the Inter-American Human Rights System" *Journal of Human Rights and the Environment*, 6(2), 177–203.

Francioni F. (2010) "International Human Rights in an Environmental Horizon" *European Journal of International Law*, 21(1), 41–55.

García A. and Varón D. (2018) "La sentencia del río Atrato: un paso más allá de la Constitución Verde" in Orduz Salinas N. ed., *La corte ambiental. Expresiones ciudadanas sobre los avances constitucionales*. Heinrich Böll Stiftung, Bogotá, 297–317.

Garnett S.T., Burgess N.D., Fa J.E., Fernández-Llamazares Á., Molnár Z., Robinson C.J., Watson J.E.M., Zander K.K., Austin B., Brondizio E.S., French Collier N., Duncan T., Ellis E., Geyle H., Jackson M.V., Jonas H., Malmer P., McGowan B., Sivongxay A. and Leiper I. (2018) "A Spatial Overview of the Global Importance of Indigenous Lands for Conservation" *Nature Sustainability*, 1(7), 369–374.

Gavin M.C., McCarter J., Mead A., Berkes F., Stepp J.R., Peterson D., Tang R. (2015) "Defining Biocultural Approaches to Conservation" *Trends in Ecology and Evolution*, 30(3), 140–145.

Gearty, C. (2010) "Do Human Rights Help or Hinder Environmental Protection?" *Journal of Human Rights and the Environment*, 1(1), 7–22.

Iorns Magallanes C.J. (2015) "Maori Cultural Rights in Aotearoa New Zealand: Protecting the Cosmology that Protects the Environment" *Wideren Law Review*, 21(2), 273–327.

Kauffman C.M. and Martin P.L. (2018) "When Rivers Have Rights: Case Comparison of New Zealand, Colombia, and India" *Presentation given at the International Studies Association Annual Conference*, San Francisco, CA.

Kosoy N. and Corbera E. (2010) "Payments for Ecosystem Services as Commodity Fetishism" *Ecological Economics*, 69, 1228–1236.

López Vargas S.L., Hernández Albarracín J.D. and Méndez Castillo C.S. (2019) "Desarrollo jurisprudencial de la protección ambiental en Colombia: aportes desde la perspectiva neoconstitucionalista" *Opera*, 24, 49–65.

Macpherson E., Ventura J.T., Ospina F.C. (2020) "Constitutional Law, Ecosystems, and Indigenous Peoples in Colombia: Biocultural Rights and Legal Subjects" *Transnational Environmental Law*, 9(3), 521–540.

Martin A. Coolsaet B., Corbera E., Dawson N.M., Fraser J.A. Lehmann I., Rodriguez I. (2016) "Justice and Conservation: The Need to Incorporate Recognition" *Biological Conservation*, 197(9), 254–261.

Melo Parra J.P. (2018) "Vínculo entre la Constitución cultural y la Constitución ecológica" in Orduz Salinas N. ed., *La corte ambiental. Expresiones ciudadanas sobre los avances constitucionales*. Heinrich Böll Stiftung, Bogotá, 279–296.

Millennium Ecosystem Assessment. (2005) *Ecosystem and Human Well-Being: Synthesis*. Island Press, Washington, DC.

O'Donnell E.L. and Talbot-Jones J. (2018) "Creating Legal Rights for Rivers: Lessons from Australia, New Zealand, and India" *Ecology and Society*, 23(1), 7, 1–10.

Oksanen M. (2020) "On Tackling the Environmental Crisis through Human Rights" *Rivista di Estetica*, 75, 104–119.

Raz J. (2010) "Human Rights without Foundations" in Besson S. and Tasioulas J. eds., *The Philosophy of International Law*. Oxford University Press, Oxford, 321–337.

Redford K. (1991) "The Ecologically Noble Savage" *Cultural Survival Quarterly*, 15(1), 46–48.

Roe D., Oviedo G., Pabon L., Painter M., Redford K., Siegele L., Springer J., Thomas D. and Walker Painemilla K. (2010) *Conservation and Human Rights: The Need for International Standards*. International Institute for Environmental Development Briefing.

Roncucci R. (2019) *Rights of Nature and the Pursuit of Environmental Justice in the Atrato Case*. Doctoral Thesis. Wageningen University & Research.

Ruiz M. and Vernooy R. eds. (2012) *The Custodians of Biodiversity. Sharing Access to and Benefit Sharing of Genetic Resources*. Earthscan from Routledge, International Development Centre, Ottawa.

Sajeva G. (2018) *When Rights Embrace Responsibilities. Biocultural Rights and the Conservation of Environment*. Oxford University Press, New Delhi.

Sajeva G. (2019) "Inside-Out. Internal and External Limits to Rights: Does It Matter?" *Diritto & questioni Pubbliche*, XIX(2), 201–223.

Sajeva G., Borrini-Feyerabend G. and Niederberberger T. (2019) *Meanings and More...* Policy Brief of the ICCA Consortium no. 7. The ICCA Consortium and Cenesta, Tehran.

Sands P. (2012) "On Being 40: A Celebration of 'Should Trees Have Standing?'" *Journal of Human Rights and the Environment*, 3, 2–3.

Taylor P.E. (2008) "Ecological Integrity and Human Rights. Introducing the Rights Versus Responsibilities Debate" in Westra L., Bosselmann K. and Westra R. eds., *Reconciling Human Existence with Ecological Integrity*. Earthscan, Sterling, VA, 93–108.

Villavicencio Calzadilla P. (2019) "A Paradigm Shift in Courts' View on Nature: The Atrato River and Amazon Basin Cases in Colombia" *Environment and Development Journal (LEAD Journal)*, 15, xiii–xvi.

Waldron J. (1993) "Rights in Conflict" in Waldron J. ed., *Liberal Rights. Collected Papers. 1981–1991*. Cambridge University Press, Cambridge, 203–224.

Whitt L.A., Roberts M., Norman W., Grieves V. (2001) "Indigenous Perspectives" in Jamieson D. ed., *A Companion to Environmental Philosophy*. Blackwell Publishing, Marston Gate, 3–20.

7 Human Rights and Rights of Nature

Prospects for a Linkage Argument

Daniel P. Corrigan

Introduction

Rights of nature (RoN) are increasingly being recognized in legal systems around the world. However, whether such rights can be justified is a matter of debate. These rights give legal standing to objects or entities that have not traditionally been considered deserving of rights. Fundamentally, this involves the debate between anthropocentric and non-anthropocentric views of what has non-instrumental value or deserves direct moral consideration.[1] Anthropocentrists hold that only human beings have non-instrumental value or direct moral standing, while non-anthropocentrists hold that entities other than human beings can have non-instrumental value or direct moral standing. This chapter considers a possible way to overcome this debate, by exploring the prospects for a "linkage argument" between human rights and RoN. Linkage arguments are based upon showing that one right (or type of rights) supports another right (or type of rights), so that if one is committed to the supported right (or type of rights), then one is also committed to the supporting right (or type of rights). Typically, both anthropocentrists and non-anthropocentrists will endorse human rights, which recognize a set of basic moral entitlements of all human beings.[2] Thus, human rights offer a type of right that is embraced by both sides in common. This chapter considers the prospects for developing a linkage argument that shows that RoN provide some type of support for the realization or implementation of human rights, so that if one endorses human rights, then one also has reason to endorse RoN. If such an argument is successful, then it will show that anthropocentrists, like non-anthropocentrists, have reason to recognize RoN.

While the approach taken in this chapter is primarily a philosophical exploration, it will also give some consideration to legal developments in this area, as these developments can offer valuable input and guidance for thinking about the topic. The first section of the paper attempts to identify exactly what rights are involved, particularly in the case of rights of nature. The second section presents a paradigm model of a linkage argument, along with conceptual apparatus for assessing such arguments. The third section examines the prospects for developing a linkage argument between human rights and RoN, and the extent to which we can offer an assessment of such arguments.

Human Rights and Rights of Nature

Before we consider the prospects for a linkage argument between human rights and rights of nature, it is important to first identify exactly what rights are at issue. In the case of human rights, this task is easier. We have relatively well-developed and widely agreed-upon sources for identifying a list of human rights, in particular the International Bill of Human Rights, which includes the Universal Declaration of Human Rights (UDHR), the International Covenant on Civil and Political Rights (ICCPR), and the International Covenant on Economic, Social, and Cultural Rights (ICESCR). However, in the case of rights of nature, identifying a list of rights is more challenging. The idea that nature can or should have rights is more recent, and only a handful of jurisdictions have adopted such rights. There is no general agreement about the content of these rights, nor any definitive source for a list of such rights.

As we attempt to identify the RoN, it should be noted that this chapter assumes a "cosmopolitan" conception of these rights. A cosmopolitan conception of RoN holds that if there is justification for ascribing a right to a particular part of nature, then all similar parts of nature are justified in having the same right. The cosmopolitan conception contrasts with a "domestic" conception of RoN, which holds that a right may be justified for a particular part of nature, or within a particular jurisdiction, but this has no implications as to whether similar parts of nature in the same or other jurisdictions should also have the right. For example, the domestic conception allows that a certain society may grant a right to a particular river, but this has no implications as to whether other rivers in that society, or other rivers in other societies, should also be granted the right. The cosmopolitan conception understands RoN as having the same form as human rights, which are characterized as universal rights that are equally possessed by all humans everywhere. Since this chapter considers the prospects for a linkage argument between human rights—which are cosmopolitan rights—and RoN, the form of the argument necessitates that the RoN in question also be cosmopolitan rights.[3]

Several countries have adopted RoN in their legal systems, so let us consider whether these examples can offer guidance for identifying a list of rights. Among the countries that have recognized RoN are New Zealand, which has granted rights to a national park, a river, and a mountain; India, where the High Court of Uttarakhand has recognized two rivers as having rights; and Colombia, where the Supreme Court recognized the Colombian Amazon as having rights. While these are certainly examples of granting rights to nature, the problem is that in each case rights have been granted to just a few particular natural entities. For example, in the case of New Zealand, adoption of these rights resulted from a treaty settlement with the Māori peoples and was motivated by the fact that these entities have special significance for the indigenous people of the country. Since these examples involve granting rights to just a handful of particular natural entities, they do not provide criteria for systematically identifying the parts of nature that should be right-holders. Therefore, these examples fail to offer guidance for determining a general list of RoN.

Another country to adopt RoN is Ecuador, which has incorporated these rights into its constitution (Republic of Ecuador 2008). The Ecuadorian constitution recognizes a right of nature to "integral respect for its existence, and for the regeneration and maintenance of its cycles, structure, and processes" (Article 71), as well as a right to be "restored" (Articles 72). In addition, it recognizes a duty of the state to "apply preventative or restrictive measures on activities that may lead to extinction of species, destruction of ecosystems, or the permanent alteration of natural cycles" (Article 73). While the Ecuadorian constitution provides a more generalized account of the RoN, the right-holder in this case—nature—may be too abstract. What is "nature," and how do we determine the particular entity (or entities) that is (are) the right-holder(s)? The constitution defines nature as "all elements comprising an ecosystem" (Article 71). However, this approach seems to present a problem in the opposite direction of that found in the cases of New Zealand, India, and Colombia. Whereas those countries granted rights to just a few particular natural objects, which is too specific and fails to offer guidance for identifying a general list of RoN, the Ecuadorian constitution offers a conception of nature that is too broad for identifying such a list. "Nature," and "all elements" of an ecosystem, seems to grant a right to everything. This raises concerns about how we would identify particular right-holders, and in turn, how the rights of an indeterminate or all-encompassing right-holder could be practically implemented.

Yet another country to adopt RoN is Bolivia, which has a national statutory law based on the idea of the rights of Mother Earth. In addition, Bolivia drafted and presented the Universal Declaration of the Rights of Mother Earth (UDRME) to the United Nations for consideration. The UDRME conceptualizes nature, or "Mother Earth," as "a unique, indivisible, self-regulating community of interrelated beings" (Article 1). Thus, the UDRME treats the Earth itself as the right-holder. It then recognizes various rights of the Earth, including a right "to life and to exist," a right to "regenerate its biocapacity," a right to "water as a source of life," a right to clean air, a right to "integral health," a right to be free from pollution, and a right to "full and prompt restoration for violation of the rights," among others. While the UDRME certainly offers an identifiable right-holder, the Earth itself, this right-holder is so massive and complex that it remains unclear how to practically implement the rights on its behalf. Even if we set aside any metaphysical concerns that may arise, such as what it means for the Earth itself to have a "right to life," we are confronted with serious practical problems. How would we implement a right of the Earth itself to be "free from pollution"? Human activities, on both the collective and the individual level, will inevitably produce some kinds of pollution. However, it seems absurd to claim that every instance of pollution, anywhere on Earth, is a rights violation. If RoN should be capable of practical implementation, this is far more likely to be achieved if we treat discrete parts of the Earth as right-holders, as was done in New Zealand, India, and Colombia, where rivers, parks, mountains, or forests have been granted rights.

Each of the examples considered so far involves some problem for identifying a general list of RoN. In many ways, these challenges revolve around what can be called the "Ontological Problem," which concerns how we are to divide up nature in order to identify particular right-holders.[4] In contrast to the cases discussed above, a more promising approach may be found in Stone's book-length development of his landmark article "Should Trees Have Standing?" (Stone 2010). While Stone entertains the possibility of rights for a broad range of entities, he offers an extended discussion of the climate, oceans, agricultural landscapes, and non-agricultural landscapes.[5] Each of these entities can be treated as a type of right-holder, which has a corresponding family or class of rights: climate rights, ocean rights, agricultural landscape rights, and non-agricultural landscape rights. By classifying right-holders at this level of abstraction, we identify more discrete entities than those granted rights in Ecuador, Bolivia, or the UDRME, yet more generalized types of entities than the particular natural objects that have been granted rights in New Zealand, India, and Colombia. Furthermore, we can treat each type of right-holder as having a certain class or set of rights, which allows for the differentiation of entitlements (as well as corresponding obligations) that are most relevant and appropriate to each type of right-holder (rights of oceans, rights of the climate, rights of non-agricultural lands, etc.).

We should also have some idea of the entitlements and obligations created by RoN. The obligations corresponding to human rights are often divided into duties to respect, protect, and fulfill those rights. We can rely on this same framework to discuss the obligations corresponding to RoN. This chapter will assume that RoN primarily involve a duty to respect the right-holder, which is often interpreted as a duty of non-interference. If an agent, such as a person, a corporation, or a government, violates this obligation of respect for (non-interference with) the right-holder, then compensatory obligations may arise, which require the offender to repair, restore, or otherwise compensate the right-holder.[6] Furthermore, there are generally obligations to ensure that others comply with the duty to respect the right-holder, which involves a duty to protect the rights. In most legal systems, the duty to protect rights falls on the state.

There remains a question about how demanding the duty of respect, or non-interference, will be. The following comment from Stone speaks to this issue: "To say that the natural environment should have rights is not to say anything as silly as that no one should be allowed to cut down a tree"[7] (Stone 2010, 10). This comment draws attention to the fact that humans will inevitably act upon and alter the natural environment in various ways, and therefore RoN must take this into account and not be unreasonably demanding. If RoN preclude humans from doing anything whatsoever to the natural environment, these rights will be rendered completely implausible. In general, each class of rights offers protections that ensure the health and integrity of the right-holder, and demand a level of non-interference consistent with those aims. For example, agricultural lands have a right to be used sustainably, in a way that does not cause collapse from over-intensified use. This may place limits on the use of fertilizers or pesticides, and demand measures for preserving topsoil (Stone 2010, 82, 84–85). Non-agricultural lands, which can include everything from forestlands and grasslands to wetlands and more, have a right against conscription for agricultural purposes, so the integrity of these types of landscape is protected and preserved (Stone 2010, 82–83).

Let us now proceed with the rough idea that RoN will apply to "mid-sized" parts of nature, where this means something in between, on the one hand, Earth or nature as a whole, and on the other hand, individual trees, plants, rocks, etc. The right-holders will be entities like non-agricultural lands, which can include areas such as forests, swamps, prairies, and the like. Furthermore, RoN will primarily involve duties of respect for, or non-interference with, the right-holder, but can also entail duties to protect the rights, which ensure compliance with the duty to respect. Now that we have at least a rough outline of a cosmopolitan conception of RoN, and the sorts of rights that are at issue, we can turn to the idea of a linkage argument and how these arguments may be assessed.

Linkage Arguments

Perhaps the most prominent advocate of linkage arguments is Henry Shue. In his seminal book *Basic Rights*, Shue (1980 [1996]) argues for what he calls "basic rights," which are human rights whose enjoyment is necessary for the enjoyment of any other human right. Hence, if one endorses any human right at all, then one is committed to the basic rights, because the basic rights are necessary for the enjoyment of the favored human right. The structure of Shue's linkage argument is as follows:

1) Everyone has a right to something.
2) Some other things are necessary for enjoying the first thing as a right, whatever the first thing is.
3) Therefore, everyone also has rights to the other things that are necessary for enjoying the first thing as a right.

(Shue 1996, 31)

According to Shue, the things that are necessary for the enjoyment of any other thing as a right are security, liberty, and subsistence. Therefore, basic rights include the rights to security, liberty, and subsistence. Since most people believe that everyone has a right to at least something or other, Shue's argument aims to show that they are therefore also committed to these three basic rights.

The basis of any linkage argument is the supporting relation between rights. Therefore, the success of a linkage argument will be determined in large part by the quality of the supporting relation(s) upon which the argument rests. For example, the success of Shue's linkage argument for basic rights depends on demonstrating that rights to security, liberty, and subsistence are necessary for supporting the enjoyment of anything else as a right.

James Nickel (2008) offers a useful conceptual scheme for assessing supporting relations. When a supporting relation exists between two things, "one of them contributes to the functioning or stability of another," and in the absence of the supporting thing, the supported thing will "function less well or be less stable" (Nickel 2008, 987–988). Nickel offers a set of concepts that aim to conceptualize supporting relations. First, he distinguishes "strong" and "weak" supporting relations. A strong supporting relation exists between two rights when one right is indispensable to the other right. In this case, "it is inconsistent—as a logical or practical matter—for a person to endorse the implementation of the assisted right without also endorsing the assisting right" (Nickel 2008, 988). A weak supporting relation exists between two rights when one right is merely useful to the other right. In this case, "the supporting right is useful but not indispensible to the supported right" (Nickel 2008, 989). Second, he distinguishes "unidirectional" and "bidirectional" supporting relations. A unidirectional supporting relation means the support holds in only one direction, with just one of the rights providing support to the other. A bidirectional supporting relation means the support holds in both directions, with each right providing support to the other. These concepts are overlapping, so that both bidirectional and unidirectional supporting relations can be described as either strong or weak. If two rights provide weak bidirectional support to each other, the rights are said to be "interdependent." In the case of interdependent rights, each right is useful for realizing the other right. If two rights provide strong bidirectional support to each other, the rights are said to be "indivisible" (Nickel 2008, 990). In the case of indivisible rights, you cannot undermine or destroy one right without also undermining or destroying the other right. Indivisibility is the most comprehensive supporting relation that can exist between two rights.

Nickel also introduces the notion of "quality of implementation," which he argues is critically important for analyzing the strength of supporting relations. Quality of implementation concerns how well a right functions, or the degree to which it has been implemented, within a particular society or political system. This concept admits of a range, which spans from non-implementation ("the right is unrecognized or exists only on paper"), to low-quality implementation, to high-quality implementation. The level of quality of implementation is determined by two factors: 1) the extent to which "major threats to the right have been adequately blocked or neutralized" (Nickel 2008, 992), and 2) the percentage of people for whom the right is effective in blocking such threats. Blocking or neutralizing threats is accomplished through actions such as "gaining recognition and compliance with the right's associated moral and legal duties, providing protections and other services, and providing legal and other remedies for noncompliance with the right" (Nickel 2008, 992). It is not uncommon to find societies where a right may effectively block or neutralize major threats for some people, while failing to block, or ineffectively blocking, such threats for others (Nickel 2008, 993). High-quality implementation requires that the right effectively block or neutralize all major threats, for all people. Failure to block or neutralize any of the major threats to a right, or the failure to do so for all people, will constitute something less than high-quality implementation. For example, suppose the government of a country is able to maintain law and order in urban areas and keep city-dwellers safe, but the government is unable to control more remote rural areas, where people are regularly attacked, robbed, and killed. In this case, there is low-quality implementation of the human right to security, because while threats to this right have been neutralized for citizens living in urban areas, these threats have not been neutralized for citizens living in remote rural areas.

Quality of implementation is important because it influences both the degree of support that a right can offer to other rights, as well as the degree of support it requires from other rights. More specifically, high-quality implementation of a particular right requires more and stronger support from other rights, while also enabling this right to provide more and stronger support to other rights. A right with low-quality implementation provides less support to other rights, but also requires less support from other rights (Nickel 2008, 994). In general, a right needs at least medium-quality implementation—both in terms of blocking threats and in terms of coverage of right-holders—before it can effectively provide any support to another right (Nickel 2008, 993).

While Nickel's conceptual scheme is helpful for assessing the quality of supporting relations, Pablo Gilabert (2010) introduces a typology for categorizing different types of supporting relations. Gilabert suggests four types of supporting relations: conceptual, normative, epistemic, and causal. A conceptual supporting relation exists when the implementation of one right is conceptually required as part of another right. An example of conceptual support exists between equality rights and other human rights, because if human rights are not implemented equally for everyone, then these rights are not fully implemented (or have not achieved high quality implementation, to use Nickel's terminology). A normative supporting relation exists when the implementation of one right normatively enhances the implementation of another right. An example of normative support exists between political rights and socioeconomic rights, because there is normative value in implementing socioeconomic entitlements through a legitimate political process based on the exercise of political rights, as opposed to, say, authoritarian implementation of such entitlements. An epistemic supporting relation exists when the implementation of one right can contribute to knowledge of how best to implement another right. For example, the exercise of political rights, such as public deliberation, helps to identify which socioeconomic policies are most effective in providing the entitlements of socioeconomic rights. Finally, a casual supporting relation exists when the implementation of one right helps to ensure or guarantee the implementation of another right. For example, the exercise of political rights, such as the right to democratic participation, helps to ensure that government officials are responsive to the people and actually provide their socioeconomic entitlements (Gilabert 2010, 429).

In light of this model linkage argument and conceptual apparatus for assessing such arguments, we can now examine the prospects for a linkage argument between human rights and RoN.

Prospects for a Linkage Argument

Scholars have (explicitly) recognized for quite some time that there is a relationship between the environment and human rights (for example, Nickel 1993; Nickel & Viola 1994; Hayward 2005; Woods 2010). This has led to the development of a "human rights and the environment" agenda, which seeks formal recognition of this relationship and attempts to identify the environmental obligations that are entailed by human rights. Among other things, it has led to advocacy for, and in many cases the adoption of, the human right to a healthy environment.[8] This right entitles people to an environmental quality that is conducive to the enjoyment of human rights, or at least, to the rights to life and health.

In 2017, the Inter-American Court of Human Rights (IACtHR) issued a landmark Advisory Opinion on this issue (IACtHR 2017). The opinion reiterates the importance of the environment for human rights:

> The Court has recognized the existence of an undeniable relationship between the protection of the environment and the realization of other human rights, in that environmental degradation and the adverse effects of climate change affect the real enjoyment of human rights.
>
> (IACtHR 2017, para 47)

However, in what is perhaps the most significant aspect of this opinion, the court recognizes RoN as part of the human right to a healthy environment.

> The Court considers it important to stress that, as an autonomous right, the right to a healthy environment, unlike other rights, protects the components of the environment, such as forests, rivers and seas, as legal interests in themselves, even in the absence of the certainty or evidence of a risk to individuals. This means that it protects nature and the environment, not only because of the benefits they provide to humanity or the effects that their degradation may have on other human rights, such as health, life or personal integrity, but because of their importance to the other living organisms with which we share the planet that also merit protection in their own right. In this regard, the Court notes a tendency, not only in court judgments, but also in Constitutions, to recognize legal personality and, consequently, rights to nature.
>
> (IACtHR 2017, para 62)

Here the court refers to "rights to nature," as opposed to "rights of nature." Nevertheless, the characterization of these rights makes it clear that the court is referring to RoN. First, the court recognizes nature as having its own "legal personality," and entities such as forests, rivers, and seas as "legal interests in themselves." In other words, nature *itself* is a legal entity with protected legal interests. Second, it is clear that the legal interests protected by these rights are the interests of nature, not the interests of humans, because the Court emphasizes that nature is entitled to protection even when there is no certainty or evidence that harm to it will result in harm to humans or human rights.[9] Third, the justification of the independent legal standing (and rights) of nature is based not merely upon its importance for a range of human rights (life, health, personal integrity), but also its importance for other living organisms that deserve direct protection in their own right. The latter part of this justification may explain why the court holds nature to have rights-based protections even in the absence of evidence of harm to humans.

This presents a potentially pivotal development in the human rights and the environment agenda, because it goes beyond previous characterizations of the right to a healthy environment, and now recognizes RoN as entailed by this human right. However, one may wonder whether this development is justified. How can a *human* right entail rights for something else (e.g. nature), "even in the absence of the certainty or evidence of a risk to [human] individuals"? If there is no evidence of risk or harm to humans, then it seems no human right is at stake. And if no human right is at stake, then it is not clear how a human right can provide justification for the rights of something other than humans. As pointed out above, the court indicates that part of the justification for RoN is the importance that nature has for other living organisms.[10] However, even if it is true that other living organisms deserve protection, these other organisms are not humans. So once again, this justification presents no human right that is at stake, and it is not clear how a human right can provide justification for RoN. For these reasons, it remains unclear how the Court can justify including RoN as part of the human right to a healthy environment, particularly in cases where there is an "absence of certainty or evidence of a risk to [human] individuals."

I believe we can address this concern, and provide a human rights–based justification for the connection between the right to a healthy environment and RoN, by developing a linkage argument. This linkage argument will have a broader basis than that offered by the IACtHR. Rather than appeal to the importance of the environment for just the rights to life, health, and personal integrity, the argument will appeal to supporting relations between the environment and a number of different human rights.

The linkage argument is modeled on Shue's argument for basic rights, and can be referred to as Linkage Argument 1:

1) Everyone has a human right to something
2) Some aspects of nature are necessary for enjoying that thing as a right, whatever that thing is

3) Rights of nature are necessary (or at least useful) for protecting and preserving these aspects of nature [11]
4) Therefore, everyone has a human right to the implementation of rights of nature necessary (or at least useful) for enjoying that thing as a human right

Notice that this argument introduces an innovation into Shue's model argument by adding an additional premise that recognizes rights for something other than humans. The success of this argument depends on establishing two things: 1) certain aspects of nature are necessary for enjoying particular human rights (Premise 2), and 2) implementing RoN is necessary, or at least useful, for protecting and preserving the aspects of nature that are necessary for enjoying those human rights (Premise 3).

Let us begin by focusing on the second issue (Premise 3). The primary challenge here is likely to be the claim that there is no need to grant RoN, because we can simply grant a human right to the aspects of nature necessary for enjoying other human rights. Indeed, that has traditionally been the aim of the human right to a healthy environment, at least to some degree. This right is focused on protecting people against environmental impacts that are detrimental to life and health. However, there has been a tendency to narrow the scope of these concerns by placing an emphasis on immediate environmental impacts on life and health, in an effort to prevent the right from becoming overly expansive and demanding.[12] This makes it doubtful whether the human right to a healthy environment alone is adequate for protecting and preserving the environment to the degree necessary for enjoying human rights in general, especially rights other than those to life and health.

Human rights have always had the potential to broaden the scope of environmental concerns and obligations because the environment is such a complex and pervasive background condition for enjoying these rights. This potential for a broader scope was recently given explicit recognition by John Knox, who served as the U.N. Special Rapporteur on human rights and the environment from 2015–2018. In 2017, Knox issued a report on the relationship between human rights and biodiversity (United Nations Human Rights Council 2017). The report contends that "the full enjoyment of human rights…depends on biodiversity, and the degradation and loss of biodiversity undermine the ability of human beings to enjoy their human rights" (United Nations Human Rights Council 2017, 3). The significance of this report lies in its potential to decidedly broaden the human rights and the environment agenda because recognition of the importance of biodiversity for the enjoyment of human rights introduces at least two innovations. First, it focuses on longer-term and more distant environmental impacts relating to human rights. The role of biodiversity in the enjoyment of human rights is likely to be realized over time, rather than as an immediate impact. Second, it incorporates concern for the wellbeing of other species into the human rights agenda.[13] Once concern is extended to biodiversity, which involves the sheer number of species that exist, this invites a radical broadening of the environmental matters relevant to human rights. If supporting biodiversity is a human rights concern, then the general wellbeing of the environment also becomes relevant, since this is necessary for supporting biodiversity.

Knox's report, and its expansion of the human rights and the environment agenda to include concern for biodiversity, was followed by an even more recent report from the U.N. Intergovernmental Science-Policy Platform on Biodiversity and Ecosystem Services (IPBES 2019a). The IPBES report finds an unprecedented and accelerating rate of extinction of species. More specifically, the report finds the current rate of extinction is higher than the average rate of extinction over the past ten million years, and this rate is accelerating. An average of 25% of the plant and animal species assessed face extinction. This includes "around 1 million species [that] already face extinction, many within a decade" (IPBES 2019b, 12). The report also recognizes the impact this loss can have for human beings: "The average abundance of native species in most major terrestrial biomes has fallen by at least 20 per cent, potentially affecting ecosystem processes and hence nature's contributions to people" (IPBES 2019b, 11). Furthermore, the report identifies and ranks the leading drivers of these trends (starting with the most impactful): changes in land and sea use, direct exploitation of organisms, climate change, pollution, and invasive species (IPBES 2019b, 12). In terms of the top driver, changes in land and sea use, agriculture accounts for the most widespread change in land use, with over one-third of the Earth's land surface now being used for crops or livestock. The second leading driver, direct exploitation of organisms, includes the over-harvesting of wood from forests and the over-exploitation of fish, shellfish, and other species from the oceans, with many species threatened with collapse.

Given this alarming rate of extinction, and the recognition of biodiversity as a human rights issue, we are faced with the question—from a human rights standpoint—of how best to protect biodiversity and prevent the continuation of this dire trend. We might look to environmental ethics for guidance in thinking about possible solutions. One approach is the animal liberation or animal rights movement, which advocates rights for various non-human animals. However, this approach endorses rights only for sentient animals. We have identified and described around 1.3 million species, but it is estimated that there may be as many as 8.7 million species on Earth. While all of these species are included in the concept of biodiversity, many of them are non-sentient species, including plants and microorganisms, among others. Furthermore, not all of these species will be of equal importance to maintaining biodiversity. Among those that are most important for this purpose, not all of them will be sentient. So if protecting biodiversity is our goal, sentience is a poor criterion, and the animal liberation or animal rights approach is clearly inadequate. Alternatively, the biocentric approach advocates recognition of the moral worth of all living things. Perhaps we could grants rights, or some other type of protection, to all living things. The problem with that approach is that it seems a practical impossibility to recognize and exercise a right on behalf of every one of these species, or even more implausibly, each member of every species. Nevertheless, all of these species are constituent parts of the biodiversity of our planet. Given the problems with each of these approaches, it may be better to turn from biodiversity itself and focus instead on the underlying support for biodiversity. Since biodiversity is dependent on a broadly healthy environment, perhaps the most plausible and effective way to protect biodiversity is to recognize rights for the underlying environment upon which biodiversity depends. In this way, we grant legal standing, in the form of rights, to various parts of nature that support biodiversity. These rights can facilitate the protection and preservation of these parts of nature, which in turn protect and preserve biodiversity.

This line of thought suggests a second type of linkage argument, which can be referred to as Linkage Argument 2:

1) Everyone has a human right to something
2) Biodiversity is necessary for enjoying that thing as a right, whatever that thing is
3) Rights of nature are necessary (or at least useful) for protecting and preserving biodiversity
4) Therefore, everyone has a human right to the implementation of rights of nature necessary (or at least useful) for enjoying that thing as a human right

Notice that this argument also adds an extra premise not found in Shue's model argument. The extra premise involves using biodiversity as a bridge between RoN and human rights. The success of this linkage argument depends on establishing that 1) biodiversity is necessary for enjoying particular human rights (Premise 2) and 2) implementing RoN is necessary, or at least useful, for protecting and preserving biodiversity (Premise 3).

The previous discussion, which led up to Linkage Argument 2, defended the second issue (Premise 3), so let us now turn to the first issue (Premise 2). In his report, Knox offers a number of arguments to support the claim that biodiversity is necessary for enjoying certain human rights, including the rights to life, health, an adequate standard of living, and non-discrimination rights. Biodiversity supports life and health in a number of ways, including biodiversity as an irreplaceable source for the derivation of medicinal drugs, the contribution of microbial diversity to the development of the human immune system, the contribution of biodiversity to diluting the transmission of pathogens to humans, and preserving the contribution of nature to human mental health (United Nations Human Rights Council 2017, 6–7). In the case of the right to an adequate standard of living, biodiversity makes significant contributions by generally supporting food security through increasing the yield of commercial crops and supporting more robust fisheries. Biodiversity also contributes to this right by supporting access to clean and safe water, as diverse animals, plants, and algal species help to draw excess nitrogen and phosphorus from the aquatic ecosystem (United Nations Human Rights Council 2017, 8).Biodiversity also plays an important supporting role in the case of non-discrimination rights, as some people depend more heavily on ecosystems than others. "For indigenous peoples, forest-dwellers, fisherfolk, and others who rely directly on the products of forest, rivers, lakes, and oceans for their food, fuel, and medicine," loss of biodiversity can have a devastating effect and reinforce existing patterns of discrimination (United Nations Human Rights Council 2017, 9). The marginalization of these people often means they have no access to political decision-making or legal remedies when their interests are at stake. Thus, Knox offers an array of reasons in support of the claim that biodiversity is necessary for enjoying some human rights.

Next, let us return to the claim that implementing RoN will protect and preserve biodiversity. While it was argued above that RoN offer the best approach to protecting and preserving biodiversity, there is little evidence available to determine whether RoN can actually achieve this. A primary reason for the lack of evidence is that RoN have not yet been fully implemented. At this point, only a handful of countries and jurisdictions have adopted RoN, and in those that have, there has so far been little exercise of these rights. This thin track record of implementation precludes us from offering empirical evidence to support the claim, and therefore we are limited to offering conceptual arguments about what these rights might achieve. If RoN are fully implemented, there is some reason to believe this would contribute to protecting and preserving biodiversity. For example, the IPBES report found that 85% of global wetlands have already been lost. Furthermore, between 2010 and 2015, 32 million hectares of tropical forest—areas of very high biodiversity—were lost (IPBES 2019b, 11). This habitat loss is a leading cause of the loss of biodiversity. High-quality implementation of RoN should stem such habitat loss, and presumably will contribute to the protection and preservation of biodiversity. More specifically, protecting non-agricultural landscape from agricultural development, by granting RoN to non-agricultural lands, seems likely to help protect and preserve the species that depend on these habitats.

Now that we have considered some grounds for the claims that 1) biodiversity is necessary for the enjoyment of human rights and 2) implementing RoN will help to protect and preserve biodiversity, we can examine the application of our two linkage arguments to particular human rights and RoN. Let us focus on the human rights discussed by Knox, and some of the RoN suggested previously.

Rights of Oceans and Non-Agricultural Lands

Linkage Argument 2, which uses biodiversity as a bridge between RoN and human rights, will be especially applicable in the case of rights of oceans and rights of non-agricultural landscapes. When I say the argument is "applicable," I mean that we can plug certain RoN and certain human rights into this model, in order to produce a linkage argument that is applicable to those particular rights. There is some commonality between these two classes of right-holders since oceans and non-agricultural landscapes are both primarily natural areas that have not been developed by humans. First, consider these rights in relation to the human rights to life, health, and an adequate standard of living. There is unidirectional support from rights of oceans and rights of non-agricultural landscapes to these human rights. The health of the oceans and non-agricultural landscapes is crucial for supporting biodiversity, and the contributions that biodiversity makes to life, health, and an adequate standard of living. In fact, these areas of nature are the primary source for biodiversity. So degradation of these areas will diminish biodiversity, and cause the loss of the important contributions that biodiversity makes to human life and health, through the natural cleansing of water and providing a barrier to the spread of pathogens to human beings. These areas are also the most likely to hold natural organisms that can be a source of medicinal drugs. Furthermore, the contribution of nature to our mental health is typically associated with these more "wild" areas. In addition, the biodiversity in these areas also makes a significant contribution to the human right to an adequate standard of living. Forty percent of the global human population lives in coastal areas. Loss of ocean biodiversity threatens the human right to an adequate standard of living for many of these people, both those who have a formal job that depends on this biodiversity, as well as those who depend on it as a source of food and other resources.

It is difficult to assess whether the unidirectional support from the rights of oceans and non-agricultural landscapes to these human rights is strong or weak. Recall that strong means indispensable, while weak means merely useful. The difficulty is due to two factors. First, as previously discussed, since RoN have yet to be fully implemented, we lack empirical information about what these rights can accomplish in terms of protecting and preserving biodiversity. We do know that destruction of these habitats diminishes biodiversity, and therefore preventing this destruction through implementation of rights of oceans and non-agricultural landscapes should contribute to protecting and preserving biodiversity. At a minimum then, these RoN should be at least useful for protecting and preserving biodiversity, which would constitute a weak supporting relation. Depending on what RoN can accomplish in terms of protecting and preserving biodiversity, it is possible they could be indispensible. However, there are many factors that impact biodiversity, and habitat protection alone will not be the only determinant. Therefore, while there is some reason to believe that implementing rights of oceans and non-agricultural landscapes will contribute to the protection and preservation of biodiversity, the protections they provide will not be the only determinant of the health of biodiversity. For these reasons, it is difficult to assess whether the rights of oceans and non-agricultural landscapes rise to the level of being indispensable for protecting and preserving biodiversity, or will be merely useful for this purpose. Thus, we are unable to fully assess the strength of this linkage argument, but can perhaps establish that the argument involves at least a weak (useful) supporting relation.

The supporting relation between these RoN and the human rights to life, health, and an adequate standard of living is causal. The protection and preservation of these natural areas, which supports biodiversity and the contribution that it makes, helps to ensure or guarantee the enjoyment of these human rights. In the absence of the protections provided by these RoN, oceans and non-agricultural habitats will likely continue to be degraded, which in turn threatens biodiversity and the contribution that it makes to these human rights.

Next, consider the relation between the rights of oceans and non-agricultural landscapes and what Knox calls "non-discrimination" rights. When discussing these human rights, he mentions "indigenous peoples, forest-dwellers, fisherfolk." I will refer to the rights of indigenous people in discussing the linkage arguments here, although these rights clearly apply more broadly to any people who are heavily dependent on the natural environment for their livelihood. Linkage Argument 1 and Linkage Argument 2 are both applicable in this case, because some relations between these RoN and non-discrimination rights require biodiversity as a bridge, while others do not.

There is bidirectional support between the rights of oceans and non-agricultural rights and the human rights of indigenous peoples. This is because these RoN help to protect the traditional lands and areas of indigenous peoples. Furthermore, indigenous peoples typically have sustainable lifestyles and practices that protect and preserve oceans and non-agricultural landscapes. For example, the IPBES report found that while the natural environment had been significantly altered by human action, it is much less severe or completely unaltered in areas managed by indigenous peoples (IPEBS 2019b, 14). Here we can also see why both Linkage Argument 1 and Linkage Argument 2 will apply. We can explain the supporting relation by appealling to biodiversity, whose protection is certainly important for ensuring there is no discrimination against people who are heavily dependent on the environment. However, we need not only appeal to biodiversity, as indigenous people often seek to protect their traditional lands in general, for cultural and other purposes, which can fall under the description of "aspects of nature" (rather than biodiversity), the concept employed in Linkage Argument 1.

The relation between these RoN and the human rights of indigenous peoples is likely to be strong, meaning indispensable. This is because the rights of indigenous people are commonly under threat, due in part to the fact that indigenous peoples are seldom integrated into the prevailing political system and therefore often lack access to means for protecting their rights. For this reason, protection of the rights of indigenous peoples can often depend on proactive efforts of the prevailing political and legal system. Among the most common threats to indigenous people is encroachment on their traditional lands for commercial and development purposes. The implementation of rights of oceans and non-agricultural landscapes would provide a set of legal norms that protect the traditional lands and areas of these peoples. In fact, implementation of these RoN could in some ways substitute for the lack of access that indigenous peoples have for exercising their rights. On the other hand, in cases where indigenous peoples do have the access and ability to exercise their rights, this will often realize the same objectives as the rights of oceans and non-agricultural lands, since the exercise of indigenous peoples' rights often functions to protect the environment. This reveals bidirectional support between these two sets of rights.

The support between these sets of rights is both causal and conceptual. It is causal because the implementation of one set of rights helps to ensure and guarantee the implementation of the other set of rights. In addition, the support is conceptual because the aims of the rights are often overlapping. For example, implementing the rights of oceans and non-agricultural lands helps to protect the traditional lands and areas of indigenous peoples, which is a common objective in the exercise of indigenous rights. Similarly, the exercise of indigenous rights to protect their traditional lands and areas will often accomplish the aims of rights of oceans and non-agricultural lands.

Rights of Agricultural Lands

Next consider the rights of agricultural lands in relation to the human rights to life, health, and an adequate standard of living. Linkage Argument 1 will be applicable in the case of these rights. There is unidirectional support from the rights of agricultural lands to these human rights. The rights of agricultural lands include an entitlement of these lands to be used in a sustainable manner, so they do not collapse from over-use and depletion through excessive use of chemical fertilizers, etc. These protections for agricultural lands support the life and health of, and an adequate standard of living for, the people who work on and depend on the produce of these lands.

In terms of the strength of this supporting relation, it will certainly be strong, or indispensable, if agricultural lands were to collapse in the absence of implementing these RoN. The IPBES report found that degradation of land has reduced productivity in 23% of the global terrestrial area. Given current practices, increases in agricultural output are not sustainable, due to factors such as loss of organic carbon in the soil (IPBES 2019b, 11). It is also common to find collapse of agricultural lands in regions of the world where forest or rain forest are clear-cut or burned in order to create agricultural land. These lands are often farmed in unsustainable ways, until they are depleted of all nutrients and no longer capable of supporting agricultural life. In such cases, the rights of agricultural lands would be indispensable for supporting the human rights to life, health, and an adequate standard of living. Furthermore, the supporting relation is causal, as the rights of agricultural lands help to ensure or guarantee the implementation of these human rights.

Rights of the Climate

Finally, consider the relation between rights of the climate and all of the human rights that have been discussed, including the rights to life, health, an adequate standard of living, and non-discrimination rights (or indigenous peoples' rights). Linkage Argument 1 and Linkage Argument 2 are both applicable to the relations between these sets of rights. Linkage Argument 1 can apply, because we can treat the climate as an aspect of nature that directly supports the object of these human rights. Linkage Argument 2 is also applicable, because the state of the climate is crucial for supporting biodiversity. Extreme climate change has the potential to cause most plant and animal species on Earth to go extinct, because these species will not be able to evolve fast enough to adapt to rapidly changing climate, nor will they be able to move to more suitable areas. In this event, we might be left with only those species that can live with or off of human beings. Thus, climate change presents an extremely serious and pervasive threat to biodiversity and the contribution that it makes to the enjoyment of human rights.

There is unidirectional support from rights of the climate to all of the human rights mentioned. This is because the climate is a pervasive background condition necessary for enjoying all of these rights. Excessive climate change and warming will certainly threaten, and can even completely undermine, the enjoyment of these rights. Among the threats posed by climate change are drought, flooding, increased exposure to diseases, food insecurity and less nutritious crops, and severe loss of biodiversity.

Given the dramatic implications that climate change can have, the supporting relation from rights of the climate to these human rights is strong, or indispensable. The state of the climate is an indispensable background condition for the enjoyment of these human rights, which suggest that rights of the climate are indispensable for the implementation of these human rights. This is a casual supporting relation, because implementation of rights of the climate helps to ensure or guarantee the implementation of these human rights.

Conclusion

This chapter has attempted to sketch a set of linkage arguments between human rights and a cosmopolitan conception of RoN. In some cases, the strength of these arguments (Linkage Argument 2) is indeterminate due to a lack of empirical evidence about what RoN can accomplish in terms of protecting and preserving biodiversity. Nevertheless, there is some reason to believe that the implementation of RoN would help to protect and preserve biodiversity, which has been recognized as necessary for the enjoyment of some human rights. This suggests RoN would be at least useful to the enjoyment of these human rights, and therefore offers at least a weak linkage argument between these two sets of rights. In other cases, the argument (Linkage Argument 1) focuses directly on aspects of nature that are necessary for the enjoyment of certain human rights. The full implementation of RoN would protect and preserve these aspects of nature, which seems to present a strong supporting relation between RoN and these human rights. While this chapter cannot hope to address all of the questions and issues that may be raised, the linkage arguments sketched here offer some grounds for showing that anthropocentrists, as well as non-anthropocentrists, have reason to support the recognition and implementation of RoN.

Acknowledgments

I would like to thank Markku Oksanen and Marion Hourdequin for their comments on previous versions of this chapter.

Notes

1 Here I assume a structure that mirrors one commonly attributed to human rights: human rights are held to be ethically justified entitlements of all human beings, and in virtue of this, rights that should be instantiated in all legal systems. Similarly, I assume that if rights of nature are ethically justified entitlements, then in virtue of this, all legal systems should instantiate these rights. However, it should be noted that other reasons, apart from ethical justification, can play a role in determining whether legal rights should be adopted. For example, various pragmatic considerations, such as feasibility, justiciability, and efficiency, among others, can be taken into account. See note 3 regarding a cosmopolitan account of rights of nature.

2 It should be noted that neither anthropocentrists nor non-anthropocentrists are necessarily committed to a rights-based approach. An entity can merit direct moral consideration without necessarily being entitled to rights. However, we do find widespread support for human rights as a set of basic moral (and legal) entitlements that belong to all people.

3 Since human rights are cosmopolitan rights, the structure of a linkage implies that RoN must also be cosmopolitan rights. This is because linkage arguments are based on demonstrating that one right (or set of rights) is necessary or useful to the functioning of another right (or set of rights). Thus, if the supported rights (human rights) are cosmopolitan rights, then the supporting rights (RoN) must also be cosmopolitan rights. It would be incoherent to offer a linkage between cosmopolitan human rights and domestic RoN, because the former are held by people everywhere, while the latter might exist only in certain jurisdictions. This allows that the supporting rights may not exist everywhere that the supported rights exist, and contradicts the justificatory structure of a linkage argument.

4 Stone references this problem:

> there are large problems involved in defining the boundaries of the 'natural object.' For example, from time to time one will wish to speak of that portion of the river that runs through a recognized jurisdiction; at other times, one may be concerned with the entire river, or the hydrologic cycle—or the whole of nature. One's ontological choices will have a strong influence on the shape of the legal system, and the choices involved are not easy.
>
> (Stone, 1972: 456, note 26)

5 Stone explicitly mentions a right only in regards to the climate, and does not mention rights for these other entities. This raises questions about whether he consistently adheres to the idea of rights throughout the book, or instead shifts to a consequentialist approach to environmental policy. Nevertheless, we can treat the major entities that he discusses as potential types of right-holders.

6 A more robust account of rights of nature might include an obligation to fulfill the rights, which would most likely involve a duty of restoration. In this case, restoration is not a mere compensatory obligation, but a primary obligation. The compensatory obligation of restoration arises only when an agent violates the duty of non-interference, and

then owes compensation or repair for the violation. A primary obligation to restore, on the other hand, can arise when no agent is responsible for harming the right-holder. For example, if the right-holder has been damaged by natural causes, such as a flood, a major storm, or some other natural disaster, a primary obligation of restoration can arise, even though no agent is at fault. See Lumpalla's chapter in this volume for a discussion of the right to restoration.

7 However, see Stone's discussion of Los Angeles municipal law, which determines which particular types of trees receive protection within the city (Stone 2012, 119). Stone suggests that "age counts in favour of protection, as I imagine do other distinct features, such as size, rarity, unusual shape, spread, and sometimes association with historical events that a tree lived through before our time" (Stone 2012, 120). While Stone seems to allow that an individual tree can have rights, this will be due to particular features that make the tree special and warrants such protection.

8 The right to a healthy environment is still not included in any global human rights treaties, such as the International Bill of Human Rights, but advocates continue to push for recognition of this right at the global level. Nevertheless, this right has been included in many regional human rights treaties, including the African Charter on Human and Peoples' Rights, the Arab Charter on Human Rights, the ASEAN Human Rights Declaration, and the Additional Protocol to the American Convention on Human Rights.

9 In addition to the features mentioned, it is also worth pointing out that the IACtHR implicitly endorses what I have called a cosmopolitan account of RoN. The rights are held to apply to "forests, rivers and seas" in general, without any criteria that might limit the rights to only particular entities of these types. Furthermore, since these natural entities are held to have legal personality in themselves, with their own protected legal interests, there is no additional constraint placed upon which ones have rights (e.g. proximity to humans, importance to a certain group, etc.).

10 See Donoso's chapter in this volume for an argument that RoN should be understood as a group right that belongs to non-human animals.

11 This premise includes the parenthetical to account for Nickel's distinction between "strong" and "weak" supporting relations. Necessity refers to a strong supporting relation, while usefulness refers to a weak supporting relation. Stating the premise in this manner allows the linkage argument to accommodate either strong or weak supporting relations.

12 For example, Nickel (1993) writes, "[The right to a safe environment] is human oriented. It does not speak directly to issues such as biodiversity, the claims of animals, conservation, or sustainable development" (283). He continues, "a narrow formulation focusing exclusively on human health and safety has the best chance of gaining acceptance as a genuine human right...Threats to health are the primary focus of the [right to a safe environment]" (284).

13 While both Knox's report and the IACtHR's Advisory Opinion offer reasons for concern about other living things, the reasons are quite different. Knox's report recognizes the importance of biodiversity *for* human rights, whereas the IACtHR claims that other living things "deserve protection in their own right." In other words, Knox offers an instrumental reason or concern about other living things, while the IACtHR claims these things deserve concern in their own right. Knox's approach provides more firm footing within a human rights framework, because it appeals to their importance for humans. This is important if one if trying to provide a justification based on human rights.

References

Gilabert, Pablo. 2010. "The Importance of Linkage Arguments for the Theory and Practice of Human Rights: A Response to James Nickel." *Human Rights Quarterly* 32: 425–438.

Hayward, Tim. 2005. *Constitutional Environmental Rights*. Oxford University Press.

Inter-American Court of Human Rights (IACtHR). Advisory Opinion OC-23/13. November 2017. https://www.corteidh.or.cr/docs/opiniones/seriea_23_ing.pdf

IPBES. 2019a. *Global Assessment Report on Biodiversity and Ecosystem Services of the Intergovernmental Science-Policy Platform on Biodiversity and Ecosystem Services*. Edited by E. S. Brondizio, J. Settele, S. Díaz, and H. T. Ngo. IPBES Secretariat, Bonn, Germany. https://www.ipbes.net/global-assessment-report-biodiversity-ecosystem-services

IPBES. 2019b. *Summary for Policymakers of the Global Assessment Report on Biodiversity and Ecosystem Services of the Intergovernmental Science-Policy Platform on Biodiversity and Ecosystem Services*. Edited by S. Díaz, J. Settele, E. S. Brondízio, H. T. Ngo, M. Guèze, J. Agard, A. Arneth, P. Balvanera, K. A. Brauman, S. H. M. Butchart, K. M. A. Chan, L. A. Garibaldi, K. Ichii, J. Liu, S. M. Subramanian, G. F. Midgley, P. Miloslavich, Z. Molnár, D. Obura, A. Pfaff, S. Polasky, A. Purvis, J. Razzaque, B. Reyers, R. Roy Chowdhury, Y. J. Shin, I. J. Visseren-Hamakers, K. J. Willis, and C. N. Zayas. IPBES Secretariat, Bonn, Germany. https://ipbes.net/sites/default/files/2020-02/ipbes_global_assessment_report_summary_for_policymakers_en.pdf

Nickel, James W. 1993. "The Right to a Safe Environment: Philosophical Perspectives on Its Scope and Justification." *Yale Journal of International Law* 18(9): 281–295.

Nickel, James W. 2008. "Rethinking Indivisibility: Towards a Theory of Supporting Relations for Human Rights." *Human Rights Quarterly* 30: 984–1001.

Nickel, James W. and Eduardo Viola. 1994. "Integrating Environmentalism and Human Rights." *Environmental Ethics* 16: 265–271.

Republic of Ecuador. 2008. *Constitution of the Republic of Ecuador*. http://pdba.georgetown.edu/Constitutions/Ecuador/english08.html

Shue, Henry. 1980. 2nd edition 1996. *Basic Rights: Subsistence, Affluence, and U.S. Foreign Policy*. Princeton University Press.

Stone, Christopher D. 1972. "Should Trees Have Standing?: Toward Legal Rights for Natural Objects." *Southern California Law Review* 45: 450–501.

Stone, Christopher D. 2010. *Should Trees Have Standing?: Law, Morality, and the Environment* (3rd edition). Oxford University Press.

Stone, Christopher D. 2012. "Response to Commentators." *Journal of Human Rights and the Environment* 3: 100–120.

United Nations Human Rights Council. 2017. *Report of the Special Rapporteur on the Issue of Human Rights Obligations Relating to the Enjoyment of a Safe, Clean, Healthy, and Sustainable Environment*. A/HRC/34/49. https://documents-dds-ny.un.org/doc/UNDOC/GEN/G17/009/97/PDF/G1700997.pdf?OpenElement

Universal Declaration of the Rights of Mother Earth. 2010. https://therightsofnature.org/wp-content/uploads/FINAL-UNIVERSAL-DECLARATION-OF-THE-RIGHTS-OF-MOTHER-EARTH-APRIL-22-2010.pdf

Woods, Kerri. 2010. *Human Rights and Environmental Sustainability*. Edward Elgar Publishing.

8 Rights-Based Restoration

Linnea Luuppala

Introduction

Degraded, damaged, and destroyed not only describes the objects of ecological restoration projects, but also the current state of the Earth itself. This is shown by report after report that paint a devastating picture of the condition of nature, but also importantly, the key role that humans play in this destructive trajectory (Tortell 2020). To fix our broken world, the United Nations General Assembly announced a global initiative, the "U.N. Decade on Ecosystem Restoration 2021–2030." The initiative comes at a time when over two billion hectares have been identified as being in a degraded state and thereby suitable for restoration (U.N. Environment Press Release 2019). Even though humanity's track record of cleaning up the wreckage is not promising, let us consider the possibility that there could be an important shift in the way nature is perceived in environmental ethics as a holder of *moral rights* that require responsible actors to repair the damage.

Ecological restoration[1] as a consistent effort to restore or recreate entire ecosystems, with all of their parts and processes intact, began in the first half of the 20th century. However, it took around half a century before the value and distinctiveness of this effort were discovered by ecologists (Jordan & Lubick 2011, 85). Since the 1970s, restoration has been more systematically developed by ecologists and has become an important part of the conservationist toolbox, by increasing our understanding of ecosystem functioning. Soon after, it became a subject of critique. What is known as the "restoration debate"—a lively exchange between environmental philosophers and ecologists—was initiated by philosopher Robert Elliot in 1982. Elliot expressed his reservations and skepticism about the idea that humans can restore nature to its original value. Elliot's arguments had two crucial points. The first focuses on a conceptual/ontological problem of restoration. Elliot understands "natural" as being "unmodified by human activity" (Elliot 1982, 84), thereby making any product of human action incompatible with naturalness. This implies that restorations of nature are "fake." The second point is more practical and attacks what Elliot calls the "restoration thesis." The restoration thesis involves the idea that natural values can be transformed into tradable units. On this account, the destruction of nature can be justified by its later restoration, assuming all of the values that lie in nature can be replicated.

Despite philosophical reservations about both the value of restoration and the idea of rights of nature (see Baard's and Donoso's chapters in this volume), I explore the question of whether it makes sense to think of nature as having a right to be restored and whether there are any significant benefits of adopting a rights-based approach to restoration. My focus is on *moral*, not legal, rights. However, I recognize that there is some interplay between the two. Throughout the chapter, I will be referring to "nature" or "ecosystem(s)," which I use as shorthand for "the nonhuman (parts) of the natural world."[2] These terms can refer to individual plants or animals, species, ecosystems, or parts of ecosystems. This bifurcation of human and non-human is simply employed as an analytical tool for better assessing the arguments, and it should not be taken as a stance on the overall human–nature relationship.

I will begin with an examination of rights of nature and the restoration debate and explore why rights have not played a role in this debate. I will then sketch the contours of an approach that I call *rights-based restoration*, which examines the compatibility of rights and restoration by testing its ethical implications. The aim is to explore what a right to restoration might look like; it does not, however, offer a comprehensive account of restoration or rights of nature, but merely a starting point for developing such an account. An important caveat is that I will be taking for granted the idea that nature can have rights. Therefore, questions about the intelligibility of rights of nature or the applicability of rights to nature are not addressed. However, I hope that my exploration will help us to better understand whether rights can contribute to our ethical theorizing about nature in general and the restoration debate in particular.

Rights and the Restoration Debate

One potential explanation as to why rights have not featured in the restoration debate has to do with the debate getting stuck on the issue of what counts as "nature" or "naturalness." Many environmental philosophers understand nature or naturalness as "unmodified by human activity" (Elliot 1982, 84) or as "independent of the actions of humanity" (Katz 1992, 103). These understandings of "nature" or "naturalness" place restoration in a difficult situation, as they imply that nature is not something that can be restored. This cuts the entire restoration debate short since the very notion of restoration becomes paradoxical. In this view, restoration appears to be a "category mistake," because in talking about restored nature we are not, in fact, talking about nature at all (Light 2000, 399). If restoration is impossible, then any debate about whether nature can have a right to be restored will be pointless. However, there are other approaches that have attempted to avoid this issue, either by taking a more pragmatic approach or by focusing on the beneficial aspects of restoration and limiting any dominating aspects (see among others Light 2000; Higgs

2003; Palamar 2006; Basl 2010; Hourdequin 2013; Almassi 2017). However, even for these alternative approaches, the issue of "naturalness" is looming in the background, since the way we understand naturalness often makes restoration appear to involve domination. For instance, restoration has been accused of domination because of the way it forces human interest and desires upon nature making the process inherently anthropocentric (Katz 1992).

What is the precise aim of restoration projects? One answer is provided by the Society for Ecological Restoration (SER): "Ecological restoration is the process of assisting the recovery of an ecosystem that has been degraded, damaged, or destroyed" (SER 2004, 3). Here naturalness is not mentioned at all, but rather the aim is to restore the "ecological integrity, health, and sustainability" of the system (ibid. 1). Of course, there are competing conceptions of restoration and its goals (for discussion, see Hourdequin 2013; Higgs 2003). However, I will adopt the SER's definition, which allows plenty of flexibility and room to accommodate different views.

The concept that most closely relates to naturalness within restoration terminology is "historical fidelity." Historical fidelity attempts to capture the extent to which a system is true to its previous pre-disturbance state. The importance of historical fidelity is to gain insight and provide a kind of "blueprint" as to what the ecological integrity of the site was prior to disturbance. Hence, the ultimate aim of restoration projects is to recover the integrity of the site as it was prior to disturbance. The question of whether a restored system is "natural," however, appears to be a separate question. Even if critics of restoration are correct that it is incapable of restoring the naturalness of a site, restoration could still be capable (at least to some degree) of restoring its ecological integrity. Of course, the term ecological integrity is a complex one, which I will explore in more detail below.

In fact, in restoration projects, the damage to the area's naturalness appears to be caused by the earlier human degradation, rather than the restoration itself. If we agree with Elliot's and Katz's arguments, most damaged ecosystems were already robbed of their naturalness by destructive human activity (e.g. resource extraction). As Light (2000) points out, restorations are not necessarily linked to destructive activities.[3] Furthermore, it is not at all clear that restoration involves an attempt to restore the naturalness of an area. According to ecologists Andre F. Clewell and James Aronson (2013, 3), the aim of restoration is to reconstitute "ecological processes, but we cannot intervene and create desired outcomes directly. Instead, we manipulate *biophysical* properties of an impaired ecosystem to facilitate resumption of processes that can only be performed by living organisms." The important distinction to make is that humans are not credited with restoring naturalness, but instead with *assisting* ecosystems to regain the structures and processes that are fundamental to maintaining their integrity and perhaps eventually, even their naturalness.[4] This leaves open the question of whether naturalness is a property that can be returned to a restored ecosystem. Elliot (1997) appears to answer this question with a contingent yes, and Katz (2018) with a vigorous no. Nevertheless, Elliot and Katz are probably correct that within the context of restoration, rights of nature cannot include a right to naturalness. Instead, rights of nature should be designed to protect the conditions that might support naturalness, rather than protect naturalness itself.

The Anatomy of Rights-Based Restoration

I will now outline the basic anatomy of rights-based restoration. There are six key elements of how a right might function in the context of restoration. First, what/who is the right-holder? Second, what type of structure would such a right have? Third, what type of right would it be? Fourth, under what circumstances would a right to restoration be invoked? Fifth, what type of duties does the right create? Sixth, who are the appropriate duty-bearers?

The Right-Holder

I want to briefly consider the different options of potential right-holders despite leaving it an open question what the appropriate right-holders are. Rights of nature could refer to individuals (such as individual animals or plants), systems (such as ecosystems or the biosphere), or species (either considered as individuals or collectives). There are two main types of rights that could be assigned to nature: individual rights and group rights. Individual rights refer to those that are held by individuals. Group rights refer to "a right held by a group as a group rather than by its members severally" (Jones 2016). A holistic account of nature (ecological wholes) seems to match best with the context of restoration. Here a specific ecological whole is considered a single entity which could be considered to have certain rights. It comes with the benefit that restoration tends to sit easier with holistic environmental ethics as they both operate at the same level of ecological wholes. Such a holistic account could be defended by appealing to either individual rights, where nature would be treated as an individual with certain rights, or group rights, where nature would denote a group that embodies different entities.[5] Group identity and integrity have been considered essential features of a group that is able to bear rights (Jones 2016). However, it is debatable whether ecosystems are able to form strong single unitary entities that have strong group identity, let alone subjectivity. Therefore, I will form my account based on an individual rights account. Importantly, my account should not be interpreted as an argument against other rights accounts, even though my account will likely conflict with some other accounts such as animal rights.

Structure of the Right

The two main theories of rights—the will theory and the interest theory—leave little or no room for developing rights of nature. The will theory of rights holds that a right gives the right-holder power over another's duty. It holds that the right-holder is capable of determining and demanding their own rights, thus displaying sovereignty. This creates a demanding threshold for being a right-holder. If an individual or being is unable to exercise this sovereignty, then they are incapable of being a right-holder (Wenar 2020). For example, infants, individuals with a serious intellectual disability, animals, and nature all fail this test for being a right-holder. The interest theory, on the other hand, holds that rights protect the *interests* or *wellbeing* of the right-holder. On this account, a right-holder must be capable of having interests/wellbeing. As a result, the interest theory is more inclusive than the will theory, since it allows for right-holders who are held to be incompetent by the will theory, as long as they have interests/wellbeing that can be protected (Wenar 2020). However, even though interest theory has less demanding requirements to be a right-holder, it too will tend to leave out nature. For example, Joel Feinberg (1974) has argued that individual animals might have rights, but plants, species, and nature cannot.[6]

However, the interest theory potentially leaves room for more parts of nature to be a right-holder. For instance, according to Joseph Raz's (1984, 195) influential account, "'x has a right' if and only if x can have rights, and other things being equal, an aspect of x's well-being (his interest) is a sufficient reason for holding some other person(s) to be under a duty." The possibility of nature having rights will depend on the "the principle of capacity to have rights," according to which, "[a]n individual is capable of having rights if and only if either his well-being is of ultimate value or he is an 'artificial person' (e.g. a corporation)" (ibid.). If it can be shown that nature has interests, or on Raz's account, wellbeing that is of intrinsic value, then nature could qualify as a potential right-holder. I will develop rights-based restoration by using Raz's interest theory of rights, not only because this theory has been influential, but also because it does not immediately exclude non-human nature. In addition, it has the advantage of being compatible with a range of different ethical theories.

Before we explore the question of whether nature can have wellbeing/interests, I want to briefly examine the logical structure of the right to restoration. It would likely not be a fundamental or stand-alone right, but instead will be contingent on other right(s). Raz's distinction between *core rights* and *derivative rights* is helpful here. According to Raz (1984, 197), core rights are founded on the interests that provide the fundamental justification for their existence. Derivative rights are grounded on a core right in that their justification comes from both the "conclusion of a sound argument [...] entailing the existence of the core right" and "justification for the existence of the derivative right" (ibid.). As such, Raz clarifies, "[t]he relation of core and derivative rights is not that of entailment, but of the order of justification" (ibid. 198). For our purposes, the right to restoration appears to be a derivative right that relies on a core right(s) for its normative force. In addition, the core right will provide vital information about the content of the derivative right. In other words, in order to better understand the right to be restored, we must first understand the core right from which it derives its essential justification.

Within the environmental ethics literature, there are several contenders that could play the role of a core right, such as the right to life, existence, ecological integrity, health, autonomy, or naturalness/wildness. In this chapter, I will focus on the core right that I believe has the most promise and most consistently pairs up with restoration: the right to ecological integrity.

Ecological Integrity

Ecological integrity is not only recognized by the restoration community as a key concept for defining the practice of restoration (e.g. SER Primer 2004; Higgs 2003) but also widely recognized as an important value in environmental ethics and environmental conservation more broadly (Leopold 1949/1966; Karr 1992; Angermeier & Karr 1994, Karr 1996; Noss et al. 2000; Kandziora et al. 2013). Ecological integrity even featured directly in the 1992 SER definition of restoration (Higgs 2003, 109). However, due to the complexity and elusiveness of the concept, "which in itself required definition," it was dropped from the current definition that guides restoration projects today (ibid., 122). Nevertheless, it still remains integral to the meaning of restoration, serving as the goal or "desired" state of ecosystems according to the SER Primer (SER 2004, 1, 7). However, a more careful analysis of the term is needed in order to determine whether it can serve as a core right.

"Integrity" is an umbrella term capturing a wide range of characteristics (Westra et al. 2000; Higgs 2003). According to ecologist James R. Karr, ecological integrity is the "sum of chemical, physical, and biological integrity" (Karr 1992, 231). Importantly, it incorporates both the structural elements and the ecological processes of an ecosystem (Karr & Angermeier 1994). Therefore, not only can integrity be used to identify an unimpaired condition of an ecosystem, it also includes the central idea of "wholeness" (Higgs 2003, 122). Wholeness importantly links with a historical and natural benchmark condition for an ecosystem. In fact, the idea of wholeness is one of the key features that sets restoration apart from other environmental management practices (Jordan & Lubick 2011). It is widely held that the aim of restoration is to restore the *entire* ecosystem, not simply a part or few parts of the ecosystem. "Integrity" therefore helps to emphasize this important and defining feature of restoration.

There is another comprehensive normative concept, ecosystem health, which SER identifies as a goal of restoration (SER 2004, 1). Health denotes a state of flourishing and wellbeing of a system (Karr 1996, 101). An ecosystem that is healthy is one that functions normally (SER 2004, 7). As I see it, however, ecological integrity is a more suitable concept for our purposes, because it includes the important link to wholeness and a more nuanced understanding of the contextual aspects of a site. Even though health is an important characteristic, it is perfectly consistent with the recreation of completely novel ecosystem or focusing on only parts of an ecosystem (e.g. soil health). In addition, it seems unclear what "normal" functioning is supposed to be for an ecosystem. Furthermore, "health" seems to be vulnerable to subjectivity allowing cultural context and values to determine what counts as healthy (Angermeier & Karr 2019, 391), whereas integrity appears to be a more objective metric assessing the state of ecosystems. A more practical benefit of ecological integrity is the fact that there already exists well-developed scientific metrics for the measurement of ecological and biological integrity. For instance, the Index of Biological Integrity (IBI), developed by Karr (1991), has a strong basis in evidence and environmental policy. It provides a multi-metric measurement of biological condition, which is used to measure the scale of biological degradation in comparison to a baseline condition. The IBI has been applied in different contexts (e.g. different ecosystems, resource management, and public policy) in at least 86 different countries (Angermeier & Karr 2019, 398). Therefore, ecological integrity seems the most promising core right upon which to base a derivative right to restoration.

Many influential definitions of ecological integrity, such as those developed by Karr (1992, 1996) and Laura Westra, Peter Miller, James R. Karr, William E. Rees, and Robert E. Ulanowicz (2000), tend to equate ecological integrity with wild nature. Karr (1996, 101), for instance, advocates this idea because the "evolutionary foundation" allows integrity to serve as "a benchmark against which society can evaluate sites altered by human actions." Angermeier and Karr (1994, 693) point out that "unnatural states," meaning human altered states, "cannot provide an objective basis for assessing biological integrity." Westra et al. (2000, 25), on the other hand, defend the use of wild nature as a benchmark "so that citizens, politicians, and policymakers know the level of degradation at sites subjected to the influence of human actions." They claim that employing this challenging benchmark allows us "to measure the full extent of our impacts on nature in exploited areas, as well as our success in protecting nature's legacy in wild areas" (ibid.). However, using wild nature as a baseline also brings some disadvantages. Ultimately it makes human societies incompatible with ecological integrity. This creates a problematic divide between human and natural systems, and prevents opportunities for bringing these systems together in a more harmonious coexistence.

There are, however, ecological integrity metrics that do not require the use of wild nature as a benchmark (e.g. Regier 1993; Kandziora et al. 2013). Westra et al. (2000, 26) contend that these alternative metrics can be useful for evaluating parts of the world that have been so extensively modified by humans that the wild benchmark is no longer applicable. Nevertheless, I find the dichotomy it creates between humans and nature problematic, because it undermines any development towards more meaningful ways for nature and humans to coexist in a shared environment. I believe it is important to have a benchmark that allows for the integration of human activities with ecological realities, thus providing guidance for appropriate human action. Perhaps our focus should not be on *whether* human actions impact nature, but instead, on *how* human actions impact nature. This question of the "how" could potentially provide powerful normative support for prohibiting certain human interventions, while leaving open the possibility that humanity could harmoniously coexist with nature.

The wild nature benchmark has also received criticism from indigenous communities. For instance, Dennis Martinez, a Tohono O'odham and Chicano, also of Swedish heritage, who is the founder of the SER's Indigenous Peoples' Restoration Network, has emphasized that even though each indigenous tribe is unique and will differ in their practices and habits, "it is safe to say that for indigenous peoples, globally, *culture overlaps with wild nature*" (Martinez 2003, 248).[7] Martinez points out that the range of ideas about nature held by many indigenous communities, such as "the distinctly wild, the feral, and the 'cultivated,'" when taken together, could encompass ecological integrity (ibid.). Martinez worries, as expressed in a research interview, that ecological integrity "downplay[s] the role of the people who in many cases both shaped and maintained the ecosystems being restored" (Jordan & Lubick 2011, 143). In fact, Martinez emphasizes, many fire-adapted ecosystems that were "created and maintained by a history of anthropogenic burns, are often more stable than so-called climax ecosystems" (ibid.). It seems to me that some problematic segregating aspects of the concept of "nature" have been needlessly carried over to "ecological integrity."

Even though Karr and others are reluctant to include humans as part of ecological integrity, they also seem to acknowledge and allow that restorations can serve as a tool to repair past degradation, which seems contradictory. If they believe that active human restoration can help bring back the area's ecological integrity, then surely human actions are not *per se* contradictory to ecological integrity. And if restorations are permissible, then surely there are other ways humans could live within ecosystems without being detrimental to their integrity. In fact, excluding humans from ecological integrity prevents us from accurately seeing how all living organisms are interlinked and interdependent on each other. Ecological integrity should therefore not exclude humans by definition, but rather, in terms of impact. If human action can be found to negatively impact several integrity metrics, then that action should be deemed inappropriate. Of course, many conservation ecologists are correct in their judgments that the majority of human impacts, especially among western societies, have predominately negative consequences for ecosystems. Nevertheless, humans can still strive towards, and even achieve, more harmonious coexistence with the rest of the natural world.

When Would the Right Be Invoked?

As previously explained, in order to invoke the right to be restored, a violation of the core right must have occurred. Consequently, we need to determine what *type* of violation is sufficient to invoke the right to restoration. I will be focusing on the *nature* and *source* of the disturbance, and how these relate to the right to be restored. To this end, I have identified four categories of disturbance to the core right of ecological integrity, along with the correlative duties:

1) In the case of *natural* stress and moderate disturbance there is *no duty* to restore (unless there is a case for restoration not based on rights of nature) or there is a *duty not* to restore
2) In the case of *natural* impairment there is *no duty* to restore (unless there is a case for restoration not based on rights of nature)
3) In the case of *direct human* impairment there is *perfect duty* to restore
4) In the case of *collective human* impairment there is *perfect duty* to restore

This classification is based on Clewell and Aronson's (2013, 35–36) tripartite categorization of ecosystem disturbances[8] consisting of stress, moderate disturbance, and impairment. Let us begin with the first category of natural disturbance, which causes stress or moderate disturbance to an ecosystem. Stress is a natural and often regular feature of ecosystems. Even though stress events temporarily disrupt and impede ecosystem processes, the ecosystem can easily recover from these disturbances. Moreover, stress often helps maintain the ecosystem's integrity (ibid.). For instance, pyrogenic ecosystems are an example where fire, as a stressor, maintains the ecosystem dynamics. Moderate disturbance, on the other hand, is a more severe form of disturbance, but not so severe that it renders the ecosystem unable to recover from its effects. Over time the ecosystem will be able to recover without assistance. Therefore, moderate disturbance tests the resilience of the ecosystem (ibid. 35–37). In other words, if an ecosystem has ecological integrity, it is resilient enough to deal with both stress and moderate disturbance. Since the source of the disturbance in these cases is natural (due to non-human causes), no one is directly morally responsible. There is no actual harm to ecological integrity in this category of disturbance, and therefore, there is no violation of the core right. Since the core right has not been violated, the right to restoration is not invoked and there is no duty of restoration.

However, the core right to ecological integrity may present a different obligation with regard to restoration, namely, a "duty not to restore." In some circumstances, it is possible for the right to ecological integrity to actually demand that humans do *not* act to restore an ecosystem. This duty not to restore arises when stress and moderate disturbances make a significant contribution to ecological integrity, so that a prohibition on restoration serves to protect the integrity of the ecosystem. Furthermore, it is important to recognize that rights are only part of a broader normative assessment which should be conducted on a case by case basis. Such contextual factors involve for instance possible rights conflicts.

The second category of natural disturbance is natural impairment, or severe damage to an ecosystem from which it cannot recover without assistance. An impaired ecosystem has its ecological integrity overwhelmed and its processes significantly, if not permanently, altered. In these cases, restoration can assist an impaired system to "reinitiate or accelerate ecological processes that induce recovery" (Clewell & Aronson 2013, 37). Here the integrity of the ecosystem has been violated, and therefore the right to restoration may be invoked, even though no moral agent is directly responsible for the harm. Consequently there may be no duty to restore, at least based on the right of nature. This dilemma may be resolved by examining the contextual circumstances and/or other important rights/values. Even though the right to restoration may not demand restoration in these types of cases, other rights, values, or "prudential" factors might demand such action. For instance, if rights of nature also include a right to naturalness/wildness (or even if this value is highly regarded in an ethical system), and the area that was damaged was in a highly "natural" state, then these other factors might direct us not to intervene and to instead allow natural processes to take their course free from human intervention. This may hold true even if it means the landscape is likely to switch to a new ecological trajectory.

There may still be circumstances that urge us to restore, even when the right to restoration has not been invoked. I will call these types of cases "restoration not based on rights of nature." This type of restoration falls outside the remit of the right to be restored. Instead, it corresponds to other duties, interests, or needs that humans may have towards other humans, other species, or other types of nonhuman entities. Examples of such restoration can involve restoration after a natural disaster. For instance, perhaps a tropical storm has destroyed the habitat of a critically endangered species, and restoration of the damaged habitat will protect or promote the right/value of the species. Or perhaps the storm destroyed a forest that was considered important by the local human community, and restoration serves as not only an important performative act, but the community also lacks the luxury of waiting several decades before the area will show signs of recovery. Even though restoration might be the right course of action in all these cases, the important difference is that it would not be due to the rights of nature, but due to other justificatory reasons. As long as no rights or values demand otherwise, restoration not based on rights of nature may direct us to restore an area that has been damaged through natural impairment.

Let us then consider the two cases of human-caused disturbance. The third category involves human action that has directly led to the destruction of an ecosystem. The individual(s) who have caused the disturbance are directly responsible for the harm and now have a duty, based on the core right, to restore the damaged ecosystem. A fully developed environmental ethic and/or system of rights will provide further guidance on how this duty is to be fulfilled. The fourth category involves cases where collective human action has caused harm to an ecosystem. Collective human actions that cause environmental harm—e.g. in the form of climate change, environmental pollution, resource extraction—will obligate those who have benefitted from these practices to restore the damaged ecosystems. For instance, the luxuries enjoyed by countries with high-income economies can involve collective action that has led to natural impairment, and everyone who has benefitted from this lifestyle should be held accountable for their share of the harm.[9]

Duties

Duties are often divided into negative and positive duties (Feinberg 2014). Negative duties demand that one *not* perform certain actions, while positive duties demand that one *performs* certain actions. The right to be restored, therefore, appears to mainly refer to a positive duty to restore. Unless the 'duty not to restore' is invoked, which would be an instance of a negative duty. However, these duties are invoked only *if* the right-holder's right(s) has been violated. In this sense the duty to restore is a reparatory duty that follows a transgression of a core right. The type of duty involved depends on the core right and the type of moral theory supporting the right. For instance, if the core right is ecological integrity, then the right to be restored would need to focus on restoring the ecosystem elements and processes that maintain ecological integrity. The damaged area would be considered restored once it has regained a suitable level of ecological integrity, similar or equivalent to that which existed prior to the disturbance. The demandingness of the restoration will depend on the moral theory justifying the rights-based approach.

What if the duty involved is unattainable? Consider the duty to restore ecological integrity in a world dominated by climate change. It is possible that climate change will render restoring ecological integrity impossible, if the ecosystem being restored is no longer viable under the new climatic conditions. However, my use of "integrity" is flexible. If the pre-disturbance condition—whatever this might be—happens to be unattainable due to new climatic conditions, ecological integrity would demand the area to be restored as closely and faithfully as possible to the pre-disturbance state. The new climatic conditions may require the use of ecological knowledge to understand how the previous ecosystem would have transformed and evolved under the new conditions had the disturbance not taken place. Alternatively, we might need to assist the damaged system to switch to a new ecological trajectory under the new climatic realities. In any event, integrity will require that we keep the trajectory of the past ecosystem as intact as possible.

As alluded to in the previous question, the right to restoration can impose individual or collective duties depending on the cause of the harm. In the case of collective duties, a sophisticated account will be needed. Furthermore, modern scientific methods might offer new ways of uncovering culpability, which might facilitate our ability to assign duties to each perpetrator. In addition, we may need to consider historic harms and injustices, in which case restitutive justice could potentially offer some guidance on what type of duties are created (e.g. Almassi 2017).

Duty-Bearers

When it comes to determining duty-bearers, the distinction between moral agents and moral patients will be useful (Regan 1983). Moral agents are rational subjects who are able to make ethical evaluations and act in accordance with them, whereas moral patients can only be the objects of moral concern for moral agents. Moral agency comes with a host of potential responsibilities determined by the framework of morality. In the case of restoration, only humans can be considered (at least according to our current knowledge) moral agents, but this is merely a necessary and not a sufficient condition for being a duty-bearer. Duty-bearing also requires that the person(s) in question is responsible for the harm in one way or another. This backward-looking view on responsibility tends to be an important feature of transgression of rights.

One of the particularly challenging problems here is how to identify the appropriate wrong-doers and/or duty-bearers. The world beyond ethics literature is much more complicated, and often there is no clear single wrongdoer, like the CEO of a mining company. Rather, the culpability for environmental harms often falls on the shoulders of groups of people, communities, entire nations, or even humanity as a whole. In addition, in the case of restoration there is usually a difficult asymmetry between the harm and the restoration work, due to the highly specialized ecological knowledge and expertise required to achieve successful restoration. As such, restorationists are usually the ones that restore environmental harms created by others. Therefore, due to the ethical distance and multifaceted nature of human actions and their effects in modern societies it can be extremely challenging to make sense of patterns of culpability. One option would be to focus instead on a forward-looking account of moral responsibility, especially when it comes to the category of collective impairment. In these cases, we could drop the backward-looking attribution of blame, recognizing that many environmental harms stem from structural injustices and that efforts should collectively be directed at "transform[ing] the structural processes to make their outcomes just" (Young 2011, 96). The focus shifts from rectifying past wrongs to a forward-looking duty to create a better world.[10] In summary, there can potentially be two different ways to assign duties: 1) directly to anyone who has caused damage to ecological integrity (backward-looking responsibility) and 2) indirectly to collectives to fix structural injustices that cause damage to ecological integrity (forward-looking responsibility). Young (2011) argues that backward-looking responsibility only works well with transgressions of moral responsibility where the perpetrator(s) are easily identifiable, whereas the forward-looking account of responsibility works better with structural and historic injustices. The problem with historic injustices is that they are faced with difficult "ontological and conceptual problems" when the traditional backward-looking account of responsibility is applied (Young 2011, 174). With historic injustices, not only are most if not all of the perpetrators and victims dead, it would seem strange to blame their actions on currently living people who had nothing to do with the transgressions. As such, I suggest that the backward-looking responsibility should apply to practices where the perpetrator and the victim are easily identifiable, and the forward-looking responsibility would apply to historic and structural rights violations.

Ethical Implications of Rights-Based Restoration

Now that we have the contours of rights-based restoration spelled out, I want to briefly consider some of the most important ethical implications it may have.

First, a rights framework in general, and a rights-based restoration in particular, can help to equalize the moral landscape. Much of environmental ethics has focused on discussions about the *moral considerability* or *moral standing* of nonhuman entities.[11] However, the claim that nature has rights appears to be much stronger than the claims these discussions have involved. Indeed, there appears to be general agreement about the "special normative force" of rights language (Wenar 2020). Therefore, being a right-holder seems to involve the strongest moral recognition and protection that something can have.[12] Accordingly, if we recognize rights of nature, this significantly elevates the status of nature within our moral system.

Robert Garner (2013) has defended the benefits of a rights-based approach in the area of animal ethics. According to Garner, rights provide particularly powerful protection to the right-holder (ibid., 94). The problem with "mere moral considerability" is that it does not easily extend beyond the sphere of individual moral responsibility, whereas rights translate much more effectively to the collective sphere and the realm of state enforcement. Put simply, if Garner is right, then moral considerability cannot compete with the normative force of rights. Even though Garner's analysis is aimed specifically at individual animals, I believe his conceptual apparatus is applicable to collective entities more broadly and can provide them with sufficient protection. In a hierarchical moral system, where rights rank highly, any entity without rights will inevitably end up worse off compared to entities that have rights.

There is another way to elevate the protection of nature to the level of rights without actually granting any direct rights. Andrew Brei (2013, 395) argues for *indirect* rights of nature via the human right to health. Because human health depends in many ways on a healthy environment (via ecosystem services, medicinal products, and mental wellbeing), human health could serve as an effective justification for rights of nature. Another option is to provide a linkage argument between human rights and rights of nature (see Corrigan in this volume). Such accounts can be quite valuable for recognizing the interdependencies between humans and nature and can create, in a very intuitive way, *direct* duties to nature (via human rights). However, accounts that are dependent on human rights will still be *indirectly* attributed to nature (via humans), and thus will be inherently dependent on the convergence of nature's interests and human interests. Even though these may be direct duties *regarding* nature, they are not direct duties *to* nature. While such approaches can offer strong grounds for environmental protection, they miss the mark that many environmental philosophers argue for—that nonhuman animals, plants, and/or nature should create direct obligations for humans because they are intrinsically valuable in themselves, just like humans.

Would rights of nature denigrate the value of human rights? Of course adding a whole new group of right-holders will create several challenges to the rights framework, such as the proliferation of rights conflicts (Andersson 2013). If there is a significant increase in right-holders, this is likely to be followed by a similar increase in rights conflicts. This could potentially make the rights framework overly cumbersome, affecting its ability to guide actions and potentially having a negative impact on the moral status of rights. Here I attempt to relieve some of these worries while acknowledging that a much more thorough examination is needed in order to resolve them. It must be emphasized that rights of nature do not involve attributing *human* rights to nature. As I have tried to argue in this chapter, rights of nature (e.g. the right to ecological integrity) would be very different from the rights of humans. Even though conflicts between human rights and rights of nature will certainly occur, these conflicts are probably not as deep as one might think. Initially, human rights appear to conflict with rights of nature mainly because the human rights framework has been designed with complete ignorance of the rights or intrinsic value of nature (apart from nature serving as an important resource to satisfy human needs). The rights of nature framework, and specifically the right to restoration, is attempting to rectify this major moral blind spot in human ethical systems. The problem is that many important and fundamental concerns of human life, such as wellbeing and justice, are crucially interlinked with the state of ecosystems and "are too often abstracted from the deteriorating state of the planet" (Miller & Rees 2000, 6). Rights of nature could play a significant role in bringing these fundamental features out of abstraction, thus resolving some (but not all) of the conflicts between these different rights.

Second, the implementation of the right to restoration must be carefully conducted. First, it must be determined *what* to restore. We must carefully determine how much of nature should be restored, whether any historic damages ought to be rectified, and how these judgments can be made and measured in a just manner. Any decisions concerning how and what to restore must also be based on careful scientific analysis (e.g. Wilson 2016), to ensure that neither the rights of humans nor the rights of nature are compromised. For instance, removing indigenous peoples from their homelands is not only a violation of human rights but may also be contrary to the rights of nature. Indigenous peoples have a right to live on and make use of their lands, and if they live within the boundaries of ecological integrity, and perhaps even contribute to that integrity, then rights of nature would also support and protect their right to remain in the ecosystem. It is crucial that any decisions regarding restoration take into account and are balanced against conflicting human rights.

Furthermore, critics of restoration may worry that Elliot's restoration thesis will become a reality. Does the right to restoration imply that humans now have an obligation or license to restore most or even all of nature? The core right of ecological integrity creates a duty to restore only those ecosystems that have their ecological integrity damaged by human impacts. However, note that any historic degradation will be guided by a forward-looking account of responsibility that demands to fix structural injustices that lead to the destruction of nature. Consequently, any pristine or still wild places are safe from human exploitation and restoration. In other words, ecological integrity will in many cases provide double protection for wild nature, as it would allow restoration only in areas already damaged by humans while prohibiting any actions that damage the integrity of ecosystems. Since ecological integrity itself comes with a sense of historical fidelity, it requires humans to carefully evaluate whether and how to interact with the wilder spaces on Earth. If an area is relatively wild, ecological integrity would require humans to protect this area unless there is a significant justification for doing otherwise. As such, ecological integrity provides a strong level of protection for the wildest places on Earth. Nonetheless, the right to ecological integrity does not replace the need for additional ethical frameworks that protect wild nature.

We must also be extremely mindful of *how* the restorations are conducted. Ecological integrity demands that we restore *native* species as much as possible. This is because these species are not only an important part of the evolutionary history of the place but have also managed to establish and have proven themselves as stable parts of the biotic community (Karr 1996, 101). These species would likely still be there, had the human-caused disturbance not taken place. However, even though ecological integrity favors native species due to their evolutionary history, it should not be used as an excuse to freeze ecosystems in time. Change, even within species composition, is part of nature and ecological integrity, and thus only species or processes that threaten the integrity of an ecosystem should be addressed.[13]

Any large-scale restoration projects that may be required by the right to restoration, akin to, for example, the Decade of Ecosystem Restoration mentioned at the beginning of the chapter, must be conducted carefully and with caution. For instance, the Decade of Ecosystem Restoration has specifically received criticism for its ambitious restoration goals and the lack of evidence, research, and funding to ensure restoration success (Cooke et al 2019; Jones et al. 2018). According to a meta-analysis of 400 restoration studies across the world, it was found that even though restorations are able to assist ecosystems toward recovery, achieving full recovery is rare. In addition, active restoration (in contrast to passive restoration) rarely achieves the planned results (Jones et al. 2018). Here we can draw two lessons. The first emphasizes the importance of protecting any intact and functioning ecosystems that embody ecological integrity. The second focuses on the *way* restoration is conducted. Rights-based restoration should favor more passive restoration practices where possible and therefore always aim for the least invasive practices.

Conclusion

Western environmental ethics will soon celebrate its 50th anniversary since the first academic theories and papers began to emerge in the 1970s. But is there cause for celebration in a world where the "brief flowering of humanity" has left nature degraded, damaged, and destroyed (Miller & Rees 2000, 6)? This devastating legacy reflects the current state of the human–nature relationship, which in many ways is equally degraded and damaged, but not yet destroyed. A beacon of hope is the key message of environmental ethics: that non-human nature has moral importance. If Angermeier and Karr (1994) are correct that our ethical foundations serve as a root cause for environmental destruction, then environmental ethics has an important role to play in the current ecological crisis. Unfortunately, it seems that many theories of environmental ethics have not managed to penetrate the moral imagination of human societies. Perhaps rights of nature can deliver such transformation, as it would bring with it not only important tools to help rebuild the human–nature relationship, but also to readjust our moral architecture.

In this chapter, I have pointed to a dramatic expansion of moral consideration to the rest of nature, one that is based on rights of nature, and specifically a right to restoration. I have shown that not only is the restoration debate a meaningful discussion in environmental ethics, but one that can be extended to discussions about the rights of nature. I sketched a view of *rights-based restoration*, which shows what a right to restoration might look like. Rights-based restoration centers on the core right to ecological integrity. When this core right is violated, it creates a duty of restoration. When we assess the environmental damage caused by humanity, it is important that we acknowledge the full spectrum of temporality. The core right of ecological integrity has the power to honor the ecological memory of nature, to recognize the importance of our actions in the present, and to give us a glimpse of a more harmonious human–nature relationship in the future. Whatever difficulties rights-based restoration imposes on humanity, these issues will be dwarfed by the environmental tragedies facing humanity if the value and rights of nature are not taken seriously.

Acknowledgments

I wish to thank the editors Markku Oksanen and Daniel Corrigan for their helpful comments on this chapter. Teea Kortetmäki and Anna Wienhues also provided generous feedback on earlier drafts. The work in this chapter has been supported by the Kone Foundation.

Notes

1 Hereafter referred to as restoration.
2 Of course, defining nature is not a simple task and there are various different conceptualizations to choose from (see Soper 1995). However, for my purposes this conceptualization will suffice.
3 This problematic link only exists in Elliot's restoration thesis (where the destruction is justified by later restoration), which Light calls "malicious restoration."
4 This argument only works when the destruction of an ecosystem was caused by humans. In cases where nature has been damaged by natural processes, restoration activities can potentially be detrimental to the naturalness of an area.
5 There is also another type of group right, collective group right, according to which the right would be "shared or jointly held right of a set of individuals" (Jones 2016). This option might be open to individualistic accounts such as biocentrism or sentientism.
6 Animal rights theorists, for instance have been quite successful at expanding the group of right-holders to animals by using the interest theory of rights (e.g. Regan 1983).

7 Italics in original.
8 Disturbance here is used as a technical term used by ecologists and refers to "serious disruptions of ecological functioning and modification of biotic expression, especially at population and community levels" (Clewell & Aronson 2013, 35). The tripartite categorization of disturbances used here does not include normal disturbance regimes.
9 Of course, attributing responsibility for rights violations is a large topic that needs elaboration in itself and involves a range of different aspects in order to connect the harm with the benefit.
10 Here the forward-looking approach refers only to responsibility and blame, not to restoration itself. Also note that it is possible to have a forward-looking account of responsibility which does not require a rights account at all.
11 See Goodpaster (1978) for a classic work on the question of the moral considerability of natural entities.
12 Of course, the type of rights theory will determine how demanding the particular theory actually is. In addition, conflicts between rights and other moral norms will affect the overall outcome of what one has a right to and what duties are produced.
13 This means that non-native species should only be removed if they are harmful to ecological integrity of the ecosystem (see Palamar 2006).

References

Almassi, B. (2017) "Ecological Restorations as Practices of Moral Repair" *Ethics and the Environment, 22*(1), 19–40.

Andersson, A. (2013) "Choices, Interests, and Potentiality: What Distinguishes Bearers of Rights?" *The Journal of Value Inquiry, 47*(3), 175–190.

Angermeier, P. L. and Karr, J. (1994) "Biological Integrity versus Biological Diversity as Policy Directives: Protecting Biotic Resources" *BioScience, 44*(10), 690–697.

Angermeier, P. L. and Karr, J. (2019) "Ecological Health Indicators" in Fath, B. D. ed., *Encyclopedia of Ecology* (2nd ed.), Elsevier, Oxford, Volume 1, 391–401.

Basl, J. (2010) "Restitutive Restoration: New Motivations for Ecological Restoration" *Environmental Ethics, 32*(2), 135–148.

Brei, A. T. (2013) "Rights and Nature: Approaching Environmental Issues by Way of Human Rights" *Journal of Agricultural and Environmental Ethics, 26*(2), 393–408.

Clewell, A. F. and Aronson, J. (2013) *Ecological Restoration: Principles, Values, and Structure of an Emerging Profession* (2nd ed.). Island Press, Washington, DC.

Cooke, S., Bennett, J., and Jones, H. (2019) "We Have a Long Way to Go if We Want to Realize the Promise of the 'Decade on Ecosystem Restoration'" *Conservation Science and Practice, 1*(e129).

Elliot, R. (1982) "Faking Nature" *Inquiry, 25*(1), 81–93.

Elliot, R. (1997) *Faking Nature: The Ethics of Environmental Restoration*. Routledge, London.

Feinberg, J. (1974) "The Rights of Animals and Unborn Generations" in Blackstone, W. T. ed., *Philosophy and Environmental Crisis*. University of Georgia Press, Athens, GA, 43–68.

Feinberg, J. (2014) *Rights, Justice, and the Bounds of Liberty: Essays in Social Philosophy*. Princeton University Press, Princeton, NJ.

Garner, R. (2013) *A Theory of Justice for Animals: Animal Rights in a Nonideal World*. Oxford University Press, New York.

Goodpaster, K. E. (1978) "On Being Morally Considerable" *The Journal of Philosophy, 75*(6), 308–325.

Higgs, E. (2003) *Nature by Design: People, Natural Process, and Ecological Restoration*. MIT Press, Cambridge, MA.

Hourdequin, M. (2013) "Restoration and History in a Changing World: A Case Study in Ethics for the Anthropocene" *Ethics and the Environment, 18*(2), 115–134.

Jones, H., Jones, P., Barbier, E., Blackburn, R., Rey Benayas, J., Holl, K., McCrackin, M., Meli, P., Montoya, D., and Mateos, D. (2018) "Restoration and Repair of Earth's Damaged Ecosystems" *Proceedings of the Royal Society of London. series B, Biological Sciences, 285*(1873), 20172577–20172578.

Jones, P. (2016) "Group Rights" in Zalta, E. N. ed., *Stanford Encyclopedia of Philosophy* (Summer 2016 ed.).

Jordan, W. R. and Lubick, G. M. (2011) *Making Nature Whole: A History of Ecological Restoration*. Island Press, Washington, DC.

Kandziora, M., Burkhard, B., and Müller, F. (2013) "Interactions of Ecosystem Properties, Ecosystem Integrity and Ecosystem Service Indicators—A Theoretical Matrix Exercise" *Ecological Indicators, 28*, 54–78.

Karr, J. R. (1991) "Biological Integrity: A Long-Neglected Aspect of Water Resource Management" *Ecological Applications, 1*(1), 66–84.

Karr, J. R. (1992) "Ecological Integrity: Protecting Earth's Life Support Systems" in Costanza, R., Norton, B. G., and Haskell, B. D. eds., *Ecosystem Health: New Goals for Environmental Management*. Island Press, Washington, DC, 223–238.

Karr, J. R. (1996) "Ecological Integrity and Ecological Health Are Not the Same" in Schulze, P. C. ed., *Engineering within Ecological Constraints*. National Academies Press, Washington, DC, 97–110.

Katz, E. (1992 [1997]) "The Big Lie: Human Restoration of Nature" in Katz, E. ed., *Nature as Subject: Human Obligation and Natural Community*. Rowman & Littlefield Publishing Group Inc., Oxford, 93–107.

Katz, E. (2018) "Replacement and Irreversibility: The Problem with Ecological Restoration as Moral Repair" *Ethics and the Environment, 23*(1), 17–28.

Leopold, Aldo (1949 [1968]) *A Sand County Almanac: and Sketches Here and There*. Oxford University Press, New York.

Light, A. (2000) "Ecological Restoration and the Culture of Nature: A Pragmatic Perspective" in Light A. and Rolston III H. eds., *Environmental Ethics: An Anthology*. Blackwell Publishing Ltd, Oxford, 398–411.

Martinez, D. (2003) "Protected Areas, Indigenous Peoples, and The Western Idea of Nature" *Ecological Restoration, 21*(4), 247–250.

Miller, P. and Rees, W. E. (2000) "Introduction" in Noss, R. F., Pimentel, D., and Westra, L. eds., *Ecological Integrity: Integrating Environment, Conservation, and Health*. Island Press, Washington, DC, 3–18.

Noss, R. F., Pimentel, D., and Westra, L. (2000) *Ecological Integrity: Integrating Environment, Conservation, and Health*. Island Press, Washington, DC.

Palamar, Colette R. (2006) "Restorashyn: Ecofeminist Restoration" *Environmental Ethics, 28*(3), 285–301.

Raz, J. (1984) "On the Nature of Rights" *Mind, 93*(370), 194–214.

Regan, T. (1983) *The Case for Animal Rights*. University of California Press, Berkeley, CA.

Regier, H. A. (1993) "The Notion of Natural and Cultural Integrity" in Woodley, S., Kay, J., and Francis G. eds., *Ecological Integrity and the Management of Ecosystems*. St. Lucie Press, Delray Beach, Florida, 3-18.

Society for Ecological Restoration International (SER), Science and Policy Working Group (2004) *The SER International Primer on Ecological Restoration.* Society for Ecological Restoration International, Tucson, AZ.

Soper, K. (1995) *What is Nature?* Blackwell, Oxford.

Tortell, P. (2020) "Earth 2020: Science, Society, and Sustainability in the Anthropocene" *Proceedings of the National Academy of Sciences—PNAS, 117*(16), 8683–8691.

United Nations, Environment. (2019) "New UN Decade on Ecosystem Restoration Offers Unparalleled Opportunity for Job Creation, Food Security and Addressing Climate Change" (Press release), U.N. website, retrieved 13.02.2020.

Wenar, L. (2020) "Rights" in Zalta, E. N. ed., *Stanford Encyclopedia of Philosophy* (Fall 2020 ed.).

Westra, L., Miller P., Karr, J. R., Rees, W. E., and Ulanowicz R. E. (2000) "Ecological Integrity and the Aims of the Global Integrity Project" in Noss, R. F., Pimentel, D., and Westra, L. eds., *Ecological Integrity: Integrating Environment, Conservation, and Health.* Island Press, Washington, DC, 19–41.

Wilson, E. O. (2016) *Half-Earth: Our Planet's Fight for Life* (1st ed.). Liveright Publishing Corporation, New York.

Young, I. M. (2011) *Responsibility for Justice.* Oxford University Press, New York.

9 Toward a New Framework for Rights of the Biotic Community*

Alfonso Donoso

E.O. Wilson described it well:

> Meanwhile, we thrash about, appallingly led, with no particular goal in mind other than economic growth, unfettered consumption, good health, and personal happiness. The impact on the rest of the biosphere is everywhere negative, the environment becoming unstable and less pleasant, our long-term future less certain.
>
> (Wilson 2016, 2)

This is how many of us, in our personal and collective endeavors, in our domestic and global interactions, have directed ourselves to bring about a relationship with the natural world that is destructive, instrumental, and immoral.

Against this wretched state of affairs, some have called for a rethinking of current social, legal, and political institutions to make them more attuned with the needs, interests, and wellbeing of natural processes and organisms. Not without reason, it has been argued that one of the paramount institutions in need of such a deep reform is our system of law. We need a new legal framework capable not only of protecting human interests but also the integrity of ecosystems and biotic communities and, more generally, a more-than-human world.

This idea is captured, almost as its logical conclusion, by the recognition of the rights of nature. It is thought that until these rights are recognized, "we cannot see [nature] as anything but a *thing* for the use of 'us'" (Stone 2010, 3, emphasis in original), that is, for us humans, with almost no other *goals in mind than economic growth, unfettered consumption, good health, and personal happiness.* As has been the case with other vulnerable groups—slaves, women, children, migrants, prisoners—who have been instrumentalized, oppressed, and dominated for the sake of others, the language of rights emerges as a step towards recognition, protection, and justice for nature.[1]

* The author would like to thank Daniel Corrigan, Sophie Halart, and Markku Oksanen for helpful comments and suggestions on earlier versions of this chapter. This research was supported by Fondecyt Project n° 11160170 and the Polar Program of the Research Council of Norway, project 144416, "Political Philosophy Looks to Antarctica."

Although I strongly support the need for progressing toward a different and less anthropocentric legal framework, in what follows I adopt a critical—yet friendly—stance toward the strategy of ascribing rights to nature. I do so on two independent but mutually reinforcing grounds. First, I raise doubts regarding the idea that rights can be adequately ascribed to nature or, more specifically, to some of its constituent parts. And second, I question the idea that the recognition of rights of nature is beneficial for all of the right-holders within nature. Despite this critical perspective, I embrace the fundamental motivation for ascribing rights to nature but contend that we should search for a different rights-based framework to protect the natural world and its members.

The chapter is organized as follows. In the first section, I introduce the idea of rights of nature by appealing to what I call the Leopoldian principle, an influential normative principle in environmental ethics, and underline a couple of its most important characteristics. In the second section, I consider the two aforementioned difficulties regarding the ascription of rights to nature. The third section presents a non-human rights framework that may avoid at least what I consider to be the most serious of these two difficulties. The final section offers a conclusion.

Rights of Nature

Although the idea of the rights of nature has juridical, political, social, and economic implications, the crucial ground and motivation for the recognition of these rights have a fundamentally moral character. In other words, the rights of nature are primarily a moral enterprise. Their recognition entails a recognition of value—the value of nature—that is considered important enough to impose duties on individuals, collectives, and institutions that, accordingly, must constrain their actions and practices as demanded by these rights. Given the moral dimensions of this enterprise, it is appropriate to turn one's attention to environmental ethics, in order to consider the grounds of—and motivation for—the rights of nature.

In one of the most quoted passages in the discipline, Aldo Leopold concisely stated what is arguably the golden rule of environmental ethics: "A thing is right when it tends to preserve the integrity, stability and beauty of the biotic community. It is wrong when it tends otherwise" (Leopold 1949, 224–225). This is the fundamental principle of his land ethic, which includes not merely land, but also animals, plants, soils, and waters, and, in later interpretations, "ecosystem relationships in riverine, estuarine, marine, and, presumably, atmospheric environments as to terrestrial environments" (Fox 2007, 40). In an effort to update Leopold's principle with later developments in the science of ecology and conservation biology, J. Baird Callicott reformulated it in the following terms: "A thing is right when it tends to disturb the biotic community only at normal spatial and temporal scales. It is wrong when it tends otherwise" (Callicott 1996, 372). Regardless of the different implications of Leopold's and Callicott's principles, what matters for present purposes is that both share a common *ethos* and motivation for the protection of nature (or, specifically, the biotic community) and, thus, taken together as a conjoined articulation, can be called the Leopoldian principle.

Even though neither Leopold nor Callicott decidedly or unambiguously embraces the language of rights to protect nature, the Leopoldian principle is of great importance both as a source of moral motivation for those who defend such rights, as well as for the normative and conceptual articulation of these rights.[2] For this reason, I now proceed to underline two constitutive elements of this principle that are helpful for understanding the general character of the rights of nature.

The first of these elements is the non-individualistic nature of the Leopoldian principle. As Callicott emphasizes in reference to Leopold's version of the principle, "the good of the biotic *community* is the ultimate measure of the moral value, the rightness or wrongness, of actions" (Callicott 1980, 320, emphasis in original).[3] This non-individualistic feature is the natural outcome of acknowledging that the "philosophical context of the land ethic and its conceptual foundation is clearly the body of empirical experience and theory which is summed up in the term *ecology*," a science focused on relationships between different entities and which "inclines its students toward a more holistic vision of the world" (Callicott 1980, 321). Independent of the details of this ecological vision, it is sufficient to underscore here that the sharp focus of the Leopoldian principle is a collective, holistic, systemic natural entity that we may represent as the biotic community.

I highlight the non-individualistic nature of Leopold's guiding principle in order to specify both the character of the right-holder and the class of rights that defenders of the rights of nature must embrace. Put simply, rights of nature—or rights of the biotic community, as I call them henceforth—are not individualistic rights, they are rights held by a whole or, in other words, by a collective entity.

Despite my critical stance in this chapter, I must emphasize that I do not find anything inherently problematic with the idea of non-individualistic rights.[4] Although historically derived from individual entitlements, these rights have an important function on their own in the organization of our societies, and they are widely and rightly recognized, for example, in the two human rights covenants—where a right of all peoples to self-determination is recognized—and also throughout the Universal Declaration of the Rights of Peoples.[5]

The second constitutive element of the Leopoldian principle that I would like to highlight is the idea that the biotic community is vulnerable to harm. Although this use of language differs from that used by Leopold and Callicott in the formulation of the Leopoldian principle, my intention is not to offer an alternative meaning than is suggested by that principle. Thus, when Callicott determines there is a wrongful anthropogenic action that disrupts the biotic community, I recognize there is a harmful act committed against that biotic community. Similarly, when Leopold calls an action that does not preserve the stability or integrity of the biotic community wrong, I recognize this is wrongful harm committed against that community. Similarly, were someone to point to the destruction, damage, or extinction of a biotic community, species, or any other natural unit, these actions would count as harm against nature here as well.[6]

The reason for this slight change of language is to bring the Leopoldian principle closer to the language of rights. Whatever rights are, they are meant to protect right-holders from actions that can correctly be described as inflicting harm (see Feinberg 1984). As I will explain in the following section, this function of rights as protections against wrongful harm connects the rights of the biotic community with interest-based theories of rights, according to which rights are to protect right-holders' interests from wrongful interference.[7] Although wrongful harm may adopt different forms and have different scopes, what matters for present purposes is that anthropogenic disruptions of the biotic community constitute such harm.

As a way to illustrate the two elements I have just underlined, consider the following examples. The Framework Law of Mother Earth and Integral Development for Living Well (*Ley Marco de la Madre Tierra y Desarrollo Integral para Vivir Bien*) is a statutory law of the Plurinational State of Bolivia adopted by the Plurinational Legislative Assembly in 2012. Among its aims is to establish principles and guidelines for access to the components, areas, and systems of Mother Earth (*Madre Tierra*), as well as the operationalization of the rights of Mother Earth. The Framework recognizes Mother Earth as a right-bearer and defines it as "a dynamic living system comprising an indivisible community of all living systems and living organisms, which are interrelated, interdependent, and complementary, and which share a common destiny" (Chapter 2, Art. 5.1). Amongst its principles, the Framework includes a principle of restoration of Mother Earth, which determines that whoever harms Mother Earth is under a legal obligation to restore or rehabilitate the adequate functioning of what has been harmed (Chapter 2, Art. 4.5).[8]

A second example is a recent decision of the Special Jurisdiction for Peace (SJP), the institution through which those who participated in the armed conflict in Colombia are investigated and prosecuted.[9] In a press release of June 2019, the Unit of Investigation and Prosecution of the SJP recognizes the environment as a victim of the armed conflict in Colombia. Furthermore, the document expresses the commitment of the SJP to finding reparatory mechanisms for the environment and ways to guarantee the non-repetition of its destruction.[10] Specifically, this commitment of the SJP is grounded in data about the enormous and harmful deforestation produced by the armed conflict and the alterations that this deforestation caused and continues to cause in the ecosystems of Colombia.[11]

It is clear that the two elements of the Leopoldian principle underlined before—the non-individualist and harm-based dimensions—are present in each of these examples. With a different language and in a variety of juridical circumstances, these cases show that when referring to the rights of nature, a biotic community, Mother Earth, the environment, a river, or any other natural unit, the subject of those rights is a whole—a systemic and collective unit—which is to be protected from anthropogenic harmful action. In each of these cases, these rights are conceived as the entitlements of a complex whole that is to be recognized and protected as a collective entity, different and independent from its constitutive parts.

In sum, from the widely influential Leopoldian principle of environmental ethics, I have underlined two basic elements that are at work in the construction of the rights of the biotic community. First, the recognition of the existence of wrongful harm against this community (or nature however defined), and second, the non-individualistic (collective, holistic) character of the right-holder. With these elements in place, it is easier to understand why the language of rights is considered the appropriate moral and juridical tool to protect the biotic community. Biotic communities are vulnerable to human action, they are subjected to anthropogenic stress, disruptions, and depletion, and rights emerge as a powerful tool to protect them.

Two Challenges for the Rights of Nature

I now consider two independent but mutually reinforcing difficulties in the idea of the rights of the biotic community. These difficulties challenge, first, the idea that the biotic community can be the proper subject of rights—the problem of ontology—and, second, the compatibility of the rights of the biotic community with other rights of members of that community—the problem of compatibility.

The Problem of Ontology

As it was argued in the previous section, one of the salient features of the rights of the biotic community is their non-individualist character. Nature, the biotic community, or however we describe the proper subject of entitlements in the rights of nature, has this collective character. This feature gives rise to the following concern: biotic communities, as collective subjects, are not sufficiently determined to allow for an adequate ascription and recognition of rights. To be efficient and coherent, advancing the entitlements of any subject of rights requires an adequate determination of the ontological outlines of the right-holder. This represents a pre-condition for both the ascription of rights as well as for the recognition of those rights by duty-bearers. Without that sufficiently clear determination of the potential subject of rights, we are blind as to what needs to be respected and how we should conduct our actions as duty-bearers.

This concern is grounded in the currently accepted paradigm in ecology and conservation biology, according to which any attempt to advance a discrete, delimited, or specified articulation of biotic communities, ecosystems, or any other natural unit is difficult to justify based on empirical evidence. In contrast to the older, classical paradigm in ecology which maintains "that any unit of nature is, in and of itself, conservable" (Pickett, Parker, & Fiedler

1992, 68), the idea that now prevails is that natural units are open, unpredictable, and defined by a strong internal heterogeneity and species superfluity or redundancy (see Allen & Hoekstra 1992; Pickett & White 1995, inter al.). Principles of conservation and ecology have evolved towards a "new nonequilibrium paradigm," which "emphasizes that ecological systems are often open to external control, frequently nondeterministic, and rarely at equilibrium" (Ostfeld et al. 1997, 4).[12] Thus, any natural units—from microsites to biomes, and including biotic communities—have a dynamic that is closer to a mosaic in constant flux and change than to a well-defined, stable, and discrete entity.[13] Patchiness, not homogeneity or stability, is what defines natural units, their interactions, and processes (see, for example, Wiens 1995).

From the perspective of the rights of the biotic community, this general feature of the relevant natural units is problematic.[14] In the law's orthodox view, subjects of rights contrast starkly with the predominant paradigm of patchiness in ecology.[15] Indeed, a pre-condition for the assignation of rights to X depends, at least partly, on the possibility to correctly conceptualize X as a single unitary entity, where subjectivity, interests, and a degree of ontological integrity could be ascribed in a generally unequivocal fashion. In contrast, the received conceptualizations of natural units by the science of ecology create serious difficulties for a recognition of rights of nature that are conceptually, morally, and juridically precise. Lacking an articulation of a single unitary entity, the ascription of rights to biotic communities becomes a difficult and contentious task, both because it is unclear what the subject of rights is and because duty-bearers are left without a clear obligation to determine their actions and practices.

The Problem of Compatibility

The absence of a sufficiently determined right-bearer is a serious difficulty for anyone embracing the idea of the rights of the biotic community. Yet some may think that it is plausible to address this issue by means of a different strategy of construction of the subject of these rights. Although I do not deny that such a strategy may exist, I cannot entertain here what it could be and, instead, I am going to concede this possibility and move onto a second and independent problem. Thus, even if those who embrace the rights of the biotic community believe that there is a viable way to respond to the problem of ontology—and, therefore, to avoid the lack of determination of natural units in the construction of the rights of the biotic community—they must confront a second independent, and more serious, challenge.

This second worry is concerned with the compatibility between the rights of the biotic community and a different set of rights, namely, those rights held by individual members of that community. The core of this challenge is that the recognition of the rights of the biotic community may pose a serious threat to the rights of individual members of those communities. The concern is that if we give rights to biotic communities as such we may leave individual rightholders off the moral radar, or worse, we may end up directly opposing those individuals, making them especially vulnerable *because* of our commitment to the collective rights of the biotic communities. A typical example of this problem is the permissibility of culling within the framework of the Leopoldian principle, which allows the selective killing of non-human animals for the sake of protecting the integrity of the biotic community (see, for example, Regan 2004, 359). This may be an acceptable outcome when one denies the existence of non-human animal rights, but it becomes deeply unpalatable once those rights are recognized.

The question, of course, is whether those who embrace the rights of biotic communities must recognize the rights of individuals within these communities. In what follows I elaborate on this question, answer it in the positive, and maintain that the recognition of the rights of the biotic community entails the recognition of the rights of some of the individual members of this community.

To begin, a preliminary is in order. Notice that when justifying the rights of the biotic community, theorists will naturally lean towards some version of an interest-based theory of rights. According to this theory, for someone or something to have rights they must possess some form of interests, and rights are for the purpose of protecting these interests.[16] Of course, that biotic communities, wholes, or non-sentient beings may have the relevant kind of interests to be protected through rights requires some argumentation that, for present purposes, I am taking for granted in this chapter. It may suffice to say that theoretical accounts of interest are not to be reduced to traditional mental states theories and, instead, can adopt an alternative form, such as the one elaborated by Gary Varner (1998). According to Varner's psycho-biological theory of interests, the full set of relevant interests is not reducible to desires or other mental or cognitive states so, for example, an entity can have interest Φ without having a desire to fulfill Φ.[17] The crucial point is that interests are not reduceable to mental states, but include biological needs and functions that, with some adjustments to Varner's theory, can be recognized in biotic communities. Insofar as interest-based theories are grounded on the possession of interests and not, for example, on some more demanding capacity for mental states—which is not to be found in biotic communities as such—interest-based theories are the obvious theoretical alternative for those who ascribe rights to non-human natural entities.[18]

Keeping this in mind, consider now my claim that if someone is committed to the rights of the biotic community, she must also be committed to the rights of at least some of the members of the biotic community. Notice that this is something that proponents of the rights of nature do not find especially problematic. Article 2 of the Universal Declaration of the Rights of Mother Earth, for example, establishes that "Mother Earth and all beings of which she is composed have [...] inherent rights," which expresses the same point I am making here. As I understand it, the kind of implication contained in the Universal Declaration is not a logical inference, but rather a moral and political one. The assumption is not that because someone believes in the rights of the biotic community she must then necessarily believe that the organisms within the biotic community have rights. Rather, the point is that to be morally and politically persuasive, defenders of the rights of biotic communities must be also committed to the defense of rights of at least some parts of these communities.[19] In particular, I shall argue, they must be committed to the idea that individual non-human sentient animals have rights.[20]

To explain why, consider the paradigmatic class of potential right-holders for the interest-based theory of rights, namely, "adult human beings with sound mental faculties" (Kramer 2010, 36). Simply put, the paradigmatic case implies that if someone has rights, human adults of sound mind must have rights. Hence, if the interest-theory of rights is the account of rights to which defenders of the rights of biotic communities must appeal to in order to ground rights, as I think it is, then they must accept that the paradigmatic case—human adults of sound mind—also have rights.

The recognition of the paradigmatic case is plausible for those who endorse the rights of biotic communities because accepting it does not amount to accepting an equivalence between the complete set of right-holders and the exclusive set of human adults of sound mind. Nothing forces us to reduce right-holders to the paradigmatic case. On the contrary, part of the attractiveness of the interest-based theory is its capacity to recognize rights in cases different from the paradigmatic case, including young children, the mentally ill, and, important for present purposes, non-human entities. This is consistent with the interest-based perspective because if an entity X has relevant similarities with the paradigmatic group of right-holders, then interest-based theorists would agree that we have good reasons to recognize X as a right-holder. Amongst the non-human entities, and because of their being subjects with basic interests, many sentient non-human animals fall within those entities who are relevantly similar to the paradigmatic case and, thus, we have good reasons to ascribe rights to them.[21]

Before closing, note that I have contended that this is a moral and political implication, not a logical one. Such is the case because supporters of the rights of biotic communities could defend a different conclusion from the one I am drawing here without falling into any kind of contradiction. Defenders of these rights could argue, for example, that only the rights of biotic communities should be recognized, meaning that apart from the biotic community, no other right-holder exists. Or, instead, they could recognize the paradigmatic case of adults of sound mind and maintain that the biotic community (and nothing else) is relevantly similar to that paradigmatic class of right-holders. These are alternatives that do not seem to violate any principle of non-contradiction, although they are utterly unpersuasive. They fail morally—they do not value everything we have strong reasons to value—and they fail politically—they bypass the paradigmatic case, which is the most reasonable starting point to discuss rights in a political community.

In sum, I have argued that if the rights of the biotic community are recognized, then the individual rights of the non-human animals within such communities must be recognized. This forces defenders of the rights of the biotic community to determine the order and relationship that ought to exist between these different types of rights. In the absence of such an account, collective rights may end up overriding individual rights within the biotic community. Within a rights-based framework, this possibility is seriously problematic. Rights are protections to be afforded to right-holders who, lacking these rights, are left unrecognized and vulnerable in their most fundamental interests and needs. This is an unwelcome potential consequence of the recognition of the rights of the biotic community that must be addressed.

Reframing the Rights of the Biotic Community

The recognition of tension between the collective and the individual has a long history in environmental philosophy.[22] In this chapter, I have been concerned with a specific version of that problem, the one taking place within a non-anthropocentric rights-based framework. In what follows, I would like to confront this tension by offering a re-articulation of that framework that allows for a harmonic co-existence between the collective rights of biotic communities and the individual rights of those within those communities. In other words, my aim is not to defend the existence or possibility of the rights of biotic communities, but to present the structure or order of rights that a non-human rights framework would have to have in order to avoid the compatibility problem.

Let us start recapitulating parts of the analysis offered so far. In the first section, I argued that rights are protections against wrongful harm and that these rights are grounded on interests of a certain kind, namely, interests in goods that are important enough to justify the creation of duties that bind moral agents. In the second section, I explained why anyone recognizing the rights of biotic communities should also recognize the rights of individual non-human sentient animals. This is what led us to consider the problem of compatibility which, in addition to the problem of ontology, represents a substantive challenge for the idea of the rights of the biotic community.

As I shall argue, I believe that there is a plausible way to articulate both kinds of rights and that this alternative depends on the recognition that important individual interests depend on some collective goods.[23] In other words, there is not a necessary antagonism between collective and individual goods and, in turn, there is not necessarily an incompatibility between individual and collective rights. On the contrary, there are cases in which individual interests are promoted by collective goods and rights. If this is correct, then the compatibility problem can be avoided. To bring these rather abstract considerations to the more specific questions considered in this chapter, let me rephrase all this in terms of non-human rights. Following the Leopoldian principle, we can identify the integrity of the biotic community as a collective good that, with some plausible stipulations, could give rise to collective rights and duties, namely, the collective right to the integrity of the biotic community and the correlative duties of moral agents to respect that right.[24]

Yet, the question concerning how this construction of collective rights contributes to a harmonic framework that combines both non-human individual and collective rights remains unanswered. To respond to this query one must focus on the kind of relationship that these different rights—individual and collective—would have to have in order for them to co-exist harmonically. To put this differently, the difficulty of compatibility considered in the previous section represents an adversarial characterization of individual and collective non-human rights. In contrast to that characterization, I propose here a framework of rights ordered by two considerations found in Joseph Raz's analysis of rights, namely, the distinction between core and derivative rights and, second, the cumulative conception of collective rights.[25]

The distinction between core and derivative rights refers to the idea that there are rights that are derived from other rights. A right that is derived or grounded in another right is, in Raz's language, a derivative right (Raz 1986, 168). The following example explains this distinction:

> My right to walk on my hands is not directly based on an interest served either by my doing so or by others having duty not to stop me. It is based on my interest in being free to do as I wish, on which my general right to personal liberty is directly based. The right to walk on my hands is one instance of the general right to personal liberty.
>
> (Raz 1986, 169)

This example is sufficiently clear as to illustrate the distinction between core and derivative rights, but needs to be complemented with the following precision: "The relation of core and derivative rights is not that of entailment, but of order of justification" (Raz 1986, 169). Hence, the core right to personal liberty is prior in the order of justification to the derivative right to walk on my hands. This priority implies that without the existence of a core right—a right which is based directly on the appropriate interest of the right-holder—there is no derivative right and, more importantly, that the existence of a derivative right is justified by the interests upon which a core right is based. This means that, even though all rights are ultimately grounded in fundamental interests, derivative rights relate only indirectly to the interests that ground core rights.

The second element in Raz's account of rights that is relevant for current purposes is his conception of collective rights.[26] For Raz,

> A collective right exists when the following three conditions are met. First, it exists because an aspect of the interest of human beings justifies holding some person(s) to be subject to a duty. Second, the interests in question are the interests of individuals as members of a group in a public good and the right is a right to that public good because it serves their interest as members of the group. Thirdly, the interest of no single member of that group in that public good is sufficient by itself to justify holding another person to be subject to a duty.
>
> (Raz 1986, 208)

Thus, according to Raz, collective rights result when a sufficient number of individuals within a collective have a strong interest in a public good, yet, if we focused only on one of these individuals' interests, that interest could not ground a duty on others. What grounds the collective duty is the aggregate of individual interests. As Raz puts it when referring to the collective right of self-determination,

> though many individuals have an interest in the self-determination of their community, the interest of any one of them is an inadequate ground for holding others to be duty-bound to satisfy that interest. The right rests on the cumulative interests of many individuals.
>
> (Raz 1986, 209)[27]

Individual members of a collective jointly possess a right that is grounded in their individual interests and that none of them possesses individually. This is what can adequately be called a collective right.

I think this account of rights can contribute to overcoming the compatibility problem. This is done through the recognition of a derivative order of rights. In this non-adversarial, derivative view of non-human rights, the biotic community is defined as the collective arising from the aggregation of non-human individuals with similar basic interests in continued existence, health, and wellbeing. Put together, these interests give rise to a collective right to a healthy environment, a right derived from the strong individual interests of the constituents of that collective. Thus, the identification of a series of individual and sufficiently strong basic interests gives rise to a collective right to a healthy environment, a right that can be presented as the biotic community's collective right to its own integrity. The interests of individuals to a healthy environment is thus protected through a collective right to the integrity of the biotic community.

This non-adversarial, derivative view of rights avoids the compatibility problem. It does so by identifying individual interests as the ground for collective rights or, in other words, by justifying the existence of a collective right by the good of individual members of the collective. More concretely, the right to integrity of biotic communities is understood in light of the interests to a healthy environment and continued existence of the non-human individual members of that community. When considering the integrity of that community, the interests and rights of the individual members of the community—the non-human sentient animals who inhabit the biotic community—have paramount importance and priority. In simpler terms, the right to integrity of the biotic community is a function of the good of these individual members of the community.[28]

Of course, this framework of non-human rights comes at a cost for the idea of the rights of the biotic community. The recognition of the right to integrity is afforded under the condition that the articulation of this right be determined in a way that gives normative priority to one constituent part of the biotic community, namely, non-human sentient animals. This may give the impression that the original motivation for these rights, captured in the Leopoldian principle, is diluted if not simply eliminated in the proposed framework. Indeed, in this view, as Raz himself puts it, the collective interests that give rise to collective rights are a mere *façon de parler* (Raz 1986, 208).

In spite of this perception, it should be noted that precisely in virtue of the systemic view and interdependence of nature (strongly defended by those who embrace a version of the Leopoldian principle), the idea that the interests of non-human sentient animals work as a justification of the rights of the biotic community should not be seen as a radical departure from the environmental goals expressed in the Leopoldian principle. Individual animal rights and interests are not alien to the idea of the integrity of the biotic community. Indeed, there is substantive space for convergence between animal rights and rights of nature theories. This area of convergence must not be underplayed especially since, as noted by Dale Jamieson, "many of our most important issues involve threats to both humans and animals as well as to the nonsentient environment" (Jamieson 1998, 51). This area of convergence is captured by pointing out that biotic communities are where non-human animals live, interact, and develop. Biotic communities are their home and, as such, their interests are in multiple ways harmonic, and mutually supporting, with the integrity of that community.

But of course, there will be plenty of circumstances in which that idea of integrity of the biotic community will conflict with individual non-human animals' interests. In those cases, the rights of the biotic community will have to cede to the normative priority of those animals.[29]

Conclusion

In this chapter, I have adopted a critical yet friendly stance towards the idea of the rights of nature. I have presented two independent challenges that this idea must confront—the ontology problem and the compatibility problem. Whilst I have simply assumed that there can be a solution to the ontology problem, I offered a general non-human rights framework that can avoid the compatibility problem. This framework is not a direct defense of the rights of nature, but an inchoate exploration of the kind of non-human rights order that would be required for a more complete justification for the rights of nature.

Notes

1 For a similar idea, see Burdon 2010.

2 To be sure, both Leopold and Callicott do use the word "right," for example, when Leopold says that "A land ethic [...] does affirm their right [of 'resources'] to continued existence" (Leopold 1949, 204) or when he claims that "birds should continue as a matter of biotic right" (Leopold 1949, 211) or when Callicott affirms "that bird species should have a biotic right to continuance" (Callicott 2013, 67). However, it is difficult to conceive of these uses of the term as moral and legal justified claims proper rather than as rhetorical expressions to strengthen their message. Be this as it may, however, nothing in my argument hinges on whether Leopold or Callicott can aptly be described as non-human rights theorists.

3 May this community be understood as a specific ecological niche or an ecosystem, and may these be conceived of as super-organisms, quasi-organisms or organisms, is beyond the point I am making here. Rather, what matters is the non-individualistic entity—nature—with which the principle is concerned.

4 For a strong individualist account of rights, see Michael Ignatieff, for whom "rights exist to protect individuals. Rights language cannot be parsed or translated into a nonindividualistic, communitarian framework. It presumes moral individualism and is nonsensical outside that assumption" (Ignatieff 2003, 67).

5 In political philosophy, group or collective rights are normally presented as a third-generation type of rights, which emerged after both classical individual liberty rights and positive rights. See Griffin 2003.

6 This portrays an inclusive account of harm, consistent with the canonical works of Mill 1978 and Feinberg 1984. Furthermore, this use of the term is consistent with the use of harm by some legal and environmental scholars, as in Sagoff 2009, White 2008, and Hall 2015, and by Callicott himself in more recent publications. See Callicott 2013, 234, where he explicitly says that the biotic community can be subject to harm.

7 Interests are here understood as a relationship between an object and the subject of the interest, where that object is a good for that subject in the sense that makes the life or existence of that subject go better.

8 For a critical approach to this law, see Villavicencio & Kotzé 2018.

9 This is the justice component of the Comprehensive System of Truth, Justice, Reparation and Non-Repetition created by the 2016 Peace Agreement of the country and active since 2017. See https://www.jep.gov.co/JEP/Paginas/Jurisdiccion-Especial-para-la-Paz.aspx (last accessed on October 13, 2020).

10 See https://www.jep.gov.co/SiteAssets/Paginas/UIA/sala-de-prensa/Comunicado%20UIA%20-%20009.pdf (last accessed on October 13, 2020).

11 This decision of the SJP occurs some years after a landmark sentence by the Colombian Constitutional Court which, in 2016, granted legal rights to the Atrato River, its basin, and its tributaries. Also, the court ordered to design a plan to clean the basin of the river and its tributaries, recuperate its ecosystems and avoid further harms to the environments of the region. See https://justiciaambientalcolombia.org/wp-content/uploads/2017/05/sentencia-t-622-de-2016-rio-atrato-1.pdf (last accessed on October 13, 2020).

12 The contrast between the new and the old paradigm is rather a complex contrast of multiple ideas and themes. The set of old ideas replaced by the new ones is well captured by the equilibrium paradigm, characterized by stability, the closure and internal regulation of ecological systems. The balance of nature is a usual metaphor concerning the natural world that reflects this old ecological paradigm. For a general contrast between the old and the new paradigm, see Pickett, Parker, & Fiedler 1992.

13 See Bormann & Likens 1979 and Milne 1991.

14 Note, however, that this is problematic not just for the idea of the rights of nature but for any form of regulation that is based on ecological understanding and that is meant to evolve as the science of ecology evolves. For a good analysis of this issue, see Arnold & Gunderson 2013. Thanks to Markku Oksanen for this observation and reference.

15 For an alternative view of legal personhood, see Kurki 2019.

16 For the classical formulation of the interest-based theory of rights, see Jhering 1877. See also Raz 1986; Feinberg 1984; Kramer 1998.

17 I have adapted and defended a version of Varner's non-conventional account of interest in Donoso 2017.

18 Interest-based theories of rights are generally opposed to will theories of rights, according to which human adults of sound mind are the *only* potential right-holders. See Kramer 2010, 35; Hart 1955, 175. For will theories, the function of rights is to secure for right-holders spaces of choice where they are sovereign to act without interference from others.

19 For two recent examples of an explicit endorsement of interest-theories of rights applied to non-human animals, see Cochrane 2012 and Mañalich 2020.

20 To be sure, I take this conclusion to be valid as a consequence of the belief in the *rights* of nature, a belief which is not necessarily embraced by all environmental ethicists. For example, Leopold and Callicott themselves are not strictly speaking *rights of nature theorists*, even though they are deeply committed to the moral standing of nature.

21 This is especially the case if we are ready to ascribe rights to non-sentient beings, let alone biotic communities, all of which represent more difficult cases for the interest-based theory of rights. To be sure, I am not denying that a case can be constructed for the ascription of rights to nature, I am only defending the idea that when rights of nature are recognized, rights of at least some non-human animals should also be recognized.

22 For a general overview of the issue, see Hargrove 1992.

23 For the connection between goods and interests, see note 7.

24 The plausibility of these stipulations for the construction of nature as a right-bearer is a critical step for anyone defending the rights of nature. Despite my doubts about how successful this construction of nature can be (see the ontological problem in the second section), here I am simply assuming that, say, the biotic community can be aptly construed as a right-holder. As I have said, my ultimate purpose in this section is not to defend the existence of a non-human right-based framework, but to explore what form that framework would have to have to avoid the compatibility problem.

25 Strictly, what follows is a Razian (as opposed to Raz's) conception of rights. Although I use here a series of characteristic elements of Raz's account, their application to individual and collective non-human rights is not something he may be willing to consider.

26 For a critical view on collective rights and particularly against Raz's account of collective rights, see Tamir 2003.

27 The aggregative conception is also known as the collective conception of group rights. See Jones 1999.

28 It could be objected that with this move I have simply translated the conflict from one place to another. If before the conflict was between the individual and the collective, now conflict rises amongst individual right-bearers. This is a version of the so-called predation problem (for the classical statement of the problem see Clark 1979. More recently, see Milburn 2015 and Keulartz 2016). As a response to this concern it must be noticed, first, that the predation problem is orthogonal to adopting the derivative account of non-human rights. And second, within a rights-based framework, the predation problem should not be described as a problem of rights for the simple reason that there is no violation of rights between prey and predators. They are not moral agents, and only moral agents can violate rights, even though not all right-bearers are moral agents.

29 Apart from possible problems and tensions between the idea of the integrity of the biotic community and non-human sentient animals, there could also be problems and tensions between different populations of non-human sentient beings, as it is the case when an alien animal species threatens the wellbeing and continued existence of an endemic one. These are inescapable and complex issues that would also have to be confronted. I have elaborated on the resolution of these conflicts in Donoso 2017 and Donoso 2019.

References

Allen, T.F., and Hoekstra, T.W. (1992) *Toward a Unified Ecology*. New York: Columbia University Press.

Arnold, C. and Gunderson, L. (2013) "Adaptative Law and Resilience" *Environmental Law Reporter* 43: 10426–10443.

Bormann, H. and Likens, G. (1979) *Pattern and Process in a Forested Ecosystem*. New York: Springer-Verlag.

Burdon, P. (2010) "The Rights of Nature: Reconsidered" *Australian Humanities Review* 49: 69–89.

Callicott, J.B. (1980) "Animal Liberation: A Triangular Affair" *Environmental Ethics* 2: 311–338.

Callicott, J.B. (1996) "Do Deconstructive Ecology and Sociobiology Undermine Leopold's Land Ethic?" *Environmental Ethics* 18: 353–372.

Callicott, J.B. (2013) *Thinking Like a Planet. The Land Ethic and the Earth Ethic*. Oxford: Oxford University Press.

Clark, S. (1979) "The Rights of Wild Things" *Inquiry* 22: 171–188.

Cochrane, A. (2012) *Animal Rights without Liberation: Applied Ethics and Human Obligations* (New York: Columbia University Press).

Donoso, A. (2017) "Representing Non-human Interests" *Environmental Values* 26: 607–628.

Donoso, A. (2019) "A Territorial Mediation in a Triangular Affair. Towards an Ecological Territorial Sovereignty" in E. Rivera-Lopez & M. Hevia (eds.), *Controversies in Latin American Bioethics*. Cham: Springer Nature, pp. 219–236.

Feinberg, J. (1984) *Harm to Others*. Oxford: Oxford University Press.

Fox, W. (2007) *A Theory of General Ethics: Human Relationships, Nature, and the Built Environment*. Cambridge, MA: MIT Press.

Griffin, J. (2003) "Collective Rights" in L. Meyer, S. Paulson and Th. Pogge (eds.), *Rights, Culture and the Law: Themes from the Legal and Political Philosophy of Joseph Raz*. Oxford: Oxford University Press, pp. 161–182.

Hargrove, E. (ed.). (1992) *The Animal Rights/Environmental Ethics Debate. The Environmental Perspective*. Albany, NY: State University of New York Press.

Hart, H.L.A. (1955) "Are There Any Natural Rights?" *The Philosophical Review* 64: 175–191.

Hall, M. (2015) *Exploring Green Crime*. London: Palgrave.

Ignatieff, M. (2003) "Human Rights, Sovereignty, and Intervention" in N. Owen (ed.), *Human Rights and Human Wrongs: The Oxford Amnesty Lectures 2001*. Oxford: Oxford University Press, pp.49–88.

Jhering, R. (1877) *Geist des Römischen Rechts*, Third part, 3rd ed. Leipzig: Breitkopf & Härtel.

Jamieson, D. (1998) "Animal Liberation is an Environmental Ethics" *Environmental Values* 7: 41–57.

Jones, P. (1999) "Human Rights, Group Rights, and Peoples' Rights" *Human Rights Quarterly* 21: 80–107.

Keulartz, J. (2016) "Should the Lion Eat Straw Like the Ox? Animal Ethics and the Predation Problem" *Journal of Agricultural and Environmental Ethics* 29: 813–834.

Kramer, M. (1998) "Rights without Trimmings" in M. Kramer, N. Simmonds and H. Steiner (eds.), *A Debate over Rights*. Oxford: Oxford University Press, pp. 7–112.

Kramer, M. (2010) "Refining the Interest Theory of Rights" *The American Journal of Jurisprudence* 55: 31–39.

Kurki, V. (2019) *A Theory of Legal Personhood*. Oxford: Oxford University Press.

Leopold, A. (1949) *A Sand County Almanac and Sketches Here and* There. New York: Oxford University Press.

Mañalich, J.P. (2020) "Animalhood, Interests, and Rights" *Journal of Human Rights and the Environment* 11: 156–172.

Milburn, J. (2015) "Rabbits, Stoats and the Predator Problem: Why a Strong Animal Rights Position Need not Call for Human Intervention to Protect Prey from Predators" *Res Publica* 21: 273–289.

Mill, J.S. (1978) *On Liberty*. Indianapolis, IN: Hackett Publishing.

Milne, B. (1991) "Heterogeneity as a Multiscale Characteristic of Landscapes" in J. Kolasa and S. Pickett (eds.), *Ecological Heterogeneity*. New York: Springer-Verlag, pp.69–84.

Ostfeld, R.S., Pickett, S., Shachak, M., and Likens, G. (eds.). (1997) *The Ecological Basis of Conservation. Heterogeneity, Ecosystems, and Biodiversity*. Dordrecht: Springer Science+Business Media.

Pickett, S., and White, P. (eds.). (1995) *The Ecology of Natural Disturbance and Patch Dynamics*. San Diego, CA: Academic Press, Inc.

Pickett, S., Parker, T., and Fiedler, P. (1992) "The New Paradigm in Ecology: Implications for Conservation Biology above the Species Level" in Peggy Fiedler and Subodh Jain (eds.), *Conservation Biology*. London: Chapman and Hall, pp. 65–88.

Raz, J. (1986) *The Morality of Freedom*. Oxford: Oxford University Press.

Regan, T. (2004) *The Case for Animal Rights*. Berkeley, CA: University of California Press.

Sagoff, M. (2009) "Environmental Harm: Political not Biological" *Journal of Agricultural & Environmental Ethics* 22: 81–88.

Stone, Ch. (2010) *Should Trees Have Standing? Law, Morality and the Environment*. 3rd edition. Oxford: Oxford University Press.

Tamir, Y. (2003) "Against Collective Rights" in L. Meyer, S. Paulson and Th. Pogge (eds.), *Rights, Culture and the Law: Themes from the Legal and Political Philosophy of Joseph Raz*. Oxford: Oxford University Press, pp. 183–204.

Varner, G. (1998) *In Nature's Interests? Interests, Animal Rights, and Environmental Ethics*. Oxford: Oxford University Press.

Villavicencio, P., and Kotzé, L. (2018) "Living in Harmony with Nature? A Critical Appraisal of the Rights of Mother Earth in Bolivia" *Transnational Environmental Law* 7: 397–424.

White, R. (2008) *Crimes against Nature. Environmental Criminology and Ecological Justice*. London: Willan.

Wiens, J. (1995) "Landscape Mosaics and Ecological Theory" in L. Hansson, L. Fahrig, and G. Merriam (eds.), *Mosaic Landscapes and Ecological Processes*. Dordrecht: Springer, pp. 1–26.

Wilson, E.O. (2016) *Half-Earth. Our Planet's Fight to Life*. New York: Liveright Publishers.

10 Fundamental Challenges for Rights of Nature

Patrik Baard

Introduction

This chapter will assess different arguments for ascribing (moral and/or legal) rights directly to nature. The general idea will be referred to as the *Rights of Nature* (henceforth RoN) *Position*, and can be formulated as follows:

RoN: natural entities such as, but not limited to, ecosystems, forests, and rivers have rights, resulting in *direct* demands on moral agents.

RoN concern natural objects that include many different entities, such as rivers, forests, or ecosystems. This is consistent with the primarily holistic approach of RoN proposals, both in legislation and those offered by non-governmental organizations (NGOs).

My main argument is that common propositions in favor of RoN should be rejected. The argument has the following structure: first, I will stipulate propositions derived from NGOs, legislatures, and scholarly literature in defense of RoN, from which RoN follows; second, I will formulate objections to those propositions, derived from both (environmental) jurisprudence and environmental ethics; third, I will attempt to offer responses to those objections that will provide reasons to maintain confidence in the propositions, and thus in RoN. Ultimately, I will suggest that neither of the propositions succeeds and that consequently, there are no reasons to have confidence in RoN.

Fundamentally, RoN encompass entities that lack the properties which warrant moral standing in the specific form of rights. For RoN to be reasonable, it is necessary to endorse one or more of the following faulty assumptions:[1]

1) Assumes a substantial plasticity of rights, such that rights can be based on properties other than conventional ones for justifying rights-claims, such as autonomy, agency, interests, or dignity
2) Assumes conventional properties to be flexible enough to apply to natural entities and processes, for instance that a river has autonomy, agency, interests, or dignity

Additionally, accepting RoN has the following problematic practical implications, which ought to make one wary of doing so:

3) Results in conflicting claims between the rights of natural entities or processes and the rights of humans
4) Renders rights trivial since all entities and processes have rights, and calls for demarcation to distinguish valid claims of right-holders from non-valid ones

I will proceed as follows. After providing a short background on RoN, the main section of the chapter will stipulate and test different propositions from which RoN follow. Objections to those propositions will be formulated, to see if reasonable responses can be provided. All of these stipulated propositions and responses will be derived from relevant sources, such as NGOs, legislatures, and Earth jurisprudence. While striving for completeness, the section will be limited to the most common and strongest arguments. For instance, an argument that will not be discussed concerns the position that the very idea of personhood is vague as the very idea of self is contingent, thus rendering it reasonable to ascribe personhood to the environment (Gordon 2018). To do justice to such an argument, more space is required than can be offered here, including discussions of personhood and metaphysics. Following the discussion of various arguments for RoN, some possible counter-objections to my overall treatment of them will be considered. However, it will be suggested that reasonable responses can be formulated to these objections, and therefore we are warranted in rejecting RoN. Finally, a summary remark will be offered.

Background

Recent years have seen a growth in calls for accepting RoN, often referred to as a "paradigm shift" or "revolution" in jurisprudence (Chapron, Epstein, & López-Bao 2019; La Follette & Maser 2017; Boyd 2017). For instance, granting the Whanganui River in New Zealand the status of legal personhood entitled the river to "all the rights, powers, duties and liabilities of a legal person" (Te Awa Tupua Act 2017, 14.2). Some examples of ascribing legal rights to nature are most likely pragmatic compromises by a respective state in order to recognize the interests of indigenous peoples and seeks to rectify past wrongs (Te Awa Tupua Act 2017, §3, §8). Strengthening environmental protection as part of respect for the rights of indigenous peoples is more consistent with conventional moral and legal frameworks than granting rights to an entity such as a river. In the former case, environmental protection is conducive to the interests of right-holders recognized by conventional moral and legal criteria. The latter approach results in *direct* duties to the river *per se*, rather than indirect duties to sustainably maintain the river due to its importance to non-controversial right-holders.

Other claims to RoN are motivated by the calls of NGOs for greater environmental protection. Organizations such as the Community Environmental Legal Defense Fund in the U.S., as well as several communities in the U.S. and NGOs in Europe, have made efforts to establish legal rights of nature, often by way of granting legal personhood to nature. One example is the Lake Erie Bill of Rights, seeking to establish "irrevocable rights for the Lake Erie Ecosystem to exist, flourish, and naturally evolve," in addition to providing a healthy environment for the residents of Toledo (Toledoans for Safe Water 2019).

Since RoN are generating more attention, these rights are increasingly being incorporated into legal systems without a corresponding growth in analyses of the concept and the arguments by which they are justified, producing a gap between the social and political discourse and legal and moral philosophy. This chapter will contribute to bridging this gap by analyzing some of the central arguments in favor of RoN.

Testing Propositions in Favor of RoN

To test the reasonableness of RoN, arguments in favor of it will be surveyed. Each argument will be stipulated as isolated propositions, from which RoN follow. Next, objections to these propositions will be formulated, and it will be determined whether valid responses to those objections can be provided, or whether the proposition should be rejected. Ultimately, it will be argued that each reply is committed to at least one of the problematic assumptions or implications listed as 1-4 above, and therefore fails.

Overly Permissive Views of Right-Holders

One position from which RoN follow relies upon a very permissive account of what entities have legal rights:

P1: rights can be conferred on any entity whatsoever that an appropriate authority recognizes as having rights.

Another possibility is to ascribe rights to any existing thing, which is the first principle of Thomas Berry's principles of Earth jurisprudence (Rights of Nature 2019):

P1:* rights are warranted for all existing things.

However, it would be very problematic to permit the ascription of moral and legal rights solely by appealing to authority (P1) or existence (P1*). P1 permits the arbitrary ascriptions of rights if there is no appeal to any other recognized criteria. It is consistent with a remark made by John Dewey, related to corporate personhood, that "'person' might legally mean whatever the law makes it mean," prompting analysis of the likely social consequences of such a recognition (Dewey 1926, quoted in Gordon 2018, 68). Yet, few legal systems are this permissive, as establishing the validity of a law entails assessing criteria of formal, procedural, and substantive kinds (Waldron 2016). A rule of law should adhere to formal requirements such as consistency, stability, and intelligibility. Procedurally, establishing law requires bodies, such as judges and legislators, who are impartial. Finally, and somewhat more controversially,[2] substantive requirements refer to the content of the law, such as morality and ultimate political ideals to which laws are conducive. Together, these requirements restricts the ability of legislators to create law, and by doing so rejects unrestrained flexibility.

Adding to the objection, legal rules must be coherent with existing material such as precedents, conventions, and a corpus of rules, or judges' discretion with appeal to legal principles (Dworkin 2019; Kramer, Simmonds, & Steiner 2002). Yet, in most legislation, there are few, if any, precedents to support RoN, and few legal principles by which RoN could be justified. However, relying solely on existing precedents would exclude legal innovations. If the existing corpus of rules provides uncertain or no guidance, that is, when a case cannot be brought under a clear rule of law, a judge is then granted discretion to decide the case. However, such discretion is not unrestrained, as one party may still have the right to win, and the judge's duty is then to discover which party should be the rightful winner (Dworkin 2019, 105). In such cases, appeal to moral principles such as justice and fairness are warranted and, ideally, provide a "coherent justification for all common law precedents" (Dworkin 2019, 143), as discretion is not open to a judge's own preferences (Dworkin 2019). This also goes for rulings that are perhaps consistent with precedents, but which lack the support of ethical and political principles, as is the case of unjust laws, or in instances where an individual may have a right *against* a state or government (Dworkin 2019). In both of these cases, it is possible to expand or change the body of law by appeal to moral principles, which enable legal innovations through appeal to rules that are extraneous to the existing legal corpus. The rights of corporations may offer an example. Initially without precedents, it is now common and rather uncontroversial to regard corporations as right-holders and as having personhood. Yet, the idea is not as novel as one may think, as it was allegedly present as a metaphor in Roman law (Gordon 2018, 63). This requires accepting a "legal fiction," which will be further discussed below. Here it suffices to say that while the flexibility of legal systems exists, it is not unrestrained. Furthermore, it is questionable whether accepting RoN is within the boundaries of what is reasonable and consistent with precedents, constitutions, moral principles, or public sentiment.

P1*, the idea that all things that exist have a right to life, would be highly demanding, at least if the concept of rights is to play any meaningful role. An example of this objection to P1* is found in criticism of Albert Schweitzer's radical form of biocentrism, which holds that *all* living things have a will to live that ought to be respected. This claim is unsubstantiated, and furthermore it has wildly demanding implications that would likely stifle even the most mundane activities.

Most legal and moral frameworks are more restrictive than P1 and P1*. P1 and P1* would succeed if it could be shown that any entity that a specific authority confers rights to, or which exists, can meaningfully be granted legal personhood. Rights are often restricted to legal persons. For some legal scholars, legal personality can be ascribed to just about any entity whatsoever.[3] However, this view is a fringe position as legislating bodies do not have unrestrained flexibility regarding what can be established (Kurki 2017, 139).

A strong objection to P1 and P1* is that it is unreasonable to consider any entity a right-holder, if it does not fulfill the minimal conditions of having interests or legal personhood, which justify valid claims for legal protection. In sum, both P1 and P1* require assuming substantial plasticity of rights and departing from conventional criteria, while P1* poses the additional risk of making rights trivial.

Applying Interest-Based Accounts to RoN

One conventional way in which right-holders are often restricted is through the notion of interests. Interests come in many forms, illustrated by Tom Regan's distinction between "one's interest in" and "being in one's interest," the latter referring to welfare interests, whereas the former refers to agent-relative preference interests (Regan 2004, 87). Joseph Raz considers that "well-being (interests) is a sufficient reason for holding some other person(s) to be under a duty," providing the foundation for claim rights, noting that capacity for possessing rights requires that an individual's "well-being is of ultimate value or he is an 'artificial person' (e.g. a corporation)" (Raz 1986, 166).

Many who argue for RoN refer to interest-based accounts of rights in practical cases (Stone 1972; Chapron et al. 2019; Johnson 1991; Te Awa Tupua Act 2017, §19.2a). That is, they make use of conventional criterion for moral standing in general, and rights in particular, and suggest that this criterion can also encompass entities and processes such as rivers, forests, and ecosystems. Christopher Stone has provided one of the most influential attempts to justify the ascription of legal rights ascribed to "forests, oceans, rivers, and other so-called 'natural objects' [...] to the natural environment as a whole" (Stone 1972, 456) based on three criteria (Stone 1972, 458):

i. The right-holder can institute legal actions *at its behest*
ii. The court must take *injury to the right-holder* into account when determining legal relief
iii. That relief must run to the *benefit of the right-holder*

An entity fulfilling these three conditions "has a legally recognized worth and dignity in its own right, and not merely to serve as a means to benefit 'us'" (Stone 1972, 458). Based on these claims, we can identify:

P2: rights can be conferred to any entity where legal actions can be instituted at its behest, and where injuries and benefits to the right-holder can be considered. Nature, and natural objects and processes, fulfill these conditions.

Ultimately, P2 is justified by reference to interests. Stone writes that: "natural objects *can* communicate their wants (needs) to us [...] The lawn tells me that it wants water by a certain dryness of the blades and soil—obvious to the touch" (Stone 1972, 471). Yet, he also states that "the more encompassing the entity of concern, the less certain we can be in venturing judgment as to the 'wants'" (Stone 1972, 472). That is, we may be somewhat certain of the interests of a lawn, but less certain about the interests of a large ecosystem. The harms and benefits must not rely on an appeal to human harms or benefits, but rather to those of the natural object itself (Stone 1972, 473).[4] Thus, it is suggested that the concepts of harms and benefits are applicable to natural objects and processes themselves, resulting in direct duties on others to avoid imposing harms upon and to provide benefits to these entities.

Stone's appeal to the relative condition of an entity as a sufficient condition for having an interest does not hold. An entity merely being in a worse or better condition does not warrant the conclusion that the entity as such has a need or want, nor *interest* in a wider sense. The Taj Mahal may need repair or sink into decay if neglected, depriving all humanity of something of great value (Feinberg 1974, 49), but it would most likely not be meaningful to state that it *communicates its wants* to us, nor to say that the Taj Mahal has a *interest* in being in a specific condition, even though the building can obviously be in a worse or better condition, obvious to the senses. The reason, however, why the Taj Mahal does not have an interest and therefore not a right *per se*, is that it has no conative life, "no conscious wishes, desires, and hopes; or urges and impulses; or unconscious drives, aims and goals; or latent tendencies, direction of growth, and natural fulfilments" (Feinberg 1974). That lack of conative life also applies to ecological systems and other natural objects. This does not imply that there are no good moral reasons to care for cultural heritages, but those reasons are not necessarily for the heritages *per se*, but rather to future generations and for commemoration.

The third condition refers to the benefit of the right-holder. A reasonable interpretation of this condition involves the idea that a damaged ecosystem should be restored, therefore "making the environment whole" (Stone 2010, 15). But can one identify a morally relevant, non-arbitrary baseline to which to measure ecosystem restoration, thus making it whole? Is it the ecosystem as it was immediately prior to being polluted? Or perhaps such a baseline does not have to be historical, but can instead relate to properties, but then *what* properties (Siipi 2017)? This is a central problem in restoration ethics (Elliot 1997; see also Luuppala in this book). Restoration ethics also raises additional concerns regarding to what extent the restored natural object would have the same natural value as before, and whether it is even empirically *possible* to restore such a complex system. Neither of these concerns about restituting past wrongs is discussed, but they are highly relevant to restituting past wrongs and raise a central issue if we are concerned with meaningfully benefitting a right-holder. Thus, P2 assumes conventional criteria for considering something a right-holder but assumes that such criteria are flexible enough to also encompass natural objects and processes. This error entails faulty assumption 2 listed above.

The Response From Goal-Directedness

An ecosystem or natural object differs from a building or monument such as the Taj Mahal. We use the concept of ecosystem health as if entities such as rivers and adjacent ecosystems have a specific form of wellbeing or a goal to be in a specific state. Thus, maybe we can modify the argument by lowering the bar for moral relevance, and state that RoN and the entities encompassed by them are goal-directed. That is, they strive toward something particular, being in a specific state or condition, analogous to an interest. This idea suggests:

P2⋆: natural objects strive towards goals, such as equilibrium, and the moral relevance of those goals warrant the ascription of rights.

It would seem as if many ecosystems are goal-directed, allowing us to predict such properties as population sizes (Woods 2017, 158). The goal, we can then surmise, would perhaps be to withstand change and to remain stable, or return to a prior stable state after disturbances, allowing for physical continuity.

The view that an ecosystem reaches toward equilibrium or a natural balance is an old one, dating back at least to antiquity (Woods 2017). Yet, the equilibrium view of ecosystems is now mostly considered irrelevant, as ecosystems are regarded as dynamic systems filled with stochastic events that limit predictions, with a non-equilibrium paradigm having replaced the equilibrium paradigm (Woods 2017, 160). At best, one could perhaps state that most ecosystems *tend toward* equilibrium, but that changes, disturbances, and stochastic events are characteristics of ecological systems. The non-equilibrium view of ecosystems is a hard blow, even to the goal-directedness version of interest-based theories of claims, because such an entity would lack the physical continuity required to constitute a goal-directed entity. Even if equilibrium does emerge, it would be questionable to characterize this as the goal of the ecosystem *per se*. Rather, the equilibrium would be more aptly described as a residual product of the individual specimens residing in that ecosystem.[5]

Commonly, only individuals, perhaps only conscious individuals, and in some cases groups can meaningfully be said to have interests (Varner 1998, 6). From restricting rights to the protection of interests, it follows that natural objects, such as rivers, forests, and ecosystems, do not have rights as they do not have interests. Thus P2 and P2⋆ fail to provide the necessary justification for RoN. Similar to P2, P2⋆ seems to entail faulty assumption 2 listed above, but also assumes that the conventional criteria are insufficient, which entails faulty assumption 1.

The Response From Marginal Cases and Representatives

In later clarifications, Stone admits that the interest-based account does not work, noting that "fundamental notions of *interests* and *equivalent welfare* become difficult to apply, even all but incoherent, depending upon the particular 'thing' bringing suit," when we consider natural entities (Stone 2010, 168). He proposes two other solutions, namely guardianship and that other entities have rights that cannot be meaningfully said to involve interests.

Consider other right-holders, such as marginal cases. Even if beings cannot make their claims heard, they can meaningfully be said to be harmed by, or to benefit from, actions. Perhaps, therefore, a modification to P2 could enable a response to the above objections:

*P2**:* others can protect the goodness of a (voiceless) entity meriting rights, serving in the role of guardians or custodians.

What P2** accomplishes is to allow that natural entities that do *not* have interests, but can still be considered right-holders, because they have some form of goodness that ought to be protected. A right-holder does not have to understand that it has rights in order for the right to be valid. If that were the case, then for instance, the senile, infants, and children would be excluded as right-holders. However, legal proceedings can be started on their behalf by those who represents their interests or wellbeing (Feinberg 1974, 47). In other words, it is possible to defend their rights via representatives and custodians. But would not such a widening of rights also provide support for RoN? After all, something that can follow from having rights, both in principle and in practice, is guardianship (Stone 1972; Te Awa Tupua Act 2017).

As previously argued, this claim must appeal to interests in order to be meaningful. The notion of "goodness" is too wide and would include such properties as justice, pleasure, and knowledge. We could either surmise what the interests typically are, as in the case of children or the elderly and some animals, and make sense of how they are harmed or benefitted, or interests could take the form of a prior expressed wish of what is to be done. Neither alternative is available regarding the entities encompassed by RoN, and thus this response is not as strong as it might have seemed. It is also vulnerable to problems, such as how we are to resolve conflicting recommendations from two different guardians.

Furthermore, and even more problematic, is that *if* we have a system of guardianship for protecting or promoting the good of a natural object, we would have to have some measure for avoiding anthropocentrism to ensure that guardianship is granted not only to those natural objects that some groups of humans feel strongly attached to and are prepared to take on guardianship for, but also for those natural objects that garner no such human attachnments.

But how can we define something that no human would find objectionable as “damage”? Stone offers two ways of doing this; one that appeals to intrinsic value, and one that relies on transcendentalism (Stone 1987; Bunzl 2015, 51 ff.). While the first approach is appealing to many environmental ethicists, intrinsic value as such does not warrant rights, as will be discussed below. Second, for some ecocentric environmental ethicists, such as Arne Næss, the intrinsic value serves as an axiom, which is supported by intuition, but not by proof (Næss 2002, 65). This does little to convince skeptics for whom such value is not self-evident. Third, can we find some non-arbitrary way to distinguish those entities in nature that have intrinsic value from those that do not? Or, does *all* of it have intrinsic value and merit respect? If that is the case, then objections similar to those against P1* above will arise, which concern a lack of robustness of foundations and troublesome implications. The other approach that Stone proposes is transcendentalism, entailing an effacing of boundaries between one’s self and other entities. However, this is a very questionable strategy. First, it is questionable whether one even *can* imagine being an entity such as a river, due to its radical otherness. Second, even if one could do this, it is be questionable what normative guidance that can be provided. As this reveals, P2** entails faulty assumption 1, and ultimately fails to justify RoN.

The Response from Corporations as Legitimate Right-Holders

Maybe we could defend RoN by appealing to entities that currently have legal standing but do not have interests. In some cases, we have entities that are so unlikely to be legal persons that a strong response could be provided to the objections to P2 above. Corporations are very distant from what we would commonly call natural persons, but if corporations can be given rights, then why not nature? Granting rights to corporations is based on a widely accepted concept of *legal fiction* (O’Donnell & Talbot-Jones 2018). However, to make a valid claim in this regard requires showing that nature is similar enough to corporations. This suggests:

*P2***:* entities such as corporations have legal rights, and ecological systems are similar to corporations in morally relevant ways.

If P2*** holds, then it would seem sensible to ascribe rights to nature. A corporation has legal personhood, and thus rights, as well as liability. In contrast to the legal rights of humans, the rights of corporations do not have the same basis in some special characteristics, such as having interests and wellbeing, or similar, beyond a fictional sense.[6] If they are similar enough, it would be incoherent not to recognize the rights of nature while recognizing the rights of corporations. We need only show that the reasons for granting rights to corporations also holds in the case of nature and natural objects.

Some take this analogical argument even further, and claim that the environment is a *better* candidate for rights than corporations since it has a "more convincing claim to personhood as it is socially understood," in contrast to how corporations are socially understood (Gordon 2018, 71). Consequently, nature has a more convincing claim to personhood than corporations and is "more legitimately the recipient of rights to personhood than the corporation" (Gordon 2018, 71). We may for instance more easily imagine nature as a person, and consequently a right-holder, than a corporation. This may hold for various reasons, such as the law running with the land, not with human persons, in regards to property rights (Gordon 2018, 61), whereas personhood in the case of corporations requires more constructive work. An additional reason may be that the concept of the individual, and the ontological status of the individual person, are increasingly questioned (Gordon 2018). Moreover, a case could possibly be made for the personhood of nature based on holistic reasons. However, this would suffer from objections similar to those presented above against the argument from goal-directedness.

Even if P2*** has intuitive appeal, it is questionable whether the relevant similarity obtains. Feinberg uses this very analogy to show how it is *not* reasonable to confer the same rights and duties on species as on corporations. He writes: "Unlike a biological species, an institution has a charter, or constitution, or bylaws, with rules defining offices and procedures, and it has human beings whose function it is to administer the rules and apply the procedures" (Feinberg 1974, 56). A species, ecosystem, or other entity encompassed by RoN lacks these features that establish continuity, rights, and liability. As discussed in relation to P2**, there must to be some system that prevents the anthropocentric tendency to merely take on guardianship for environmental areas that are favored by non-controversial right-holders such as natural persons. In some cases, it may be very difficult to find representatives for an environmental area. For instance, an aesthetically pleasing or historically meaningful environmental area or characteristic umbrella species is perhaps more likely to garner representatives than a neglected niched ecosystem or a swamp.

In contrast, however, there are successful campaigns that have utilized RoN-like arguments to end environmentally disastrous decisions. An example is found in Pennsylvania, where the small borough of Tamaqua passed a bill that protected their river following the work of local grassroots organizations. As with P2**, the need for representatives restricts rights to environmental entities and properties that have willing representatives or guardians, which usually means entities that are valued by some specific group of people. But that argument succeeds only by appealing to the group of people as conventional right-holders and the environmental entity as something specifically valuable to them. Furthermore, the mere fact that an entity can have guardians does not necessarily determine who is a *rightful* and *legitimate* guardian, and by what criteria guardianship is assessed as legitimate. Who has the right to voice the concerns? As with hierarchies of rights discussed below, there are also issues concerning how to weigh different, possibly conflicting, voices against each other. For example, what criteria or principles determine that an NGO is a more legitimate guardian of an environmental area than a logging company? This is especially problematic given the difficulties of weighing RoN against property rights (which, as was recounted above, often give precedence to the latter over the former).

In sum, P2** and P2*** both make appeals to entities that do not have interests, but which nevertheless have rights conferred on them. This entails faulty assumption 1 listed above. Furthermore, these propositions make it questionable whether it is actually nature *per se* that is accorded rights, or rather, just those environmental areas deemed important by some humans. Finally, it is also questionable whether nature is similar enough to corporations to establish these claims.

Counterintuitive, or Trivial, Implications of RoN

If a river has a right, under what conditions would the rights of this river trump other rights? That is, can we meaningfully explain the implications of treating a river as a right-holder? Would the rights of a river trump the subsistence rights of people or animals living nearby? An affirmative answer subsumes the rights of individual organisms to the rights of the river. This is akin to environmental fascism since it rejects the rights of individuals by appeal to a collective good (Regan 2004, 359 ff.). Of course, the mere fact that the rights of a collective, as such, trump individual rights does not merit fascism. The group-rights of indigenous people could, for instance, rightfully trump individual property rights. A central question is rather how to balance the group rights with individual human rights of human beings. What is meant by the accusation of environmental fascism is the rejection of the relevance of individual rights by appeal to, for instance, the intrinsic value of a collective species or ecosystems, which in turn has a substantially less robust foundation than human group rights, such as those of indigenous peoples.

One way to avoid the counterintuitive conclusion that the rights of a river would trump the rights of animals or even humans is to soften the implications of the rights of a river. This suggests:

P3: the rights of nature would not supersede the rights of basic human welfare.

Instead of identifying a reasonable ground for RoN, as did the previous propositions, P3 justifies RoN by claiming that no counterintuitive implications follow. This can be considered a pragmatic defense of RoN. It is also supported by Stone, who states that RoN do not imply "anything as silly as that no one should be allowed to cut down a tree" (Stone 1972, 457) and that hierarchies of rights can be established, and no rights are absolute (Stone 1972, 457 ff., 482).

Nothing more follows from RoN than a duty to analyze and investigate what the possible consequences or risks of a decision may be, and "to really *think about* what [one] is doing" (Stone 1972, 484). An additional procedural consequence also follows, so that "those who would infringe on [rights] must go through certain procedures to do so" (Stone 1972, 488 ff.), and "those procedures are a measure of what we value as a society" (Stone 1972, 482). But impact analyses are already mandatory in countries such as Sweden and elsewhere, without any appeal to RoN.[7] This makes RoN redundant in many cases. Of course, one could perhaps insist on stronger or more robust procedures to reflect their value, but that is a practical matter. Furthermore, being valuable *per se* does not establish rights. We can make the processes that permit infringing on something valuable cumbersome, to deter those who would infringe on those things, without appeal to rights.

There are additional challenges posed by P3. First, if we assume that rights are absolute and should never be infringed, it is likely that rights conflicts will emerge if we accept RoN. That is, the rights of a river will come into conflict with human rights, or perhaps even animal rights. It is possible to escape such conflicts, as is evident by the discussion of environmental fascism within environmental ethics (see Callicott 2013), but it usually requires a view of rights as moderate—that is, that most rights can be overridden if conflicting with stronger rights. That view is not a given, as some deontological perspectives hold that, for instance, a deontological right to life is inviolable no matter how much good would result from infringing upon that right, whereas others hold more moderate views according to which it is right to infringe upon a right if there is, on balance, more reason for doing so than refraining from it (Kagan 2019, 174 ff.). But accepting a moderate view of rights begs criteria for creating a hierarchy of rights. That is, the mere fact that one needs to create a hierarchy of rights, which may permit infringements on rights, does not entail the rejection of rights. Rather, guidelines as to when such infringements are permissible or recommended need to be provided. Stone, for instance, regards no rights as absolute, but suggests that infringements are justified only if appropriate processes that reflect the appropriate values are in place. But that procedural suggestion does little to provide a substantial answer regarding what criteria such processes should embody. It also has the unfortunate implication that all rights can be overridden, even the right to life (see Stone 1972, 482). Moreover, practical cases from Ecuador and Bolivia, where RoN-like norms have been included in legislation, have resulted in rights of nature often being trumped by other rights, especially when large extractive interests are involved (Gordon 2018, 85). However, establishing a reasonable hierarchy of rights in a disciplined manner could offer a possible way forward that makes RoN a sensible position.

If RoN entails absolute rights of nature, then highly counterintuitive implications follow. However, if the implications of being a right-holder is that infringements of rights are permissible when certain procedures are met, then RoN becomes a redundant concept, because such procedures are already required.

Intrinsic Values as a Foundation for Rights

Another possibility to make RoN reasonable lies in an appeal to the intrinsic value of nature. Basing RoN on appeal to intrinsic value has been attempted from several perspectives.[8] This approach suggests:

P4: nature has intrinsic value, and entities with intrinsic value have rights.

That nature has intrinsic value is a view held by many environmental ethicists (Rolston 2012). However, even if it is true that nature has intrinsic value, this does not warrant the inference that nature has rights. Having intrinsic value is not a sufficient condition for rights. If that were the case, then we would need an explanation of how properties that are traditionally held to have intrinsic value, such as beauty or knowledge, have rights (see the objection to P2** above). Furthermore, it should be noted that intrinsic values come in many different forms, ranging from subjective and agent-relative to objective and agent-neutral.[9] For example, an agent may cherish some specific entity that lacks any extrinsically valuable features, while in other cases, artifacts such as works of art may have an intrinsic value that is less agent-relative. However, an appeal to intrinsic value *per se* is not instructive as to which of these forms of intrinsic value would merit rights.

Having intrinsic value is also not a necessary condition for rights. Humans have a right to health care, which is not due to health care having intrinsic value, but rather to its instrumental value for human wellbeing. Chapron et al. argue that RoN follows from intrinsic value by appealing to legal philosopher Joseph Raz (Chapron et al. 2019). However, Raz bases rights on *ultimate values* conferred to humans, and explicitly states that not even a dog has ultimate value, and thus cannot be granted rights, making this a questionable ground for supporting RoN (Raz 1986, 177 ff.). Raz also mentions the case of the rights of plants, imagining for instance "some scientists hav[ing] a duty to preserve certain rare species of plants because they are the only source of a medicine for a rare and fatal disease." However, he denies that the plants have a right to the benefit, because "the benefit is to be conferred on a thing whose existence and prosperity are not of ultimate value" (Raz 1986, 177).

An additional problem that emerges if we accept P4 is the question of how far down the phylogenetic scale obligations to right-holders reach (Norton 1982). If it includes *all* species for instance, then objections similar to those against P1* are relevant. It becomes questionable whether it is even meaningful to speak of rights, not to mention that it would lead to paralysis of actions to satisfy one's needs, even subsistence needs, as we would have to consider an infinite chain of other claimants (Norton 1982, 333). It therefore seems unlikely to support RoN, even if intrinsic value of nature and its radical otherness can perhaps provide us with *other* reasons for acting. But those reasons are not justified by appeals to rights. It is difficult to categorize P4 in term of the taxonomy of problematic assumptions and implications listed above, but it seems to propose other criteria for rights other than conventional ones, which entails faulty assumption 1, and it also risks rendering rights trivial, which entails problematic implication 4.

The Theological Argument

One of the more curious arguments for RoN could be labeled the theological argument. It is somewhat similar to, although more conditional than, P1* above (Chapron et al. 2019: Vatican 2015). It could perhaps be formulated as follows:

P5: rights are granted to those entities that are valuable, or have a special status, in different religions. Nature has such a status.

We find an example in Pope Francis' address to the U.N. which invoked the rights of nature based on two grounds: 1) that we are a part of nature, and so harm done to the environment "is harm done to humanity," and 2) because all living creatures have intrinsic value, in their existence, life, beauty, and interdependence with other creatures (Vatican 2015). The second reason faces objections similar to those that confronted P1* and P4 above. The first reason does not really affirm RoN, but rather states that such rights are contingent on the rights of humans, since we are a part of nature. Harming the environment would constitute harm to other humans; that is, harm to non-controversial right-holders. A right *to* nature for conventional right-holders should not be conflated with RoN.

Chapron et al. make the somewhat curious statement that "rights arguments stem from religion or spirituality," and that "enlightenment human rights theories often identified the biblical God as a source of human rights" (Chapron et al. 2019, 1392). The latter is patently false if by "enlightenment" they mean the type of philosophy recognizing reason as the sole authority. Immanuel Kant is instructive in this regard, calling religious matters "the most pernicious and disgraceful" of all the forms of immaturity that the enlightenment would remove, instead basing duties on reason (Kant 1996).

There is no reason why one should not confer a higher status on some entities that are specifically valuable to a group or to correct past wrongs. Such was the motivation for granting rights to the Ganges River in India, as well as the Whanganui River in New Zealand (O'Donnell & Talbot-Jones 2018). However, those rights are contingent on the interests and faith of human groups, not conferred directly on the object, or based on a status or characteristics that make the object a right-holder by its own merits. Similarly, some arguments advocate RoN by appeal to their supposed consistency with the worldview of indigenous and local people (Chapron et al. 2019). However, respect for the worldview of indigenous and local people does not require the adoption of RoN. Rather, such respect is consistent with conventional views of regarding natural persons as right-holders and recognizing that some things, such as for instance a river, hold a special status for a significant number of people. But this can be accommodated by conventional accounts of right-holders and does not require RoN *per se*. To put this more clearly, it might follow from RoN that a specific river is worthy of greater protection should it have rights. However, that conclusion may follow for other reasons and does not necessarily require accepting RoN. That the river is worthy of increased protection may follow from its special status to a community, or from the rights of an indigenous group, assuming the river holds a special status for them. Given that the acceptance of RoN comes with many additional costs, as suggested above, there is good reason to rely more closely on such conventional conceptualizations of right-holders, which do not bring such costs.

Some Possible Reasons to Refute the Overall Argument

Despite the discussion above, we may not be ready to accept my argument and conclude that there are good reasons to, if not reject, then at least be very skeptical about, RoN. One objection is that RoN primarily concerns *legal*, not *moral*, rights. This point also concerns the criteria in the taxonomy of faulty assumptions (1-4), namely that the criteria are not as conventional and do not have the same authority for establishing something as a right-holder. However, I believe that the criteria are some of the most robust criteria for assessing right-holders. For instance, autonomy and agency are both central to will theories of rights, according to which rights have the function of protecting the autonomy of agents (Kramer, Simmonds, & Steiner 2002; see Kagan 2019). Interests, on the other hand, provide a foundation for both legal rights (Raz 1986) and animal rights (Regan 2004) and provide the foundation for interest theories of rights (Waldron 2016). Dignity, on the other hand, refers to Kant's notion of substitutable value and which ones are above such tradeoffs (Kant 1997). Furthermore, these criteria are also quite generous. For example, animals can be accommodated by appeal to autonomy (Kagan 2019), interests (Regan 2004), and dignity (Korsgaard 2018). Including such disparate criteria, which are commonly separated, such as the usual divide between will and interest theories of rights, provides completeness. However, when we find that the propositions discussed above are insufficient in light of these criteria, despite their completeness, this is a strong signal that RoN provide an unsatisfactory position.

But the charge does not end solely with criteria such as autonomy, interests, or dignity. As is well known, and indeed a philosophical issue unto itself, legal and moral rights differ. It could be argued that the criteria are sufficient, because they primarily apply to moral rights, whereas RoN concern legal rights. Roughly, the distinction between these two types of rights can be made useful by examining how each type of right is warranted. Legal rights depend on appeal to convention and consistency with materials such as precedents and constitutions. In contrast, moral rights are validated by appeal to valid moral principles (Regan 2004). For instance, environmental ethicist Paul W. Taylor states that animals and plants have legal rights "in those societies whose legal systems contain laws that protect their good in various ways," but that they do not have legal rights in the absence of such laws, and he rejects the idea that animals and plants have *moral* rights (Taylor 2011, 224, 246 ff.). He bases this conclusion on four criteria for being a bearer of moral rights, none of which is fulfilled in the case of individual plants and animals: 1) a right-holder is a moral agent, 2) there is a necessary connection between being a right-holder and self-respect, in the sense of regarding itself as a person of inherent worth, or others doing so, 3) it must make sense to say that a being is able to choose to exercise its right, and 4) a bearer of moral rights has certain second-order entitlements, such as claims to restitution or justified grievance for the violation of one's rights, in virtue of being a right-holder (Taylor 2011, 246 ff.). Of course, none of this this precludes individual animals and plants from being worthy of respect, but that respect does not necessitate or justify the ascription of rights. Furthermore, Taylor also argues that societies which recognize legal rights for wild animals will more completely cohere with valid moral principles (Taylor 2011, 224). This observation is relevant because appeals to moral philosophy are warranted in the cases where a corpus of rules and existing legal material such as constitutions, conventions, and precedents provide uncertain guidance (Dworkin 2019). Given that RoN involves a revolution in law (Boyd 2017; Chapron et al. 2019), they lack precedents and the existing corpus of legal rules is ill-suited to support or accommodate RoN. Therefore, appeals to moral rights are warranted to make a reasonable case for RoN. But, as argued above, this appeals fail and moral philosophy is unable to validate RoN.

One final objection to the argument is that we should maintain RoN for pragmatical reasons, in order to strengthen environmental legal protections. It is an unfortunate misconception to identify the set of entities owed respect with the set of entities that are right-holders, and to equal the distinction of "rights" and "no rights" with "moral standing" and "no moral standing" or "valuable" and "worthless". The concept of "moral standing" is not equivalent to the concept of rights. Right-holders, surely, deserve specific forms of respect, such as respect for their claims or liberties. Legal right-holders generate an even more specific form of respect, which is recognized in law. But there are *other* reasons for respect and reverence. For instance, intrinsic values provide us with reasons to care for the good of an entity, even if it has no rights. Investigating the reasons that make sense of our intuitive judgment that nature, and individual organisms within nature, are owed respect, and how they should be valued, is a key task of environmental ethics. But environmental ethics do not necessitate rights of nature, as suggested by environmental ethicist Richard Routley:

> An environmental ethic does not commit one to the view that natural objects such as trees have rights [...] For moral prohibitions forbidding certain actions with respect to an object do not award that object a correlative right. [...] Thus, although any person may have a right by no

> means every living thing can (significantly) have rights, and arguably most sentient objects other than persons cannot have rights.
>
> (Routley 1973, 209)

Acknowledging wrongs does not necessitate an appeal to rights. Given that it is most likely difficult to accommodate RoN within rights-based jurisprudence, and given that RoN is ill-suited for our conception of moral rights, it is questionable whether rights is an appropriate norm to employ when it comes to nature and natural objects. Furthermore, we already have *other* reasons to care for nature and natural objects that do not necessitate rights, so the difficult task of defending RoN is merely redundant.

Ultimately, the attempt to make RoN reasonable comes at a price. That price is the risk of trivializing the very concept of rights. Alternatively, the price is to accept a very complex system of faulty assumptions and problematic implications (1-4). When other, simpler arguments can fulfill the task of providing reasons as to why environmental protection ought to be strengthened, there remains little reason to defend RoN. Rejecting RoN does not entail accepting that only humans have rights. There are good reasons to believe that animals have rights, to various extents (Regan 2004; Taylor 2011; Korsgaard 2018; Kagan 2019). Rejecting RoN, however, does mean rejecting an overly expansive accounts of rights.

Concluding Remark

This chapter has sought to analyze the strength of some common arguments in favor of RoN. The propositions can be shown to involve a range of faulty assumptions and problematic implications (1-4), which leave little reason to have confidence in RoN. Most arguments in support of RoN, as discussed above above, entail faulty assumption 1, by assuming a substantial plasticity of rights. This is consistent with the "revolutionary" character of RoN, in that it seeks foundations for RoN that appeal to criteria other than those established in the corpus of legal rules and ethical theory. However, some common arguments, such as P2 with its appeal to interests, entail faulty assumption 2, insofar as it assumes that conventional properties for identifying right-holders can be flexible enough to also include natural entities and processes.

If it is correct that conferring legal and/or moral rights on nature and natural objects is unlikely to succeed in any meaningful way, then it would be better to strengthen other arguments in favor of stronger environmental protection. After all, if strong arguments can be provided for environmental protection, even without appeal to rights, then legislative and regulatory bodies have good reasons to support this. In other words, we should strengthen and apply ethical arguments in favor of environmental protection, rather than attempt to awkwardly modify a certain normative and legal concept in order to also include nature.

Acknowledgment

I would like to thank the editors Daniel Corrigan and Markku Oksanen, as well as Helena Siipi and the participants of the philosophy seminar at the University of Turku, who have given comments on earlier versions of this chapter.

Notes

1 I would like to thank Helena Siipi for pointing this out.
2 For a critical discussion on the substantive requirement, see Raz (1979). See Dworkin (2019) for a discussion on ethical aspects in law and jurisprudence.
3 See Kurki (2017, 140 ff.) for a critical discussion.
4 See also Stone (2010, 168 ff.) where this is clarified.
5 For an instructive and critical discussion on the notion of goal-directedness as meriting moral relevance, see Cahen (1988).
6 An additional possibility, which will not be discussed here is that if RoN cannot be accepted due to natural objects failing to fulfill the necessary conditions for being right-holders, then neither should corporations have rights since they also fail to fulfill these conditions. However, there are some differences between the environment and corporations, identified by Feinberg (1974) that will be discussed below.
7 See for instance ch. 6 § 3 of The Swedish Environmental Code. https://www.riksdagen.se/sv/dokument-lagar/dokument/svensk-forfattningssamling/miljobalk-1998808_sfs-1998-808 (19 March 2019).
8 Both Chapron et al. (2019), and NGOs such as the Swedish LODYN make such appeals. See LODYN (2019).
9 See Sandler (2012) for an instructive overview of intrinsic values.

References

Boyd, D. R. (2017) *The Rights of Nature: A Legal Revolution That Could Save the World*. ECW Press, Toronto, Canada.

Bunzl, M. (2015) *Uncertainty and the Philosophy of Climate Change*. Routledge, New York.

Cahen, H. (1988) "Against the Moral Considerability of Ecosystems" *Environmental Ethics*, 10, 195–216.

Callicott, J. B. (2013) *Thinking Like a Planet: The Land Ethic and the Earth Ethic*. Oxford University Press, Oxford.

Chapron, G., Epstein, Y., & López-Bao, J. V. (2019) "A Right Revolution for Nature" *Science*, 363, 1392–1393.

Dewey, J. (1926) "The Historic Background of Corporate Legal Personality" *Yale Law Journal*, 35, 655–673

Dworkin, R. (2019) *Taking Rights Seriously*. Bloomsbury Group, London.

Elliot, R. (1997) *Faking Nature: The Ethics of Environmental Restoration*. Routledge, London.

Feinberg, J. (1974) "The Rights of Animals and Unborn Generations" in Blackstone, W. T. (ed.), *Philosophy & Environmental Crisis*. University of Georgia Press, Athens, GA, 43–68.

Gordon, G. J. (2018) "Environmental Personhood" *Columbia Journal of Environmental Law*, 43, 49–91.

Johnson, L. E. (1991) *A Morally Deep World: An Essay on Moral Significance and Environmental Ethics*. Cambridge University Press, Cambridge.

Kagan, S. (2019) *How to Count Animals: More or Less*. Oxford University Press, Oxford.

Kant, I. (1996) "An Answer to the Question 'What is Enlightenment?'" in Gregor, M. J., & Wood, A. W. (eds.), *Immanuel Kant: Practical Philosophy*. Cambridge University Press, Cambridge, 11–22.

Kant, I. (1997) *Groundwork of the Metaphysics of Morals*. Cambridge University Press, Cambridge.

Korsgaard, C. M. (2018) *Fellow Creatures: Our Obligations to the Other Animals*. Oxford University Press, Oxford.

Kramer, M. H., Simmonds, N. E., & Steiner, H. (2002) *A Debate Over Rights: Philosophical Enquiries*. Oxford University Press, Oxford.

Kurki, V. (2017) *A Theory of Legal Personality*. PhD Dissertation, Clare Hall, Cambridge University.

La Follette, C., & Maser, C. (2017) *Sustainability and the Rights of Nature*. Taylor & Francis Group, New York.

LODYN (2019) "Frågor och svar om naturens rättigheter" [FAQ on Nature's Rights]. Available online: http://www.lodyn.se/fragor-och-svar-om-naturens-rattigheter/ (28 March 2019).

Næss, A. (2002) *Life's Philosophy: Reason and Feeling in a Deeper World*. University of Georgia Press, Athens, GA.

Norton, B. (1982) "The Rights of Future Generations" *Environmental Ethics*, 4, 319–337.

O'Donnell, E. L., & Talbot-Jones, J. (2018) "Creating Legal Rights for Rivers: Lessons from Australia, New Zealand, and India" *Ecology & Society*, 23. doi: 10.5751/ES-09854-230107

Raz, J. (1979) "The Rule of Law and Its Virtue" in Raz, J. (ed.), *The Authority of Law*. Oxford University Press, Oxford. DOI: 10.1093/acprof:oso/9780198253457.001.0001

Raz, J. (1986) *The Morality of Freedom*. Clarendon Press, Oxford.

Regan, T. (2004) *The Case for Animal Rights*. Chicago University Press, Chicago, IL.

Rolston, H. (2012) *A New Environmental Ethics?* Routledge, New York.

Routley, R. (1973) "Is There a Need for a New, an Environmental, Ethic?" *Proceedings of the XVth World Congress of Philosophy*. Sofia Press, Varna, Bulgaria, 205–210.

Sandler, R. (2012) *The Ethics of Species*. Cambridge University Press, Cambridge.

Siipi, H. (2017) "Unnatural Kinds: Biodiversity and Human-Modified Entities" in Garson, J., Plutynski, A., & Sarkar, S. (eds.), *The Routledge Handbook of Philosophy of Biodiversity*. Routledge, London, 125–138.

Stone, C. (1972) "Should Trees Have Standing: Toward Legal Rights for Natural Objects" *Southern California Law Review*, 45, 450–501.

Stone, C. (1987) *Earth and Other Ethics*. Harper and Row, New York.

Stone, C. (2010) *Should Trees Have Standing?: Law, Morality, and the Environment*, 3rd ed. Oxford University Press, Oxford.

Taylor, P. W. (2011) *Respect for Nature 25th Anniversary Edition*. Princeton University Press, Princeton, NJ.

Te Awa Tupua Act (2017). Available online: http://www.legislation.govt.nz/bill/government/2016/0129/latest/DLM6830851.html?src=qs (25 March 2019).

The Rights of Nature (2019) "Thomas Berry's Ten Principles of Jurisprudence" Available online: http://therightsofnature.org/thomas-berrys-ten-principles-of-jurisprudence/ (29 March 2019).

Toledoans for Safe Water (2019) "Safe Water Toledo" Available online: https://lakeerieaction.wixsite.com/safewatertoledo (28 March 2019).

Varner, G. E. (1998) *In Nature's Interests: Interests, Animal Rights, and Environmental Ethics*. Oxford University Press, Oxford.

Vatican (2015) "Address of the Holy Father to the UN General Assembly" Available online: http://w2.vatican.va/content/francesco/en/speeches/2015/september/documents/papa-francesco_20150925_onu-visita.html (20 March 2019).

Waldron, J. 2016, "The Rule of Law" *The Stanford Encyclopedia of Philosophy* (Fall 2016 edition), Edward N. Zalta (ed.) Available online: https://plato.stanford.edu/archives/fall2016/entries/rule-of-law/ (5 April 2019).

Woods, M. (2017) *Rethinking Wilderness*. Broadview Press, Peterborough, CA.

11 Close Reading Stone

Investigating the Seminal Article

Markku Oksanen and Anne Kumpula

Introduction

Most contributors in this book refer to the groundbreaking text of the field, "Should Trees Have Standing? Toward Legal Rights for Natural Objects" (hereafter, "Trees"), authored by California law professor Christopher D. Stone. Stone's influential idea about rights of nature was originally a classroom thought experiment that led to reflection on the reasonableness and possibility of expanding the community of right-holders (Stone 2010, xi). The article has been widely read in both academia (first in law,[1] later in philosophy and political theory[2]) and among the bigger audience in its trade book form (1974). There has been a slightly increasing trend of citations of the article in debates on environmental ethics and policy.[3] In 1978, prominent conservation biologist David Ehrenfeld suggested, with reference to Stone, that "the idea of rights conferred by other-than-human existence is becoming increasingly popular (and is meeting with increasing resistance)" (Ehrenfeld 1978, 208). In keeping with Ehrenfeld's observation, one of the main reasons for citing "Trees" has been its presentation of an ideal type position that is to be rejected or praised; unlike many other landmark articles, there seem to be no real rivalries over its interpretation. Another notable reason for citing the article is non-literal use of the key phrase as a catchy expression that can promote the public reflection on, and the transformation of, the moral relationship between human beings and the natural world (e.g. Nash 1989), despite certain doubts—for example, J. L. Sax characterized it "as a form of verbal overkill" (1973, 83n37) and Holmes Rolston III as "linguistically odd" (1975, 110). In general, as Stone himself put it, the academic significance of "Trees" has been "quite out of proportion to its actual impact on the courts" (Stone 2010, xi), considering the fact that U.S. lawyers have filed thousands of environmental suits over the years (Stone 2010, xvi, 159 ff.).[4]

After the turn of the millennium, however, there have been developments in different parts of the world and within different legal traditions that adopt Stone's idea in actual legislation or through judicial decisions, either as a general idea or granting specific rights to specific natural entities and processes, as discussed in various chapters of this book and elsewhere (see e.g. Rühs & Jones

2016; Clark et al. 2018; Chapron et al. 2019). Rather than examine the drivers and rationale behind the renaissance of this idea and the difficulties in operationalizing it (without disturbing compromises), the purpose of this chapter is to return to Stone's original article and to "close read" it because of its role as a primary source of inspiration.

To read closely, for our purposes, means that we want to understand the sources and consequences of its continual attraction by studying the text itself and by setting it within the larger intellectual climate of the era (cf. Rodman 1977). We employ "close reading"[5] mainly as an expression to emphasize our focus—Stone's original text and the historical context in which it was written—and the nature of our approach—historical and analytical, rather than solely critical. We also shed some light on the argumentative and rhetorical strategies that Stone uses by comparing them to those appearing in the secondary literature; especially we consider the applicability of Thomas Kuhn's notion of paradigm to understand the nature of the change concerning the implementation of rights of nature. Finally, we want to understand how he makes the idea of the rights of non-human entities plausible and appealing both to those readers who otherwise tend to be skeptical about the unorthodox use of the concept of rights and to those who reject the language of rights because of its centrality to liberal and libertarian thinking and see "rights" as belonging to ecologically harmful metanarratives or ideologies (for example, see Angstadt and Hourdequin in this book). Our way of proceeding is to ask six questions in six sections, to reflect on them, and to flesh out which branches are living and which are not in "Trees."

Are You Serious, Professor Stone?

Given the forum of publication in an academic journal and the author's credentials as a law professor, it may seem unnecessary to reflect on the genre of the text. However, both the historical context and the words Stone uses warrant asking this question. Let us consider it while at the same time introducing the structure of "Trees."

"Trees" consists of two short introductory sections and two exploratory sections. The third and most fundamental section sets up the foundations for operationalizing rights of nature in law. This is the section that has raised issues regarding environmental policy. Stone manages to formulate a kind of research agenda that covers the key issue of what it means for a natural object to be a holder of legal rights. This agenda touches upon the trickiest question: can or should the rights of natural objects be made redundant (cf. Baard in this book)? Stone answers negatively and explicates his intuition in the final paragraph of the section as follows:

> If my sense of these influences is correct, then a society in which it is stated, however vaguely, that 'rivers have legal rights' would evolve a different legal system than one which did not employ that expression, even

> if the two of them had, at the start, the very same 'legal rules' in other respects.
>
> ("Trees" 489)

Of course, most of the critical discussion on the rights of nature concentrates on examining how environmental regulation and policies might change and—nowadays also—have changed after attributing legal rights to natural objects. Since there are new laws and actual cases in various countries, this can be a subject of empirical legal research rather than a topic of mere speculation. One of those changes that Stone emphasizes is to part ways with the "homocentric" (i.e. anthropocentric) perspective of the natural world and with a legal system that "is engaged in the process of *creating* monetary worth" of natural objects ("Trees" 476).

Let us return to the first section of "Trees." It provides an account of moral progress and the expansion of the scope of right-holders. Here Stone paints a picture according to which the current normative landscape is not an unalterable natural, or brute, fact, but instead results from certain historical and legal developments. It is followed by a brief statement of the intent of the article, that he is "quite seriously" defending the rights of nature. What does "quite seriously" mean—half-seriously or tongue-in-cheek seriously or fully and genuinely seriously? The last option is probably the best way to read the article, despite the existence of much earlier satirical literature of which Stone—unlike his contemporaries in Australia—seems to be unaware. Most notably, in the late 18th century, the English (and the French[6]) discussion about women's rights was ridiculed—or even silenced as antithetical to "commonsense" —by claiming that it would lead to attributing rights to "brutes"; the Australian philosopher Peter Singer opens his *Animal Liberation* (Singer 1975) with a reference to the late 18th-century English philosopher Thomas Taylor, and earlier Singer's compatriot John Passmore had employed the same reference to characterize the historic use as "ironic" (Passmore 1974, 115).[7] More philosophically, the claim is that expanding the community of right-holders from "free men" to all human adults will lead us down a slippery slope. On the other hand, as part of the Romantic movement, numerous poets and writers did take a non-ironic, if not "provocative, prejudice-dispelling of sympathy," approach to non-human animals (Perkins 2007, 5), using the language of rights.

In fiction and some other genres of literary self-expression, it is notoriously difficult to know with certainty what is the intended meaning and tone of the text. When it comes to academic writing, the default assumption is that the author is serious and honest and should be read accordingly. There are exceptions in academic writings, but Stone's article is not such a case; it is a professional and scholarly piece of work, or a lawyer's article.

Didn't You Know About Your Colleagues, Professor Stone?

It is typical to think of Stone's article as an original contribution, although Stone himself reminds us that everyone "should always be prepared to discover one's [own] unoriginality" (Stone 2010, xi). Whether original or not, Stone's examination of the rights of non-human objects as an environmental policy instrument and as a cultural critique is sophisticated, and thus is deserving of its place in the canon of environmental literature. Nevertheless, he was influenced by the intellectual climate of the era.

To begin with, Stone came to the profession in the early 1960s when the United States was becoming the worldwide leader of environmental policies and, following the publication of Rachel Carson's *The Silent Spring* (1962), modern environmentalism as an ideology and movement started to emerge. This era produced many legal innovations that have been copied and refined in countries around the world, and that have hampered and even been rescinded by conservative U.S. governments from the Reagan administration on. These laws include the Clean Air Act (1963), the Wilderness Act (1964), the National Environmental Policy Act (NEPA 1970), the Clean Water Act (1972), and the Endangered Species Act (1973). Viewed from a distance (historically and geographically), the climate encouraged innovation; an environmentally concerned academic did not have to concentrate on defending earlier legal reforms, but rather, could unapologetically put forward seemingly crazy ideas. Most of these innovations were, however, human-centered and political (cf. Andrews 1999, 253, on the experimental nature of the U.S. environmental policy in the 1970s). For instance, in her classic work, Carson claims that people have the right to know, in this case, about the harmful consequences of DDT and other pesticides. When Carson presented her bid, the right to know was not actual legislation as it appears today in domestic and international legislation, such as the Aarhus convention (1998). Without the right to know, it can be difficult to operationalize the rights of nature framework because it presupposes the expansion of the scope of standing and it made access to information crucial in environmental battles both in the political arenas and in the courtrooms (see chapters by Gutman and by Angstadt and Hourdequin in this book; cf. Oksanen & Kumpula 2013; Andrews 1999, 240–242). Respectively, with a reference to NEPA, Stone points out that "What the environment must look for is that its interests be taken into account in subtler, more procedural ways" ("Trees" 483).

Stone's first degree was in philosophy (BA at Harvard 1959). However, to study and do philosophy was essentially insular until the 1970s if not longer. This becomes apparent with the lack of references to philosophers who were Stone's contemporaries. In addition to the aforementioned Singer and Passmore, a third Australian, Richard Routley, an eco-radical and idiosyncratic philosopher, explicitly states that the dominant rights discourse is plainly anthropocentric. In the search for "a new, an environmental ethic," Routley considered it possible that "an environmental ethic does not commit one to the view that natural objects such as trees [sic!] have rights" (Routley 1973). Based on "Trees," it appears Stone is unfamiliar with the contemporary discussion in Australia; and no wonder, since in the early 1970s, geographical distances isolated scholars from each other and historical texts were not available online

(Godfrey-Smith 2019). The same account applies to the Norwegian philosopher Arne Naess and his concerns with ecocatastrophe that motivated the development of Deep Ecology from the late 1960s on (Rothenberg 1989, 1–2). He occasionally employs the language of rights in his ecosophical vision: to cite the 1989 English translation, Naess argues, beyond the rights of animals, for "the right of all forms to live" as "a universal right" (Naess 1989, 166). Finally, the same ignorance applies even to Stone's own compatriots. In 1971, a well-known philosophical meeting took place at the University of Georgia to discuss the "environmental crisis" (Blackstone 1974). One of the participants was the legal philosopher Joel Feinberg, whose article on the rights of various non-paradigmatic entities appeared in the proceedings and became a classic in the field. Feinberg's interest-based theory of rights made it conceptually possible that individual animals could have rights, but plants, species, and non-individual natural entities could not have rights (Feinberg 1974). (Holmes Rolston's first contribution to environmental ethics also touches upon rights of nature, but not affirmatively [Rolston 1975].) This lack of references in "Trees" is conspicuous and interesting in regard to the historiography of environmentalist ideas. More specifically, the early development of philosophical research on environmental issues seems to have emerged independently in places unconnected to each other, but it is Stone's article around which more recent debate and theorization has evolved. This is significant from the perspective of environmental ethics, where the idea of rights of nature has either been rejected (Norton 1984; Taylor 1986) or has played no key role in theory building (with the notable exception of animal ethics and green political theory).

There is another side of the coin, however, and the simultaneous emergence of environmental philosophical study could be seen as an indication of certain commonalities regarding starting points, or the existence of "normal science,"[8] should the following observation from Kuhn (1962/2012, 65) apply to the emergence of environmentalism:

> The very fact that a significant scientific novelty so often emerges simultaneously from several laboratories is an index both to the strongly traditional nature of normal science and to the completeness with which that traditional pursuit prepares the way for its own change.

The emergence of environmentalism in several isolated and distinct places can be understood against a background constituted by the transfer of ideas from evolution and ecology into philosophy and law and the global interest in Carson's work. The foundations of this background were laid by naturalist authors such as George Perkins Marsh, Charles Darwin, and Ernst Haeckel in the latter half of the 19th century, and were later complemented by Gustaf Arrhenius' ideas about the possibility of global warming. The science of ecology began to spread and took shape as a discipline in the first decade of the 20th century, led several decades later to the formation of conservation biology as "a crisis discipline" (Soulé 1985).

The title of the final section of Stone's article is one that current readers may find ambiguous and somewhat bizarre: "the psychic and socio-psychic aspects." This characterization also applies to the content of this section, which has nothing to do with the paranormal, clairvoyance, or occultism, but rather, to the other primary meaning of "psychic" referring to historical mentalities or cultural atmosphere. Nevertheless, this section is rarely mentioned in the secondary literature. As Stone later stressed the rapidity of the writing process, the result is like a stream of consciousness of almost anything Stone considers relevant to capturing the environmentalist atmosphere, or *zeitgeist*, of the era and the formation of environmental consciousness. In addition, it passingly covers such topical issues as overpopulation, economic growth, and improvements in the standard of living.

Fundamentally, the article falls conveniently into a new line of thinking that critically assesses the anthropocentric view that "nature exists *for men*" ("Trees" 489; in the 2010 edition *men* has been replaced with the non-sexist expression *humans*). In retrospect, the line of thinking is consistent with now-classic authors—besides the philosophers mentioned earlier—such as Aldo Leopold, Carson, Lynn White Jr., and Garrett Hardin, none of whom are referred to in the article.[9] But, in all fairness to Stone, he was a forerunner within his own discipline. There were very limited opportunities to know about the activities of these other academics working outside of legal scholarship. Furthermore, if we ignore the much older debate on animal rights and recognize that the article was written prior to the publication of the first systematic philosophical analyses of the environmental crisis, we can see that it shares a sort of eclecticism or essayistic characteristics with many other publications of the era; in other words, the field had yet to be established or to take the form of a normal science.

Are You Revolutionary, Professor Stone?

The political and legal objectives of "Trees" are rather straightforward. Stone suggests that "natural objects" should have a right to sue and to speak for themselves in court, so as to have an opportunity to defend their fundamental interests against humans whose actions threaten to damage them. This means a natural object can obtain a kind of quasi-agency in the legal process, and due to this status, may obtain immunity against affective human actions if the court decides to grant it. "Standing [i.e. having rights] does nothing but get you through the courthouse door," as Stone (1987, 10) puts it in *Earth and Other Ethics*, his main contribution to environmental ethical theory. In court, the interests of non-human right-holders can be defended and advanced by their proxies or representatives, since trees, lakes, and rocks—just like certain human groups—are incapable of bringing suit on their own behalf. In this respect, their agency is not full agency and their legal capacity is limited. At the same time, Stone gives the impression that his theory is an alternative to the prevailing anthropocentrism, and one that is novel and radical: it provides "... a new conception of man's relationship to the rest of nature" ("Trees" 495).

Although an early commentator John Rodman (1977, 95) dubbed Stone's idea "tame," many contemporary commentators see it differently and stress that Stone's main idea is a request for change. But what should change and how? For Stone, as for most other environmentalists, the idea of conservation is to protect those elements and processes in nature that are threatened by human endeavors and vulnerable to harm and irrecoverable damage. Thus, Stone seems to argue for conservativism with respect to the natural world: "In order to protect ourselves, therefore, we ought to be conservative now in our treatment of nature. I agree" ("Trees" 490). "Conservative" may mean to be cautious, but it may also mean to preserve. To be a "bioconservative" is to be critical of many human practices and institutions that enable and justify a wide variety of nature-affecting activities. Thus, it is these acts, practices, and institutions that may harm nature that should be amended; it is revolutionary with respect to existing practices and institutions.[10] (Cf. Gutman's chapter in this book on the concept of *ch'ixi* in Andean indigenous thinking.)

In contemporary environmental policy, there are numerous terms denoting change; consider "transition" and "transformation," or kindred terms such as "(co)evolution," "(co)creation," "(co)development," or even "(policy) innovation." All of them articulate a search for changes in the human domain, legal novelties, or new policy instruments or institutions. Nevertheless, more hyperbolic statements of Stone's proposal appear frequently. Time and again the idea of rights of nature has been seen as "revolutionary" (e.g. Boyd 2017) with regard to the human/nature relationship and, more academically, as a paradigm shift or, at least, as having "paradigm-shifting potential" (see Angstadt and Hourdequin in this book). The term "paradigm" was made famous by Kuhn a decade earlier, but at the same time is extremely ambiguous; in general, those who share paradigm commit themselves "to the same rules and standards of scientific practice."[11] For example, in Earth jurisprudence and a number of publications influenced by Stone's article, the Kuhnian concepts of paradigm and paradigm shift are widely used. Rühs and Jones (2016) wrote that "our system of laws does not protect the Earth from destruction because that is not its ultimate purpose, and, for this reason, a paradigm shift is needed." The way to do this is through the creation of "substantive constitutional rights of nature" (ibid.).

Stone, however, does not refer to Kuhn's book and does not employ its core vocabulary (not even in his 2010 book). In science as well as in jurisprudence, there are changes that occur over time. Paradigm shifts in science point to the discontinuities and incommensurability between paradigms. Despite the use of the expression, it is not clear whether a legal system can manifest discontinuity, as the legal changes can be more of gradual nature and laws can be even layered. Ultimately, we are faced with the question of whether a full-fledged and clear-cut revolution in society is possible or not. One of us (Oksanen 2014) has endorsed moderate skepticism about such revolutions, but this does not imply that no social change occurs. Also, in legal thought and practice, fundamental and dramatic changes are possible. Accordingly, what was once an unthinkable idea and did not exist became normal. The normative objective of "Trees" is to influence environmental policies and environmental thinking at large, to normalize them as essential parts of national and international legislation. Given this, the Kuhnian vocabulary does not fit conveniently to describe a major legal change.

How to Think the Unthinkable, Professor Stone?

Despite our reservations above, let us think about the Kuhnian concept a bit further. There is a certain affinity between Stone's concept of unthinkable and Kuhn's concept of incommensurability. However, whereas incommensurability may entail insurmountable limits to understanding, to label something unthinkable can increase the likelihood of grasping the idea as a novelty. In other words, Stone is not waiting for a change of paradigm through the death of proponents of the old paradigm, but instead believes these proponents may revise their views through customary scientific argumentation. The introduction of "Trees" with the subtitle "the unthinkable" can be seen to consist of three argumentative components: conceptual soundness and plausibility, change, and normalization.

Let us begin with conceptual soundness and plausibility. Stone writes:

> Throughout legal history, each successive extension of rights to some new entity has been, theretofore, a bit unthinkable. We are inclined to suppose the rightlessness of rightless 'things' to be a decree of Nature, not a legal convention acting in support of some status quo.
>
> ("Trees" 253)

What does "unthinkable" mean? There are at least two possibilities. In a literal sense, unthinkable is something that cannot be thought, that is, is inconceivable and beyond imagination (though in fiction, as we saw earlier, these "beyond imagination" dimensions are being imagined if not upside down). In this sense, humans as rational beings and as language-users, reach the limits of understanding, sometimes due to the limits of language. Stone's use of "unthinkable" is more modest, as it refers to an idea that has not been seriously examined, although it would deserve, in light of the current situation, a serious consideration. From a legal perspective, the rights of nature is an unconventional idea, and to be legally viable, numerous changes would have to be made to the law and legal procedures, but there may be reasons that justify such a change. From the perspective of common morality, as a part of ordinary persons' moral resources, the attribution of rights to non-human entities is an expedient move—having rights can indicate that there are limits to the treatment of an entity and that the entity has value in its own right. Such a use of "rights" is, of course, problematic for those who rigidly want to endorse the established legal meaning of "rights." Due to the history of the concept, new developments should not be rejected without closer examination.

The opening sentence of "Trees" makes a reference to Darwin and his naturalistic account of the emergence of sociality and our capacity to sympathize with the animal kingdom. The scope of moral concern has expanded from one's own family and children, to members of one's own community, to society at large—this can be understood as the progress, or the evolution or perfection, of morality. Here one can spot a fundamental difference between Stone and Kuhn: for Kuhn, there is no linear progress in science, whereas the expansion of the scope of ethical concern standardly is linear, as previous conceptions are not being rejected but improved.

The paradigm subjects of human concern are naturally the existing living beings, or natural persons. From the 19th century on, there emerged a category of legal persons that extends beyond natural persons, to include things such as trusts, firms, municipalities and towns, and states. All of these are capable of having rights (and duties). Stone points out, "The world of the lawyer is peopled with inanimate right-holders" ("Trees" 252). These collective agents are legally recognized actors whose rights have consolidated through time and who thus became familiar elements in the social reality, despite the fact that each change in the course of time might have been deemed impossible prior to its realization. For those who lived before the emergence of the category of "legal person," it can be difficult to understand them—they were an anomaly to be contrasted with the rights of "natural persons." The modern (western) legal system is secular in principle; Rodman (1977, 92) characterizes Stone as "a kind of legal existentialist/pragmatist with no fixed ontology." However, in the late medieval or early modern period, when the rudiments of the modern understanding of law began to emerge, metaphysical conceptions were rather different: for example, issues such as the rights of angels and demons were taken seriously (see Brett 2014, 23).

The first two sections of Stone's article are examples of priming, a concept used in behavioral psychology experiments: the reader is made aware of the history of ideas about right-holders. In light of this awareness, she is better prepared to face the next question, and thus to believe "the unthinkable" may be worthy of consideration.

It is plausible to consider that making the "unthinkable" "thinkable" is an instance of a paradigm shift. But to what extent does Stone's idea embody the Kuhnian concept of "a paradigm shift"? Could the extension of rights to non-humans be just tinkering within normal science?[12] Stone's argumentation is not a radical deviation from all parts of normal science—or legal thinking—but only from the basic assumption of human centrality. His reliance on the discourse of rights is as conventional as would have been reliance on the discourse of resources with regard to natural objects. Moreover, within normal science, the divide between humanity and the rest of nature is as dominant as the divide between right-holders and non-right-holders. Some of these ideas have been questioned in the indigenous adoption of rights of nature, as have been indicated in several chapters in this book.

Stone's argumentative strategy has three aspects:

1) The refutation of conceptual unsoundness: there are already right-holders other than living human individuals
2) The argument from historical examples: the conception of right-holders changes over time
3) The argument from the transformation of values: the conception of right-holders reflects current values; as values change, so does the conception of right-holders. (This element provides the justification for change in Stone's article, although he hardly touches upon it [Rodman 1977, 93])

Overall, Stone's argument rests on the idea of change: laws have been revised, laws are revisable, and the revision of the law is justifiable. Thus, long and established legal tradition is not an obstacle to introducing change and this makes the idea that the meaning of a (legal) concept is permanently fixed unthinkable. The argument from the transformation of values can be understood as showing that the publication and reception of Stone's article provide reasons for expanding the scope of right-holders: they exemplify cultural changes. Of course, this is a very weak argument due to the vast quantity and wide range of views found in academic publishing. However, given that academic publishing tends to be rather conservative, Stone's article might be considered an instance, or signal, of cultural change.

As previously mentioned, the concept of paradigm shift was popular at the time of publication—and still is—but the epistemological distinction between externalism and internalism is also applicable to legal theory. Broadly put, externalists argue that factors external to science influence scientific work and its results; internalists rather claim that scientific truths changes because they are falsified. As to the laws, external factors can affect legal thinking. A contemporary commentator of Stone, Laurence Tribe (1974, 1342), wrote "Acceptance of the notion that some previously 'rightless' entity enjoys legal protection is largely a matter of acculturation." The notion of acculturation refers to adaptation to a new regulation by the subjects of regulation. Stone makes a similar claim when he speculates—as have many expansionist environmental philosophers, such as Tom Regan (1988)—that the expansion of the community of the right-holders is "bound to sound odd or frightening or laughable" (Stone 1972, 455). And then he points to the examples of women, indigenous peoples, and African-Americans in U.S. history. And these examples indicate, though still incomplete, normalization.

How do we recognize cultural change and who makes such changes? There are no simple answers to questions like this, as the drivers of legal and broader cultural changes can be complex. Kuhn points to more detailed socio-historical research when he states that, within a certain segment of the population, the political revolutions are triggered "by a growing sense … that existing institutions have ceased adequately to meet the problems posed by an environment that they have in part created" (Kuhn 1962/2012, 92). Kuhn also describes political revolution as a change "in ways that those institutions themselves prohibit. Their success therefore necessitates the partial relinquishment of one set of institutions in favor of another ..." (Kuhn 1962/2012, 93). Paradoxically, the expansion of the range of rights-holders can be an orderly revolution, a revolution in our relationship with the rest of nature, if done in accordance with the rules that govern constitutional change. Such a revolution is in some sense a tame revolution, but nonetheless welcome.

Is the "Scope Talk" of Rights a Jigsaw Puzzle, Professor Stone?

The British philosopher Timothy Williamson says that "progress in mathematics and science often depends on not *questioning* basic assumptions, but instead building on them. Such activity is 'normal science'..." (2019, 109). Could Stone still be a master of the normal science that he wants to revolutionize? Let's consider the revolutionary dimensions of "Trees" from a different angle. Previously, we expressed some reservations about talk of paradigm change; here we take a broader perspective on political thought. As we see it, Stone's proposal is very specific and some of its essential elements are less revolutionary than is often thought. For example, one might think that rights are just an established concept of early modern natural law and current liberal thought. Furthermore, Stone's approach to policy transformation is not particularly novel, as it relies on established legal structures.

This raises questions about the nature of social revolution more generally. It has frequently been observed that large-scale changes in culture and key institutions do not occur overnight, but instead require long periods of time, and perhaps even several generations, to evolve. With these reservations in mind, we may end up with two contrasting thoughts: on the one hand, one can identify a revolutionary idea, and through the art of persuasion make that idea—and the article itself—appealing to new generations of readers who are more inclined to make the idea not only thinkable but also realizable. On the other hand, a rights-based approach to formulating the normative ideals of the human–nature relationship is still very much working and tinkering within the existing paradigm. As Kuhn writes: "At least in the mature sciences, answers (or full substitutes for answers) to questions like these are firmly embedded in the educational initiation that prepares and licences the student for professional practice" (Kuhn 1962/2012, 5). In law, the creed of the exclusion of non-humans from the community of right-holders has traditionally been a starting point of legal education.

It is easy to think of the issue of membership in the community of rights-holders as a jigsaw puzzle. When we put forward a general, sketchy, and imperfect definition of having rights

All Xs having a property *p* have rights

we end up operationalizing the normative idea of having rights through answering the following more specific questions:

1) *What* property *p* is a sufficient and necessary condition for having rights?
2) *Why* is property *p* a sufficient and necessary condition for having rights?
3) *What* Xs have property *p*? (Or what Xs are right-holders?)

Since the early 1970s, environmental ethics has involved a systematic investigation of these questions (both in legal studies and in applied ethics). The key normative concepts are not limited to rights but include others such as moral considerability, moral significance, moral status, moral standing, moral subject, moral patient, moral agent, and moral person. In 2012, Stone responded to commentators (in a special issue of *Journal of Human Rights and the Environment*) that his goal was to advance the internal consistency of the legal system (Stone 2012, 100). It is easy to read his aims as rather conservative, and making no attempt to change the paradigm. Thus, he uses the established language of rights and suggests relying on the established ways of protecting and advancing one's rights using designated representatives and the courts. As is common with environmental ethical theorists, Stone relies on concepts and institutions that have evolved over centuries: should there be a revolution or a paradigm change, it will occur in an incrementalistic manner, which has sometimes been referred to as "ethical extensionism."

Some of the normative concepts mentioned above are enduring, while others are novel and therefore free of historical burdens that belong to rights discourse. Although assigning rights to nature is not revolutionary due to its conventional key term, rights of nature can be revolutionary when compared to optional frameworks. Namely, if the alternative of rights of nature framework is a human-centered view that justifies the customary ways of thinking and behaving, the rights of nature position rejects it. So, its revolutionary character is relative to other normative frameworks regulating nature-affecting human behavior. More precisely, the revolutionary character of rights of nature depends on its demandingness and its regulatory power in real life, where trade-offs occur and where rights of nature are as open to different interpretations as any other competing rights are.

How Democratic Are You, Professor Stone?

"Trees" is a brainchild of the civil rights movement era and Stone makes connections to it on several occasions. How would the possibility of objects of nature having rights or being legal persons expand, improve, and deepen the democratic dimensions of societal decision-making, if the idea of non-human rights is restricted to the right to sue? This concern is vital, as the early critic of Stone, Joseph L. Sax, pointed out:

> On the standing question, Stone's guardianship theory does not appear to solve the multiple suit and adequacy of representation problems [reference omitted]. For if the interests are wide-ranging enough, no single guardian is likely to defend all of them—distinct and at times conflicting—in a fully satisfactory way. Sports fishing or deer hunting guardians may have rather

> different views from those of wilderness guardians, about the needs of the natural resources they seek to protect.
>
> (Sax 1973, 83n37)

Thus, rivalries over representation arise, giving way to such questions as how to choose the representatives, how to ensure that representatives promote their "clients'" interests, and how to identify and rank competing interests in a legitimate manner. In current environmental laws, some of these questions are tackled by means of not having designated representatives or fixed ranking systems but emphasizing that anyone can act on behalf of a non-human rights-holder. Let us think in light of democratic decision-making. The issue of the democratic nature of environmental policy and the rights of nature approach has three challenges: the composition of the community of right-holders and representation; the role of the courts; and the increasing power of environmental administration.

The composition of the community of right-holders in "Trees" is regarded as resulting from human decisions and practices. Stone is not, it seems, putting forward a theory of natural or moral rights that exist independently of convention. Politically, and if we limit our focus to democratic states, there is a rich discussion on the composition of the demos (that is, who are citizens and/or who should be granted full participation in political decision-making?) and on the nature of democratic processes (how should political decisions be made?). Should trees and other natural objects have a vote or a voice so they can participate in the democratic processes? This will be decided by those who now have democratic rights and who can represent the rightless. Still, very few claim that natural entities should be granted political rights and that we should have a multispecies demos (e.g. Eckersley 2000, 118, on "democracy-of-the-affected"). But if we limit our concern to passive rights or immunities, and we consider that there are rights independent of democratic decisions and the resulting laws, then trees and other natural objects could have standing and be capable of suffering injury. Even then, some commentators believe that legal rights of non-human entities will not be recognized before a wide political consensus has been reached (e.g. Des Jardins 1993, 118). It is rather natural then to limit one's concern to humans and their opportunities and resources for participating in decision-making about the natural world (cf. Tănăsescu in this book).

In some liberal democracies,[13] the translation of the idea of rights of nature into law may not succeed—depending on the jurisdiction—if the idea or its translation into law lacks political support,[14] or they contradict the established legal framework so much so that larger revisions (e.g. in property law) become inevitable. (Since it is difficult to apprehend and foresee all of the implications of implementing a rights of nature regime, this speaks in favor of understanding it as a paradigm change.) Stone does not address this as a political issue; he does not consider whether political decision-making could be a means of enacting new legislation. In "Trees" he treats this as essentially a juridical issue, and the matter of standing as being instituted through legal or administrative action.[15] Stone's main argument attempts to justify the claim that non-human entities have rights that can be defended through legal procedures. This means that he has to answer the question of who can give voice to voiceless nature. This is as much a political as it is a legal issue. From our perspective, the question concerns public participation and participatory environmental governance. Nevertheless, in the early 1970s, discussion about the nature of environmental democracy was just beginning to take shape. For example, the Stockholm Declaration, which was adopted just a few months before Stone wrote his article, does not include participatory rights in the sense that we now understand them and of which the right to bring legal action is just one aspect.

From this standpoint, it is understandable that Stone viewed the issue of representation as a pragmatic problem. Nevertheless, he emphasizes the role of non-governmental organizations (NGOs) as trustees or guardians of nature. The reason for this is interesting; he doubts the ability of government authorities to genuinely defend non-human nature. They are "one of the bogeys of the environmental movement" ("Trees" 472). The role of NGOs is not only to improve the quality of decision-making but also to increase the transparency and civic watching of public agencies. On the other hand, he does not accept the idea of *actio popularis* i.e. a right of private citizens to bring legal action on behalf of nature. According to him, "court economy might be better served by simply designating the guardian de jure representative of the natural object" ("Trees" 470). The guardians of nature must be designated by the court ("Trees" 473). It seems that in "Trees," efficiency is more important than, for example, increasing trust and legitimacy through public participation. Even though rights of nature legislation would be enacted democratically, it creates another potential source of social conflict.

Concluding Remarks

In this chapter, we have taken a closer look at an influential academic article in environmental law and policy, an article that could be called—using today's buzzword—a "game-changer." We have argued that Stone's article is less revolutionary and paradigm-shifting than is often thought. The extension of rights to new entities is rather an organic change or reform. This being said, this is not meant to diminish the possibly growing impact of this fascinating article, which can hopefully serve as a source of inspiration for new generations of readers.

In the contests between rival theories/paradigms, Kuhn portrays the winners as follows:

> They were able to do so because they shared two essential characteristics. Their achievement was sufficiently unprecedented to attract an enduring group of adherents away from competing modes of scientific activity. Simultaneously, it was sufficiently open-ended to leave all sorts of problems for the redefined group of practitioners to resolve.
>
> (Kuhn 1962/2012, 10–11)

As for rights, though there are "paradigm" right-holders, there have always been many controversies over non-paradigmatic humans like fetuses, the comatose, and the severely brain-damaged; the idea of paradigm right-holders is not a fixed concept. In this respect, the idea of rights does not differ from basic (and thin) moral terms, such as good and bad, right and wrong. There will be rivalries.

Overall, there is an irony in the story. Although Stone is a sharp legal thinker whose ideas constitute a promising approach to the environmental predicament, at the same time he is openly cautious about the potential of putting rights of nature into practice. In "Trees" and elsewhere, he emphasizes that to have rights means to have standing and to have standing gives license to file suit. When rights are contradictory, the rights of non-human nature can lose in the court but this should not be regarded as an argument against rights, as conflicts are unavoidable. Nevertheless, access to court is an expression of recognition and may further accelerate the transformation of human attitudes to them. Even if non-human entities win a case, it may have only local implications and fail to produce long-standing transformation of policies and human behavior. Furthermore, laws can be changed, even constitutional rights, but usually, constitutional rights are not taken away once granted. In an article on climate change, Stone states bluntly that even if the climate were granted standing, the problem would not be solved in courtrooms. He writes,

> No litigation, of any sort, is going to have a major impact on climate policy—certainly not any suit on behalf of the 'climate.' The bulk of the efforts will require concerted and cooperative action among nations, of a sort that can be achieved only through diplomacy, legislation, and administrative action.
>
> (Stone 2010, 70; cf. Lazarus 2020)

Saying this may shake the non-lawyer's trust in rights, courts, and strategic litigation for the benefit of the environment, but within environmentalism, the notion of rights—both the rights of non-human nature and the environmental rights of humans—should not be considered a magic concept that can solve all or most problems. It does have a place, and a function, as part of our moral vocabulary and as a moral resource, but it is not omnipotent.

Acknowledgments

We would like to thank Daniel Corrigan, Teea Kortetmäki, and Jani Sinokki for their comments on previous versions of the chapter.

Notes

1 One of the reasons it was cited by lawyers is the ruling of *Sierra Club v. Morton*, in which Justice Douglas refers to it in his dissenting opinion.

2 Despite being anthologized, the place of "Trees" in the canon of environmental ethics and green political theory is not undisputable: for instance, such prominent books as *Oxford Handbook of Environmental Ethics* and *Oxford Handbook of Environmental Political Theory* mention him once. Instead, Stone's defense of ethical pluralism in a series of articles and in *Earth and Other Ethics* (1987) has evoked perhaps more discussion among philosophers.

3 Because "Trees" has been published in several places and editions, it is difficult to count the exact citation numbers. A google.scholar search, based on the original 1972 article provides the following results: in the 1970s there are 169, in the 80s 198, in the 90s 427, in the 00s 469, and in the 10s 984 citations; currently 2409 citations in total (as of December 8, 2020).

4 Again, it is notable that Stone's influence on the U.S. environmental policy seems minimal; for instance, Andrews's (1999) lengthy historical research does not cite Stone.

5 The notion of close reading points to New Criticism in literary theory, which evolved in the mid-20th century. Close reading instructs literary scholars to focus merely on the text under scrutiny and nothing else. We do recognize that New Criticism has features that even contradict the conventional approach to scientific texts. This includes "the intentional fallacy," according to which the meaning of a text is independent of the author's intentions. The other steps outside the original doctrines of New Criticism include our interests in the contextual and genealogical factors and in the reception of "Trees" in academia and its influence on the current rights of nature movement around the world.

6 During the height of the French revolution, the adopted idea of universal rights recognized only citizens as right-holders and only men as citizens. Famously, Olympe de Gouges opposed this and published a declaration of the rights of woman and female citizens in 1791—and there is no irony involved in her story: she was judged guilty of treason and executed.

7 Singer as a utilitarian is, of course, skeptical about the priority of rights in ethical thought; Passmore instead says that, "to suggest that animals, plants, landscapes have a 'right to exist' is to create confusion. The idea of 'rights' is simply not applicable to what is non-human." Passmore justifies this by claiming that humans, non-human organisms and soil are in the ecological sense a community, but not in the moral sense. Being a member of the moral community requires that one must be able to recognize mutual obligations (Passmore 1974/1980, 116). For a more detailed analysis of Thomas Taylor, see Bourke 2011, 170–173; Taylor was also planning to write on the rights of "vegetables and minerals."

8 Kuhn (1962/2012, 10) defines normal science as "research firmly based upon one or more past scientific achievements, achievements that some particular scientific community acknowledges for a time as supplying the foundation for its further practice."

9 Stone mentions that he learned of Leopold's land ethic a few years later (Stone 2010, 177n3).

10 In contrast, the British philosopher Roger Scruton sees environmentalism and conservativism as "natural bedfellows" that share the goal of "husbanding resources and ensuring their renewal." This also requires, among other things, to "keep in place the customs and institutions that place a break on our appetites" (Scruton 2013, 9).

11 Kuhn 1962/2012, 11. Kuhn synonymously uses the concepts of "paradigm shift" (or "paradigm change") and "revolution."

12 More broadly, in environmental and animal ethics, most systematic views are developed within the framework of established theories, be they Aristotelian, utilitarian, Kantian, pluralist, or their combinations; even Naess's (1989) vision of Deep Ecology draws on various sources, such as Baruch Spinoza, Mahatma Gandhi, and Indian philosophies.

13 As has been pointed out earlier in this book, the ways of producing rights of nature are multiple in liberal democracies. In some legal systems, the rights of nature (or animals)

become actual legislation through court decisions, in others it requires a change of law. We have not considered non-democratic political systems here.

14 Some of the lower-level court decisions, referred to also in this book, can be revolutionary and at odds with the majority views but still be adopted as laws.

15 In the 2010 book chapter on climate change and standing, Stone's analysis is much more sophisticated thanks to new legal cases and new legislation. But the fundamentals remain the same: standing has not been defined in the U.S. Constitution or other legislation, but it is part of the Division of Powers to court to decide about it (Stone 2010, 35–36).

References

Andrews, R.N.L. (1999) *Managing the Environment, Managing Ourselves: A History of American Environmental Policy*. Yale University Press, New Haven, CT.

Blackstone, W.T. (1974) "Introduction" in Blackstone, W.T. ed., *Philosophy and the Environmental Crisis*. University of Georgia Press, Athens, 1–9.

Bourke, J. (2011) *What it Means to Be Human*. Virago, London.

Boyd, D.R. (2017) *The Rights of Nature. A Legal Revolution That Could Save the World*. ECW Press, Toronto, ON.

Brett, A.S. (2014) *Changes of State. Nature and the Limits of the City in Early Modern Natural Law*. Princeton University Press, Princeton, NJ.

Chapron, G., Epstein, Y., and Vicente López-Bao, J. (2019) "A Rights Revolution for Nature" *Science*, 363, 1392–1393. doi: 10.1126/science.aav5601

Clark, C., Emmanouil, N., Page, J., and Pelizzoni, A. (2018) "Can You Hear the Rivers Sing: Legal Personhood, Ontology, and the Nitty-Gritty of Governance" *Ecology Law Quarterly*, 45, 787–844.

Des Jardins, J.R. (1993) *Environmental Ethics*. Wadsworth, Belmont, CA.

Ehrenfeld, D. (1978) *The Arrogance of Humanism*. Oxford University Press, Oxford.

Eckersley, R. (2000) "Deliberative Democracy, Ecological Representation and Risk: Towards a Democracy of the Affected" in Saward, M. ed., *Democratic Innovation. Deliberation, Representation and Association*. Routledge, London, 117–132.

Feinberg, J. (1974) "The Rights of Animals and Unborn Generations" in Blackstone, W.T. ed., *Philosophy and the Environmental Crisis*. University of Georgia Press, Athens, GA, 43–68.

Godfrey-Smith, P. (2019) "Australian Philosophy." *Aeon*. https://aeon.co/essays/why-does-australia-have-an-outsized-influence-on-philosophy (accessed 10/30/2020).

Kuhn, T.S. (1962/2012) *The Structure of Scientific Revolutions*. 50th anniversary ed. University of Chicago Press, Chicago, IL.

Lazarus, R.J. (2020) *The Rule of Five. Making Climate History at the Supreme Court*. Belknap Press, Cambridge, MA.

Naess, A. (1989) *Ecology, Community and Lifestyle*. Cambridge University Press, Cambridge.

Nash, R.F. (1989) *The Rights of Nature. A History of Environmental Ethics*. University of Wisconsin Press, Madison, WI.

Norton, B.G. (1984) "Environmental Ethics and Nonhuman Rights" *Environmental Ethics*, 6, 17–36.

Oksanen, M. (2014) "Global Warming and the Critique of Culture" *Ethical Perspectives*, 21, 539–563.

Oksanen, M., and Kumpula, A. (2013) "Transparency in Conservation. Rare Species, Secret Files, and Democracy" *Environmental Politics*, 22, 975–991. doi: 10.1080/09644016.2013.775726.

Passmore, J. (1974/1980) *Man's Responsibility for Nature*. 2nd ed. Duckworth, London.

Perkins, D. (2007) *Romanticism and Animal Rights*. Cambridge University Press, Cambridge.
Regan, T. (1988) *The Case for Animal Rights*. Routledge, London (orig. publ. 1983).
Rodman, J. (1977) "The Liberation of Nature" *Inquiry*, 20, 83–145.
Rolston, H. III (1975) "Is There an Ecological Ethic?" *Ethics*, 85, 93–109.
Rothenberg, D. (1989) "Introduction" in Arne Naess ed., *Ecology, Community and Lifestyle*. Cambridge University Press, Cambridge, 1–22.
Routley, R. (1973) "Is There a Need for a New, an Environmental, Ethic?" *Proceedings of the XVth World Congress of Philosophy*. Sofia, Varna, Bulgaria.
Rühs, N. and Jones, A. (2016) "The Implementation of Earth Jurisprudence through Substantive Constitutional Rights of Nature" *Sustainability* 8, 174. doi: 10.3390/su8020174.
Sax, J.L. (1973) "Standing to Sue: A Critical Review of the Mineral King Decision" *Natural Resources Journal*, 13, 76–88.
Scruton, R. (2013) *Green Philosophy. How to Think Seriously about the Planet*. Atlantic Books, London.
Singer, P. (1975/1990) *Animal Liberation*. New revised edition. Avon Books, New York.
Soulé, M.E. (1985) "What is Conservation Biology?" *Conservation Biology*, 35, 727–734.
Stone, C.D. (1972) "Should Trees Have Standing? Towards Legal Rights for Natural Objects?" *Southern California Law Review*, 45, 450–501.
Stone, C.D. (1974) *Should Trees Have Standing?* William Kaufman, Los Altos, California.
Stone, C.D. (1987) *Earth and Other Ethics: The Case of Moral Pluralism*. Harper and Row, New York.
Stone, C.D. (2010) *Should Trees Have Standing? Law, Morality, and the Environment*. 3rd edition. Oxford University Press, Oxford.
Stone, C.D. (2012) "Response to Commentators." *Journal of Human Rights and the Environment*, 3, 100–120.
Taylor, P.W. (1986) *Respect for Nature. A Theory of Environmental Ethics*. Princeton University Press, Princeton, NJ.
Tribe, L.H. (1974) "Ways Not to Think about Plastic Trees: New Foundations for Environmental Law" *The Yale Law Journal*, 83, 1315–1348.
Williamson, T. (2019) *Doing Philosophy*. Oxford University Press, Oxford.

Index

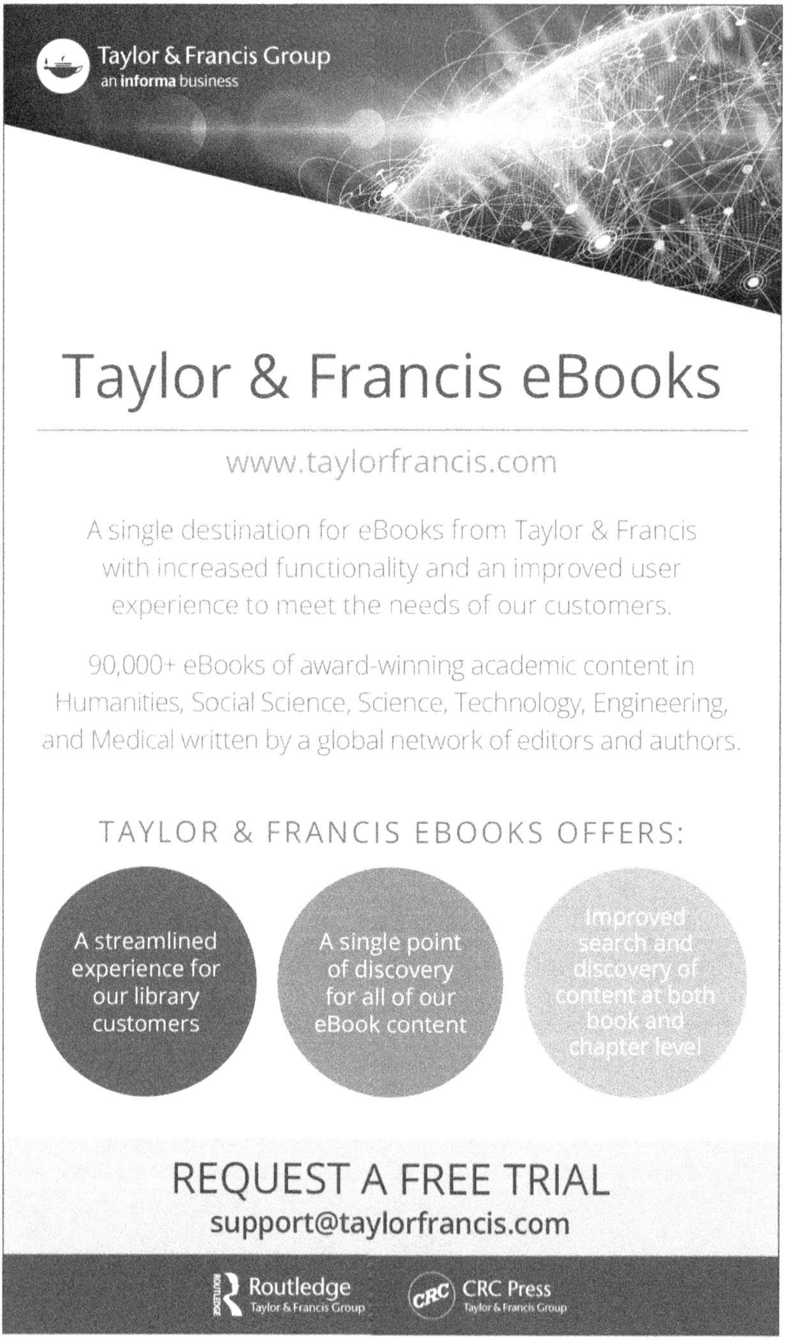
Taylor & Francis Group
an informa business
Taylor & Francis eBooks
www.taylorfrancis.com
A single destination for eBooks from Taylor & Francis with increased functionality and an improved user experience to meet the needs of our customers.
90,000+ eBooks of award-winning academic content in Humanities, Social Science, Science, Technology, Engineering, and Medical written by a global network of editors and authors.
TAYLOR & FRANCIS EBOOKS OFFERS:
A streamlined experience for our library customers
A single point of discovery for all of our eBook content
Improved search and discovery of content at both book and chapter level
REQUEST A FREE TRIAL
support@taylorfrancis.com
Routledge
Taylor & Francis Group
CRC Press
Taylor & Francis Group

For Product Safety Concerns and Information please contact our EU
representative GPSR@taylorandfrancis.com
Taylor & Francis Verlag GmbH, Kaufingerstraße 24, 80331 München, Germany

www.ingramcontent.com/pod-product-compliance
Lightning Source LLC
LaVergne TN
LVHW021127300926
849160LV00010B/902